Comprehensive Computer Learning

Adobe Photoshop

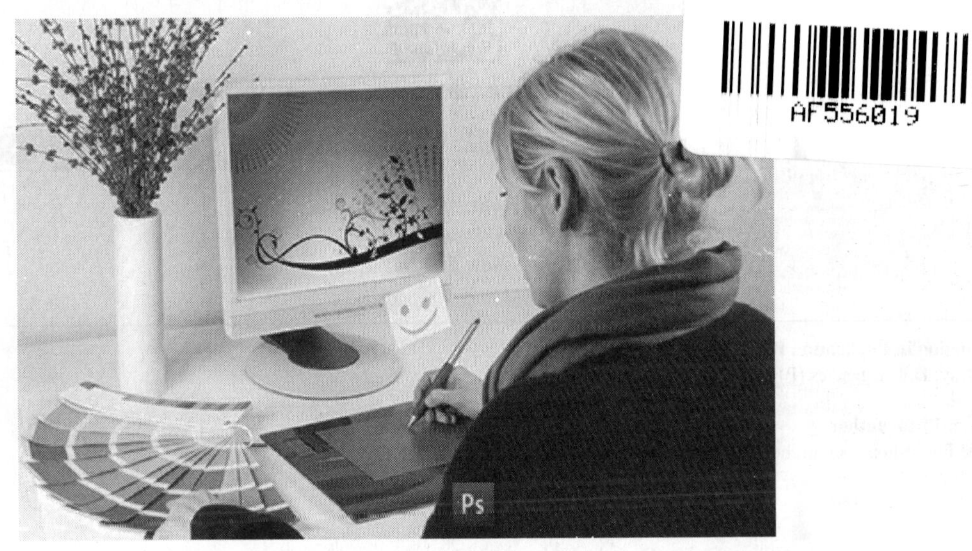

by
Bittu Kumar

V&S PUBLISHERS

Published by:

Head Office
F-2/16, Ansari Road, Daryaganj,
New Delhi-110002 ☎ 23240026, 27.
info@vspublishers.com
www.vspublishers.com

Regional Office
5-1-707/1, Brij Bhawan (Beside Central Bank of India Lane) Bank Street, Koti,
Hyderabad - 500 095 ☎ 040-24737290
vspublishershyd@gmail.com

Online Brandstore: amazon.in/vspublishers

Buy Books Online: amazon • Flipkart  **Follow us on:**  

ISBN 978-93-505701-6-6
New Edition

Cataloging in Publication Data--DK
Courtesy: D.K. Agencies (P) Ltd. <docinfo@dkagencies.com>

Kumar, Bittu, author.
Adobe Photoshop : comprehensive computer learning / by Bittu Kumar.
pages cm
ISBN 9789350570166

1. Adobe Photoshop. 2. Image processing--Digital techniques. 3. Computer graphics--Computer programs. I. Title.

LCC T385.K86 2022 | DDC 006.6 23

Printed at : Param Offsetters, Okhla, New Delhi–110020

Publisher's Note

After successfully publishing youth-oriented books and getting commendable appreciation from students, teachers and parents alike, V&S Publishers is venturing into the arena of student and job-oriented books with a series of computer books on various important subjects for readers of all ages. Written and presented in lucid language and simple terms, without any computer jargon, these books are an easy-to-follow manual for readers. For the convenience of readers the information is set out in an easy to understand, step-by-step format, with clear illustrations and detailed explanations to accompany each action. Besides, every book is accompanied by an interactive video tutorials in Youtube for better understanding of the readers.

Today we live in a world of computers. The present scenario is that computers are used in every field be it education, business, trade and commerce, home and hobby, or even our ordinary day-to-day life. The importance of computers is an undeniable fact in today's world. In fact, we can't think of a world without computers.

Realising this indisputable fact, we are coming up with the series of **"Comprehensive Computer Learning (CCL)"** books. The series currently includes –

1. Comprehensive Computer Learning (CCL)
2. Comprehensive Computer Learning – A Youngsters' Guide
3. Comprehensive Computer Learning – Microsoft Office 2010
4. Comprehensive Computer Learning – Desktop Publishing (DTP)
5. Comprehensive Computer Learning – Adobe Photoshop

Key features of these books:

- Written in simple and lucid language
- Presented in step-by-step, easy-to-understand format with detailed explanations with appropriate images & screenshots, charts & tables
- Useful tips and notes given in every chapter as additional information
- Accompanied by interactive video tutorials in Youtube for better understanding

This book **"Comprehensive Computer Learning – Adobe Photoshop"** has been explicitly written keeping in mind the needs of Youngsters and Executives. The book is a concise handbook for any one and every one who intends to learn Photoshop and play with images and photographs.

While every effort has been made to minimise printing and other errors, it may be possible that a few might have managed to escape the wakeful eyes. We would like to request the readers to bring these errors to our notice so that we can rectify the same in subsequent editions.

Contents

Introduction to Photoshop

What is Photoshop?

Photoshop is the leading digital image editing application for the Internet, print and other new media disciplines. It is embraced by millions of graphic artists, print designers, visual communicators, and regular people like you and me. It's likely that nearly every picture you've seen (such as posters, book covers, magazine pictures, and brochures) has either been created or edited by Photoshop. The powerful tools used to enhance and edit these pictures are also capable for use in the digital world including the infinite possibilities of the Internet.

Versions of Photoshop

The table below shows the various versions of Adobe Photoshop.

Version	Platform	Codename	Release date	Notes and significant changes
0.07	Macintosh	–	January 1988 (not publicly released)	❑ This demo is the first known copy of Photoshop with any public exposure.
0.63	Macintosh	–	October 1988	–
0.87	Macintosh	*Seurat*	March 1989	❑ First version distributed commercially (by the scanner company Barneyscan), though distributed as "Barneyscan XP".
1.0	Macintosh	–	February 1990	–
2.0	Macintosh	Fast Eddy	June 1991	❑ Paths ❑ CMYK Colour ❑ EPS Rasterization
2.5	Macintosh	Merlin	November 1992	❑ 16 bit per channel support ❑ "Deluxe" edition available on CD-ROM
	Windows	Brimstone		
	IRIX, Solaris	–	November 1993	

Version	Platform	Codename	Release date	Notes and significant changes
3.0	Macintosh	Tiger Mountain	September 1994	❑ Tabbed Palettes ❑ Layers
	Windows, IRIX, Solaris	–	November 1994	
4.0	Macintosh, Windows	Big Electric Cat	November 1996	❑ Adjustment Layers ❑ Actions (macros)
5.0	Macintosh, Windows	Strange Cargo	May 1998	❑ Editable type (previously, type was rasterized as soon as it was added) ❑ Multiple Undo (History Palette) ❑ Colour Management ❑ Magnetic Lasso
5.5	Macintosh, Windows	Strange Cargo	February 1999	❑ Bundled with Image Ready ❑ Save for Web ❑ Extract
6.0	Macintosh, Windows	Venus in Furs	September 2000	❑ Vector Shapes ❑ Updated User Interface ❑ "Liquify" filter ❑ Layer styles/Blending Options dialog
7.0	Mac OS 'Classic'/Mac OS X, Windows	Liquid Sky	March 2002	❑ Made text fully vector ❑ Healing Brush ❑ New painting engine
7.0.1	Mac OS 'Classic'/Mac OS X, Windows	–	August 2002	❑ Camera RAW 1.x (optional plugin)
CS (8.0)	Mac OS X, Windows	Dark Matter	October 2003	❑ Camera RAW 2.x ❑ Highly modified "Slice Tool" ❑ Shadow/Highlight command ❑ Match Colour command ❑ Lens Blur filter ❑ Smart Guides ❑ Real-Time Histogram ❑ Detection and refusal to print scanned images of various banknotes ❑ Macro vision copy protection based on Safe cast DRM technology

Version	Platform	Codename	Release date	Notes and significant changes
				❑ Scripting support for JavaScript and other languages ❑ Hierarchical layer groups ❑ 16 bit per channel layers, painting, and adjustments ❑ Support for files over 2 Gigabytes ❑ Documents up to 300,000 pixels in either dimension ❑ Type on a path
CS2 (9.0)	Mac OS X, Windows 2000 / XP	Space Monkey	April 4, 2005	❑ Camera RAW 3.x ❑ Smart Objects ❑ Image Warp ❑ Spot healing brush ❑ Red-Eye tool ❑ Lens Correction filter ❑ Smart Sharpen ❑ Vanishing Point ❑ Better memory management on 64-bit PowerPC G5 Macintosh machines running Mac OS X 10.4 ❑ High dynamic range imaging (HDRI) support (32 bit per channel floating point) ❑ More smudging options, such as "Scattering" ❑ Modified layer selection, such as ability to select more than one layer.
CS3, CS3 Extended (10.0)	Universal Mac OS X, Windows XP SP2 or later	Red Pill	April 16, 2007	❑ Native support for the Intel-based Macintosh platform and improved support for Windows Vista ❑ Revised user interface ❑ Feature additions to Adobe Camera RAW ❑ Quick Select tool ❑ Alterations to Curves, Vanishing Point, Channel Mixer, Brightness and Contrast, and the Print dialog ❑ Black-and-white conversion adjustment

Version	Platform	Codename	Release date	Notes and significant changes
				❑ Auto Align and Auto Blend ❑ Smart (non-destructive) Filters ❑ Mobile device graphic optimization ❑ Improvements to cloning and healing ❑ More complete 32 bit / HDR support (layers, painting, more filters and adjustments) ❑ Faster launching ❑ ImageReady removed
CS4, CS4 Extended (11.0)	Universal Mac OS X, Windows	Stonehenge	October 15, 2008	❑ Smoother panning and zooming and fluid canvas rotation ❑ OpenGL display acceleration in Photoshop ❑ Native support for 64-bit on Windows Vista x64 ❑ Adjustments panel ❑ Masks panel ❑ Improved Adobe Photoshop Lightroom workflow ❑ Content-aware scaling ❑ Extended depth of field ❑ Auto-blending of images ❑ Auto-alignment of layers ❑ New file display options (tabbed document display and n-up views) ❑ New file management and workspaces with Adobe Bridge CS4
CS5, CS5 Extended (12.0)	Mac OS X, Windows	White Rabbit	April 30, 2010	❑ Content Aware Fill ❑ Puppet Warp Tool ❑ 64 bit for Mac OS X ❑ Bristle Tips ❑ Mixer Brush ❑ Automatic Lens Correction ❑ Easier HDR toning for beginners ❑ Improved selection and masking controls

Version	Platform	Codename	Release date	Notes and significant changes
				❑ Camera RAW grain control ❑ GPU HUD controls for brush resize, colour picker, colour sampling ❑ Improved Ray Tracing quality and speed (Extended) ❑ Repousse 3D extrusion tool (Extended) ❑ Image based lights (Extended)
CS5.1 CS5.1 Extended (12.1, 12.0.4)	Mac OS X, Windows	White Rabbit	May 3, 2011	❑ Interacts with remote applications over TCP/IP, such as tablets and other computers. ❑ Subscription model pricing
CS6 (13.0)	Mac OS X, Windows	Superstition	May 7, 2012 (current)	❑ UI redesign (all new icons and optional dark UI) ❑ Auto and background saves ❑ Content-aware Patch and Move tools ❑ Blur Gallery ❑ Colour Range: skin tone and face detection ❑ Adobe Camera RAW 7 ❑ Enhanced crop tool ❑ New properties panel ❑ Enhanced video support ❑ Oil Paint filter now ships with the program ❑ Adaptive Wide Angle filter ❑ Paragraph and Character Styles ❑ Built in support for Middle Eastern languages ❑ Updated Printing UI ❑ 3DLUT adjustment ❑ Vector strokes, dotted/dashed strokes ❑ Overhauled vector tools ❑ Snap to Pixel for vector tools and transforms ❑ 3D UI completely redone, now easier to use

Features of Photoshop

Among various features of Photoshop the following ten features are most important and mostly used.

1. Document navigation
2. Cropping
3. Layers and Groups
4. Tool presets and the preset manager
5. Layer Styles
6. ACR – healing multiple images and setting presets and applying them in Bridge
7. Creating New Files
8. Soft Proofing and Printing
9. Resetting Photoshop's preferences and Plugin Folder when Launching
10. Alternate ways to open files

How to install Photoshop

The following steps will show you how to install Photoshop on your computer.

1. Browse for the setup.exe in your DVD/ Downloaded.

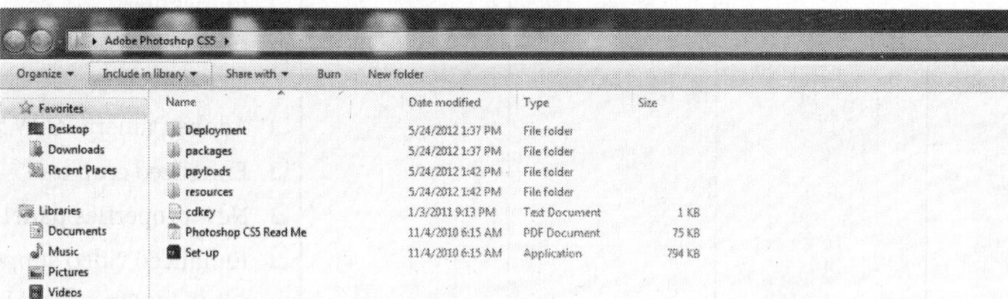

2. Run Setup.exe.

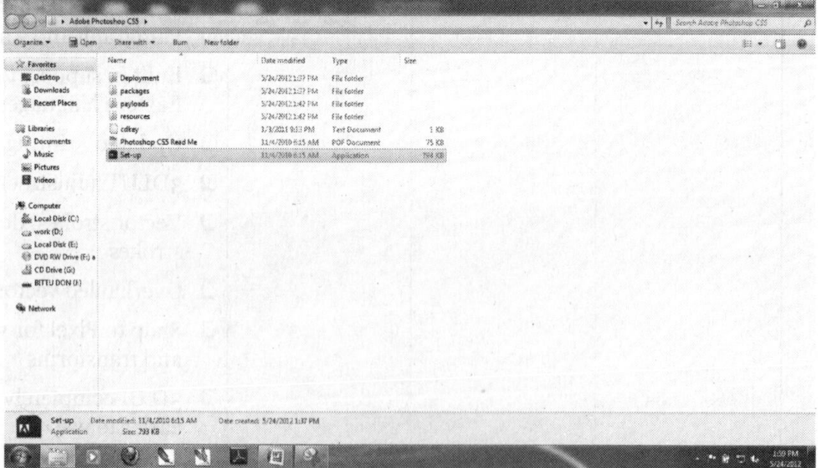

3. Wait for setup to start, a dialog box will open.

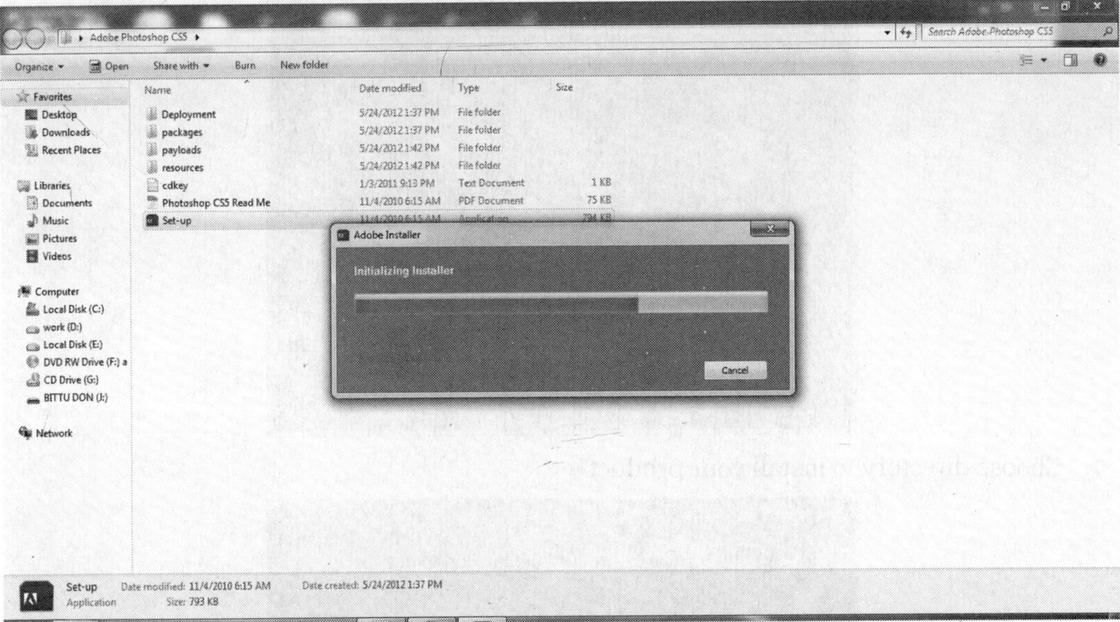

4. Read the agreement and click install.

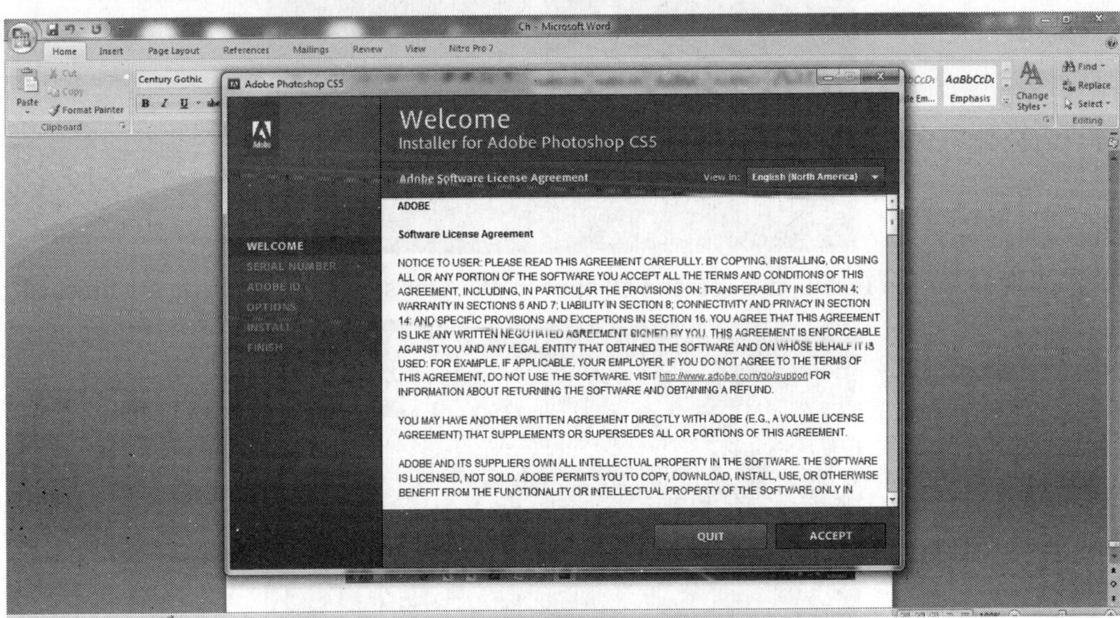

5. Enter your license number or click to install as trial, select your Language and continue

6. Create your adobe ID or skip if you want

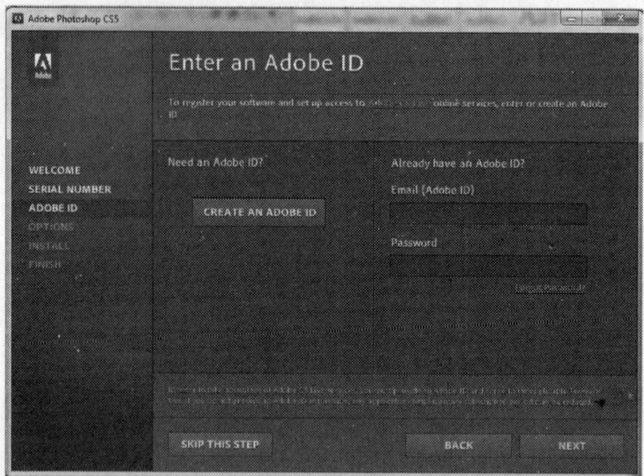

7. Choose directory to install your product

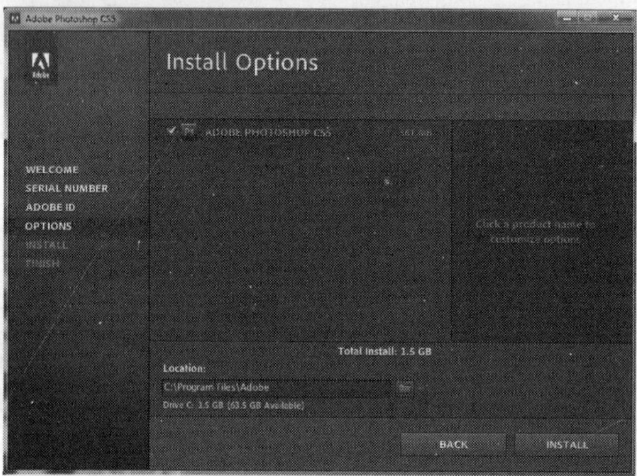

8. Click on button Install, this screen will appear. Wait for some time and you are finished.

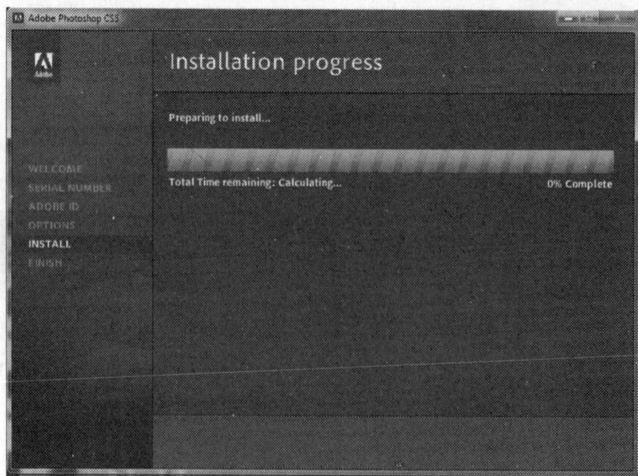

9. You are done! Now you can begin....!

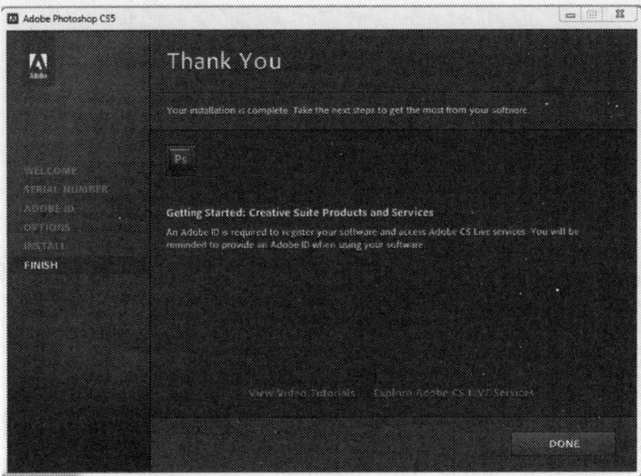

Getting started

Photoshop enables you to create, modify, combine, and optimize digital images. You can then save the images to print, share via e-mail, publish online, or view on a handheld device, such as an iPod.

You've heard of Photoshop, right? Of course you have – you wouldn't be reading this book otherwise! You've probably heard of Photoshop's sidekick, Fireworks, too, but you might not be quite sure of what it does or where it fits in. Here we will discuss all that you think of but never try yourself.

Photoshop is the most commonly used tool in the web designer's arsenal. From the preparation of initial design comps to generating optimized graphics for a web page, most web designers rely heavily on these two programs.

So what are you waiting for? Open up Photoshop and let's start!

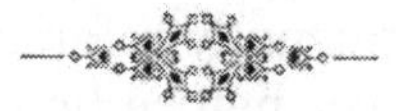

The Photoshop Workspace

In this introductory chapter, we'll cover some of the basic tools and tasks that we'll draw on in later chapters. We'll also share some of the shortcuts and time-savers that we use frequently. This chapter won't give you an exhaustive review of the many things that Photoshop can do, but it should provide the bare bones that will help get beginners started. If you're already familiar with the interface and can perform tasks like making selections, applying gradients, and working with layers, you might want to skip ahead to the next chapter.

Photoshop's "out of the box" workspace consists of the following components:

- **Menu bar** – You will probably already be familiar with the menu bar from other programs. This runs across the top of your Photoshop window, and contains various menu options for Photoshop's tools.
- **Options bar** – The options bar sits beneath the menu bar and holds contextualized options for different tools. It also contains the workspace menu, where you can save and load arrangements of palettes.
- **Toolbox** – By default, the toolbox sits to the left of your Photoshop window, and contains shortcuts to Photoshop tools.

Now that you're going to work in Photoshop, you might want to start talking like a designer. Designers, like professionals in most specialist fields, have their own terminology and words for things. A comp (short for "composite") refers to a mockup of the final solution that a designer has in mind. Traditionally, "comp" is used in the print world to refer to page layouts, but for web designers it usually refers to a static interface prepared entirely in Photoshop for the client to look over before he or she decides to proceed. You might even hear it being used as a verb: "comping" is the process of creating that mockup site.

- **Palettes** – Individual "panes" that hold information or options for working with your file, known as palettes (or panels), float on the right-hand side. Each palette is labelled with a tab, and can be minimized, closed, grouped with other palettes, or dragged in and out of a panel dock. In the example that follows, the Navigator palette contains a thumbnail of the image that allows you to zoom in or out of the image quickly, and to change the part of the image displayed on the screen.

- **Document windows** – Each open document has their own document window with a status bar along the bottom. The status bar sits to the right of the zoom percentage displayed in the bottom left-hand corner, and displays information that's specific to the document.

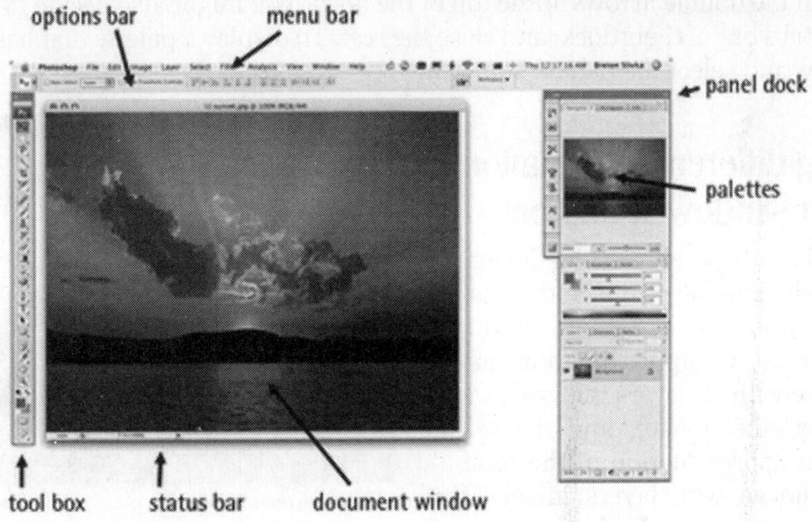

The Photoshop workspace

Customizing your Workspace

You can customize your Photoshop workspace to suit you or your project – almost everything within your workspace can be repositioned and reconfigured. You might choose to customize your workspace by:

Changing the look of the menu bar

You can change which menu items are visible in your menu bar, and even add colour to your menu items. If you wanted, you could also assign new or different keyboard shortcuts to menu commands (which I don't recommend until you feel very comfortable with Photoshop or have a compelling reason to do so!). Go to **Edit > Menus** and use the dialog box to modify the menu bar and palette menus.

Moving the options bar

If you want to move the options bar, you can do so by clicking on the handle on its left side and moving it around. The options bar will "dock" to the top or bottom of the screen automatically if moved near those areas.

Moving the toolbox

The toolbox is extremely portable, and can be moved to any location on your screen. Move the toolbox by clicking on the light gray area at the top of it and dragging it around. You can switch between different toolbox layouts by clicking the double arrow along the top of the toolbox.

Rearranging palettes

There are many ways to rearrange your palettes. You might want to separate a palette from its palette group, and move it into another group. You can do this by dragging the palette tab out of its original group and into the new group. You may want to expand or collapse a dock, by clicking on the double arrows at the top of the dock. You might also decide to drag some of your palette tabs out of their dock, and close the rest. To display a palette that has been closed, go to Window and select the palette you want to show.

Displaying different information in document window status bar

The status bar displays the document file size by default. The file size is shown as two numbers separated by a forward slash: the first number is an approximation of the image file size with all layers merged (known as "flattening" the image), and the second number is an approximation of the total file size of the image with layers intact. If all this sounds new to you, don't worry – we'll be discussing layers shortly. You can set the status bar to display different information, such as the document dimension in pixels, or the version number of the file. To do this, click on the arrow icon next to the status bar, select Show and choose the information you'd like to see.

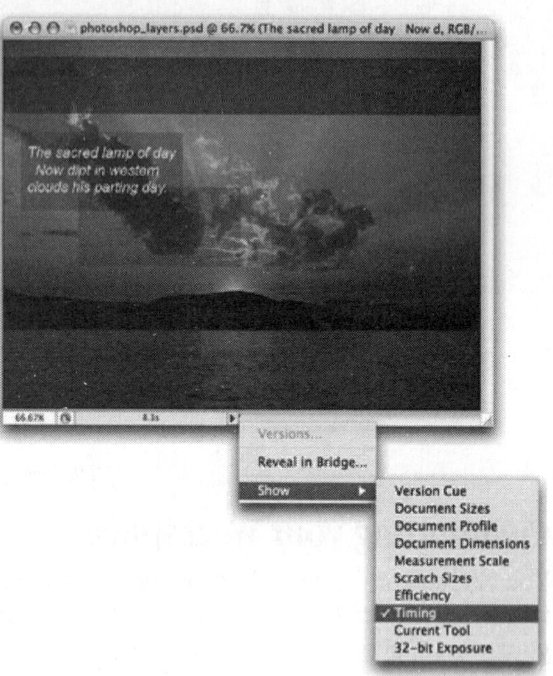

Display information in status bar

Saving your Customized Workspace

As you become more proficient with Photoshop, you may discover that you use certain sets of palettes for different types of projects, and that there are some palettes that you don't use at all. Photoshop allows you to save and load different workspaces – different arrangements of palettes, menus, and even different keyboard shortcuts – to help you work more efficiently.

After you've customized your workspace to your satisfaction, select the Workspace menu in the options bar, click Save Workspace and enter a name for your workspace, such as Creating Thumbnails or My Default Workspace. You can then load your different workspaces by opening Workspace and selecting your custom workspace from the menu list.

Working in Photoshop

Now that you've been introduced to the Photoshop workspace and have a basic idea of where everything is, let's start getting our hands dirty.

Creating New Documents

You can create a new document by selecting **File > New** from the menu bar, or pressing the keyboard shortcut **Ctrl-N** on a PC or Command-N on a Mac. The New dialog box will appear, where you can specify the document size and other settings.

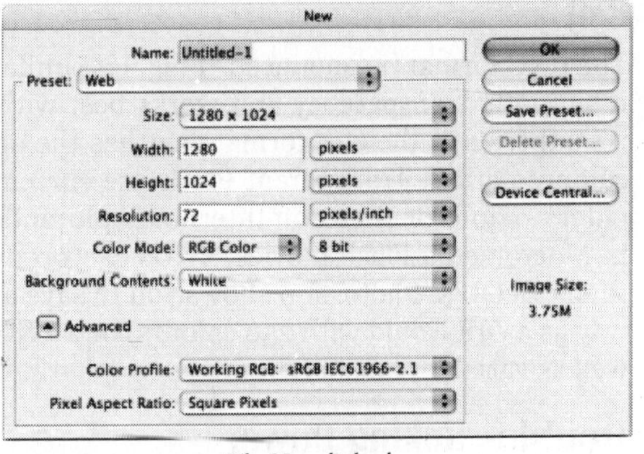

The New dialog box

Opening Files

Open files by selecting **File > Open** from the menu bar, or pressing **Ctrl-O** (Command-O on a Mac). You can select and open multiple files by holding down Ctrl (Command on a Mac) and clicking on all the files you require in the file dialog box.

Saving Files

Save a file by selecting **File > Save**, or pressing **Ctrl-S** (Command-S on a Mac). For a newly-created document, this will save your work in Photoshop Document (PSD) format.
If you would prefer to save a copy of the document, you can use **File > Save As** or pressing **Ctrl-Shift-S** (Command-Shift-S on a Mac) instead.

Snappy Presets

If you're designing for a website with a minimum screen size of 800Ã—600 pixels, I'd recommend you to start with a 750Ã—550 pixel document. The smaller dimensions give you a better estimate of your actual screen area after you take into account scroll bars and menu bars. Also, be sure to set the resolution at 72dpi to reflect the actual screen resolution. If you want easy access to these dimensions for other new documents, it's probably a good idea to click Save Preset and give the settings a name like Web Page. The next time you create a new document, you will be able to load your Web Page settings from the Preset list.

Saving Files for the Web

Photoshop files themselves can't be embedded into a web page. You will need to export your file and save it in a web-friendly format. There are three formats for web graphics: GIFs, JPEGs, and PNGs.

GIF

The GIF format (pronounced "jiff" or "giff" depending on which side of the tracks you grew up) can have a maximum of 256 colours. GIF files support transparency and animation, and work best with graphics that have large areas of the same colour.

JPEG

The JPEG format (pronounced "jay-peg") works best with photographic images or images that have more than 256 colours and gradient. Images saved in JPEG format are compressed, which means that image information will actually be lost, causing the image to degrade in quality.

Example of an image that should be saved as JPEG

PNG

The PNG format (pronounced "ping") is similar to the GIF format in that it supports transparency and works best with solid-colour images, but it's superior to the GIF format as it has the ability to support true levels of transparency for coloured areas. Transparent PNGs are currently not in widespread use on the Web because older versions of Microsoft Internet Explorer do not support them; however, they're often used in Macromedia Flash movies. PNGs can produce a better quality image at a smaller file size than can GIFs. Photoshop allows you to save an image as a PNG-8 file (which works the same way as a GIF would with 256 colours) or a PNG-24 file (which allows for millions of colours as well as variable transparency).

Double-clicking Power

As if keyboard shortcuts weren't quick enough, Windows users have even more ways to open and save files, such as: holding down Ctrl and double-clicking the work area to create new documents, double-clicking the work area to pull up the Open dialog box, to open files holding down Alt and double-clicking the work area to open existing files as new documents, holding down Ctrl-Shift and double-clicking the work area to save documents, holding down Shift and double-clicking the work area to access Adobe Bridge – Adobe's "control centre" and file browser. The work area is the gray area behind the document windows. If your shortcuts aren't working, check that you are clicking on an empty spot on the work area, and not in one of the document windows or Photoshop tools! Alas, Photoshop on a Mac does not have a work area, so Mac users won't get to enjoy the goodness of double-click shortcuts.

To save for the Web in Photoshop, select **File > Save** for Web & Devices... or press **Ctrl-Alt-Shift-S** (Command-Option-Shift-S on a Mac). This will bring up the Save For

Web dialog box shown overleaf, which will show you a preview of the image that will be exported, with its optimized size in the bottom left-hand corner. You can adjust the settings for the image using the options in the pane on the right. Choose whether you want to save the file as a GIF, JPEG, PNG-8, or PNG-24, and have a play with the other settings, keeping an eye on the optimized file size. Try to strike a balance between the quality and file size of the image. When you're happy with your result, click Save and give your image a filename.

If you tried the above exercise, you're probably quite pleased with yourself for saving an image of reasonable quality at a file size significantly smaller than the original. You managed this by altering the settings in the right-hand pane, but what do these settings actually do?

GIF/PNG-8

- **Colours** – Adjusting this setting reduces the number of colours used in the image. This will usually make the biggest difference in the final image.
- **Dither amount and type (No Dither, Diffusion, Pattern, Noise)** – This setting has nothing to do with being nervous or agitated (although it's quite possible that you may have been a few moments ago!). Dither refers to a compression technique in which the pattern of dots is varied to give the illusion of a colour gradient. Changing the dither will result in a more noticeable degradation for images that involve a large number of colours blended together.
- **Transparency** – If you want transparent areas in your graphic, check this box.
- **Matte colour** – For transparent images, the matte colour is used to help blend the edges of your image into the background of the web page. For non-transparent images, the matte colour defines the background colour of the image.

JPEG

Quality – Changing the value in the Quality drop-down box alters the level of compression for the image. Reducing the quality may result in blurring or pixelation, but too high a setting will produce a large file that will take users too long to download. A good approach is to decrease the quality value gradually until you notice the degradation of your image becoming unacceptable. A reasonable compromise will be somewhere around this point.

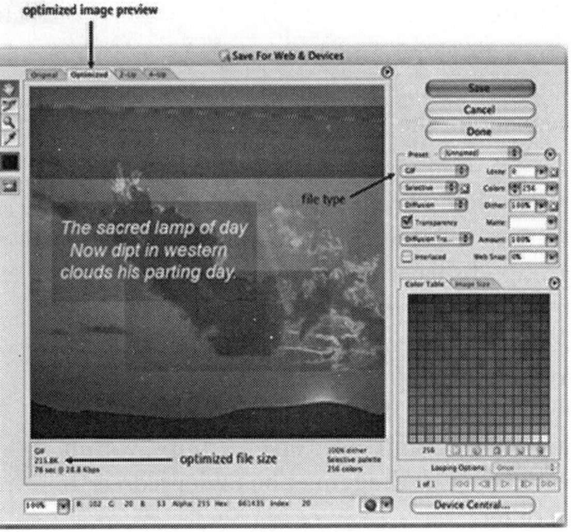

The Save for Web dialog box

Saving Files For The Web In Fireworks

The Optimize palette in Fireworks

You can optimize images for the Web in Fireworks using the Optimize palette. Set the file type and options in the Optimize palette in advance, and when you're ready to export your web image, select **File > Export** or press **Ctrl-Shift-R** (Command-Shift-R on a Mac). Fireworks will save the image based on the settings that you've defined.

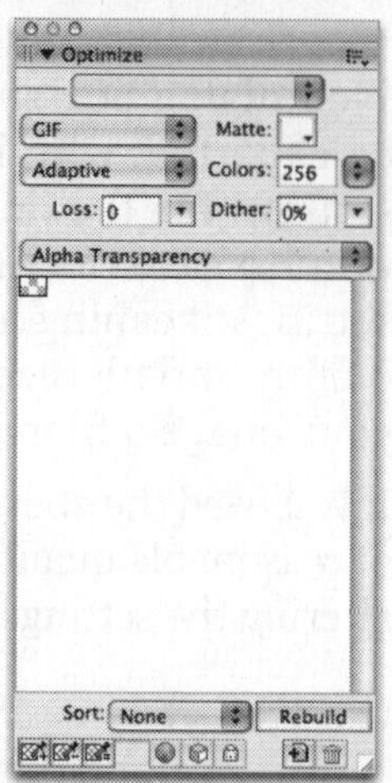

Why Two Tools?

Considering that it's possible to save files for the Web in Photoshop, it's perfectly reasonable for you to wonder why you would need Fireworks. While it's true that both programs can perform many of the same tasks, there are certain things that Fireworks can do that Photoshop can't. Fireworks also makes web-specific tasks easier, and since it's a smaller program that doesn't contain the full suite of Photoshop effects, it loads more quickly than Photoshop. As you work through this book you'll come to learn which tool is more suitable for particular tasks.

Photoshop Layers

Layers are a powerful feature of Photoshop that allow you to work on one part of an image without disturbing the rest of it. While the concept of layers may seem intimidating at first, once you get the hang of using layers you'll wonder how you ever survived without them! The examples show how the layers in the Photoshop document do to the right stack together.

A layered Photoshop document

The transparent parts of any layer, shown by the checkered grid, allow the layers beneath that layer to show through.

You can show and hide each layer in an image by clicking on its corresponding eye icon in the Layers palette.

To organize your layers, you can arrange them into layer groups by going to **Layer > New > Group....** Each layer group displays in the same way as any ungrouped layers on the Layers palette. A layer group is signified by a folder icon. You can collapse or expand layer groups by clicking on the triangle to the left of the folder icon, and nest layer groups within each other by dragging one folder icon into another.

layered group

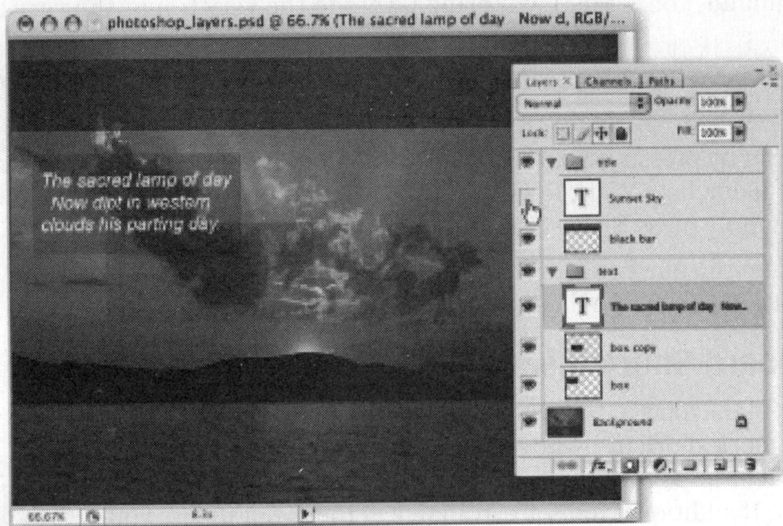

A Photoshop document with layers displayed

Hiding A Layer

Layer Shortcuts and Tasks

- ❑ Rename layers by double-clicking on the layer name.
- ❑ Change the transparency of a layer by changing its opacity with the Opacity slider, or typing a value into the Opacity box (which is visible when you have the Selection, Move, or Crop tools selected).
- ❑ Duplicate a selected layer by pressing **Ctrl-J** (Command-J on a Mac). You can also duplicate a layer by dragging it while pressing the Alt (Option) key.
- ❑ Select multiple layers by holding down Ctrl (Command on a Mac) and clicking the layer names. This forms a temporary link between the selected layers that allows you to move them as one unit, delete them all, and so on.

You can also link layers together. Select layers by clicking on them while holding down Shift or Ctrl (Command on a Mac). Once you have selected all the layers you wish to link, click the Link Layers button at the bottom-left of the Layers palette (signified by the chain). Linking layers allows the link relationship to remain even after you select a different layer (unlike the process of simply selecting multiple layers).

To unlink all the layers, select one of the linked layers and go to **Layer > Unlink Layers.** To unlink a single layer, select the layer you wish to remove from the link and click its corresponding link icon; the other layers will stay linked. To temporarily unlink a layer, hold down Shift and click on its link icon (a red "X" will appear over the link icon). Reactivate the link by holding down Shift and clicking the link icon again.

Rearrange layers by dragging the layer above or below other layers. Use the "move down" shortcut **Ctrl-[** (Command-[on a Mac) and the "move up" shortcut **Ctrl-]** (Command-]) to move selected layers up and down. **Shift-Ctrl-[** and **Shift-Ctrl-]** (Shift-Command-[

and Shift-Command-] on a Mac) will bring layers to the very top or the very bottom of the stack.

Select a layer by using the keyboard shortcuts **Alt-[** and **Alt-]** (Option-[and Option-] on a Mac). These keystrokes let you move up and down through the layers in the Layers palette.

Create a new layer by pressing **Shift-Ctrl-N** (Shift-Command-N on a Mac). This will bring up the New Layer dialog box. Want to create new layers quickly without having to deal with the dialogue box? Simply press **Shift-Ctrl-Alt-N** (Shift-Command-Option-N).

Merge a layer into the one beneath it by pressing **Ctrl-E** (Command-E). If you have selected layers, this shortcut will merge those selected layers together.

Quick Keyboard Shortcuts

Naturally, most of the tools in the toolbox have a keyboard shortcut. You can learn each tool's shortcut by hovering your cursor over a tool for a few seconds: a tooltip box will appear, displaying the name of the tool and its shortcut. If additional tools are available in the flyout menu, you can cycle through them by pressing Shift-[keyboard shortcut]. Keyboard shortcuts can save your valuable time – pressing "V" to bring up the Move Tool is certainly a lot quicker than moving the cursor over to the toolbox to select it. It may not seem all that significant right now, but the time you take to access tools will add up over the course of a project! For your convenience, whenever I mention a tool, I'll list its shortcut in parentheses, e.g. the Move Tool (V).

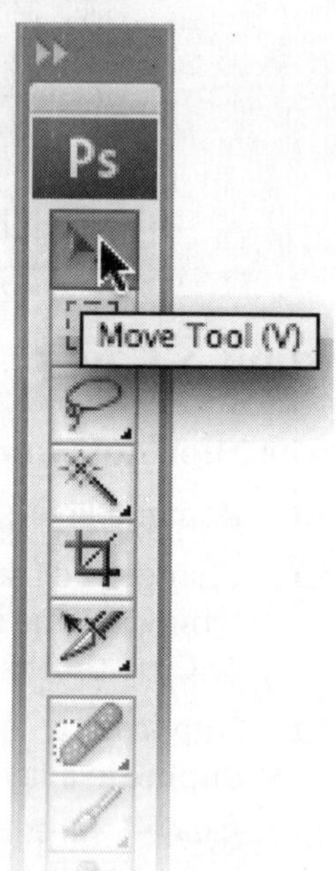

Tooltip for a keyboard shortcut

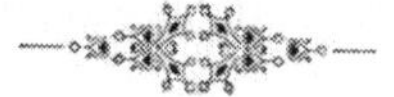

Photoshop Toolbox

You've probably been hanging out to get stuck into the very nifty Photoshop toolbox. In this section, I'll introduce some of the most frequently used tools found in the toolbox. I'll discuss some of the other tools in later chapters as we apply them to solutions.

You'll notice that some of the tool icons have small black triangles in their bottom right-hand corners. These icons contain hidden treasures! The triangle indicates that there are more related tools available; if you click on the tool icon and hold it down, a "flyout" menu will appear, displaying the additional tools.

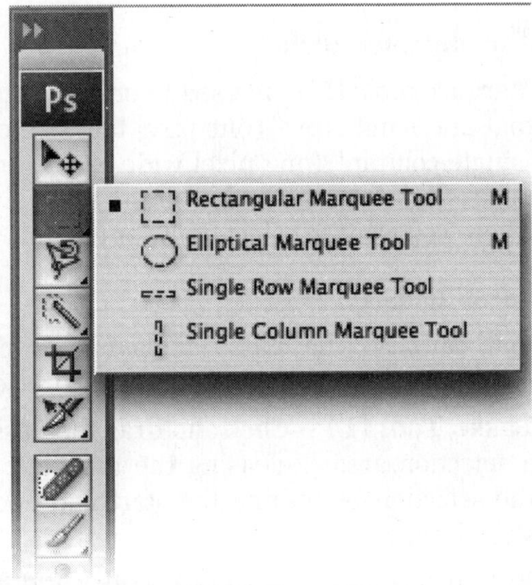

Finding the hidden tools

Secret Selections

Selections can have varying levels of transparency, known as the degree of opacity. It's actually possible to make a selection with an opacity of 100% in one area, but only 20% in another area. If a selection contains any pixels for which the opacity is more than 50%, they will be displayed with a border of dotted lines. Photoshop won't visibly outline areas with less than 50% opacity (though they will still be selected). Selection tools automatically select at 100% opacity. We'll learn about creating transparent selections using Quick Masks and alpha channels later.

Selection Tools

You can use the selection tools to select certain areas of your document for editing. If you use a selection tool, only the area that's selected will be affected by any changes you make. You can "feather" selections (specify a fuzzy radius for them) using the Feather field in the options bar. The example of the next page shows two rectangles: one created by filling in a selection with a feather of zero pixels, and one that's created by filling in the same selection with a feather of five pixels.

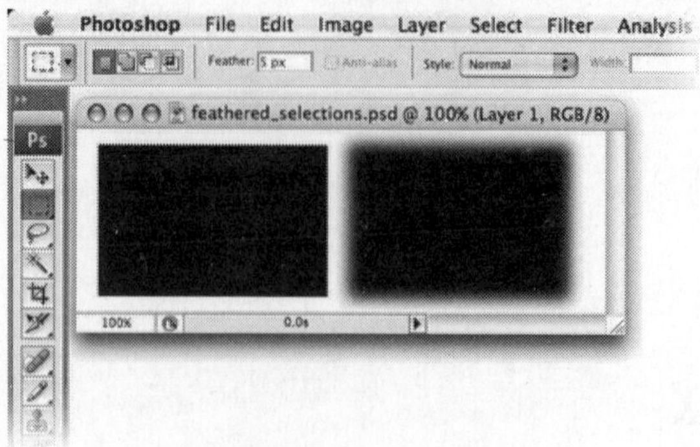

"Fuzzy" edges with feathered selections

The Marquee tools

Marquee tools (M) are used to create rectangular or elliptical selections, including selections that are "single row" (one pixel tall, stretching across the entire width of the document) and "single column" (one pixel wide, stretching through the entire height of the document). To make single-row or single-column selections, click with the appropriate tool on the image area where you want to select a row or column.

Lasso tools

You can use the Lasso tools (L) to create freeform selections. The Lasso Tool comes in three different forms:

Lasso Tool (L) – Click and drag the Lasso Tool to draw a selection area. Releasing the mouse button will close the selection by joining the start and end points with a straight line.

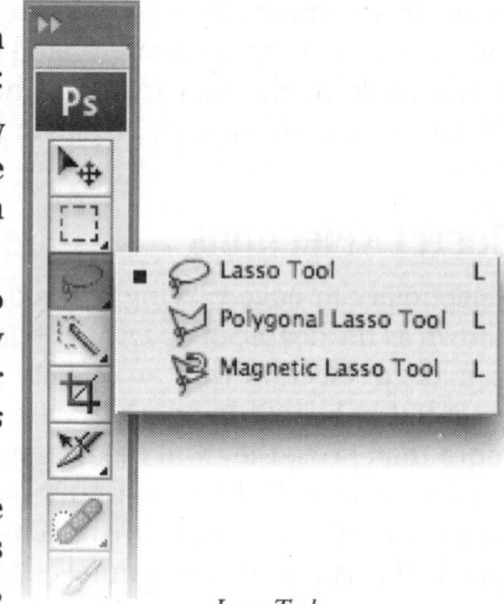

Lasso Tool

Polygonal Lasso Tool (L) – Click at different points to create vertices of a polygonal shape. Close the selection by moving your cursor to the beginning and clicking once, or pressing the Enter key. *No Selection Sometimes Equals All Selected.*

If you've made a selection, only the pixels within the selection are active and can be worked on. Some tools can be used without making a selection at all. However, be aware that if you have not made a specific selection, Photoshop will assume that you are working on the entire layer and any changes you make will affect all pixels in the layer.

Magnetic Lasso Tool (L) – If you think you need help with making your selection, try the Magnetic Lasso Tool. Photoshop will attempt to make a "smart" selection by following the edges of contrast and colour difference. Click once near the "edge" of an object and follow around it – Photoshop will automatically lay down a path. You can also click as you follow the line to force points to be created on the path. Close the selection by pressing the Enter key or clicking at a point near the beginning of the selection.

Magic Wand

The Magic Wand Tool (W) selects areas of similar colour. You can change the tolerance (how close the colour values should be to the sampled colour in order to be selected) of a Magic Wand selection, and choose whether you want the selection to be contiguous (pixels that are touching) or not (in which case, matching colours across the entire document will be selected).

Using the Magic Wand to create a selection

Selection Shortcuts and Tasks

Hold the Shift key to add another selection to the first. Hold the Alt key (Option key on a Mac) to subtract your new selection from the first. Hold Shift-Alt (Shift-Option) to select the intersection of your first and second selections. Use the arrow keys to move the selection pixel by pixel. If you feel that this doesn't move your selection quickly enough, hold down Shift and use the arrow keys to move the selection ten pixels at a time. Press **Ctrl-J** (Command-J on a Mac) to copy the selection into its own layer. To cut the selection into its own layer, press **Shift-Ctrl-J** (Shift-Command-J). If this seems familiar to you, it's because I mentioned earlier how to copy a layer using the same keyboard shortcut. Now that you know that not selecting anything sometimes means that everything is selected, it makes sense that simply by selecting a layer in the Layers palette, you can copy the entire layer by pressing **Ctrl-J** (Command-J). To deselect a selected area, click outside of it with one of the Marquee tools, or press **Ctrl-D** (Command-D on a Mac). To reactivate your last selection, press **Shift-Ctrl-D** (Shift-Command-D).

The Move Tool

The Move Tool (V) moves a selected area or an entire layer. You can invoke the Move Tool temporarily when using most other tools by holding down the Ctrl key (Command key on a Mac).

Move and Copy Shortcut

For most tools, holding **Ctrl-Alt** (Command-Option on a Mac) and dragging a selected area will temporarily invoke the Move Tool, allowing you to move and duplicate the selected layer quickly.

You can also duplicate a layer by holding down the Alt key (Option key on a Mac) while using the Move Tool, as shown in the image.

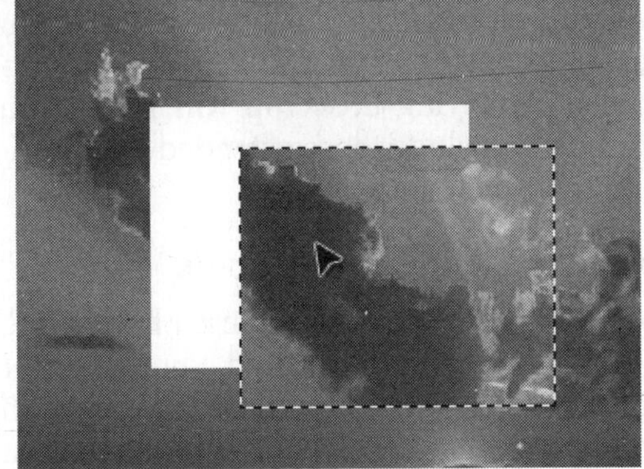

The Move Tool in action

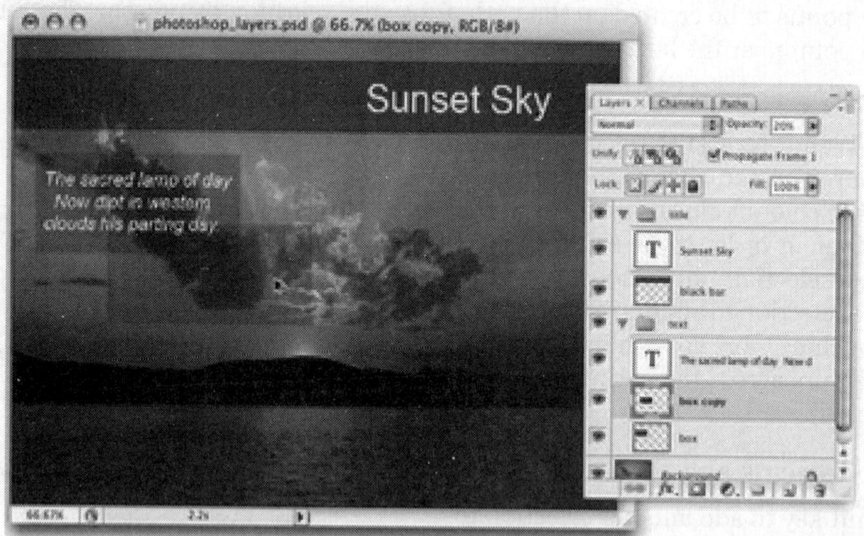

Copying a layer with the Move Tool

The Crop Tool

The Crop Tool (C) is used to trim images. Create a selection using the Crop Tool, then double-click at the centre of the selection, or press Enter, to crop the image to the size of the selection.

To cancel without cropping, select another tool or press the Esc key.

Creating a selection using the Crop Tool

Crop Outside the Box

You can use the Crop Tool to resize your canvas. Expand your document window so that it's larger than the image area, and create a crop selection that includes the image and extends onto the gray areas "outside" the image. Applying this crop will resize your canvas to include those extended boundaries, making your canvas larger.

The cropped image

Drawing and Painting Tools

Apart from its extraordinary photo editing abilities, the multi-talented Photoshop also provides drawing and painting tools that allow you to create your own shapes and backgrounds.

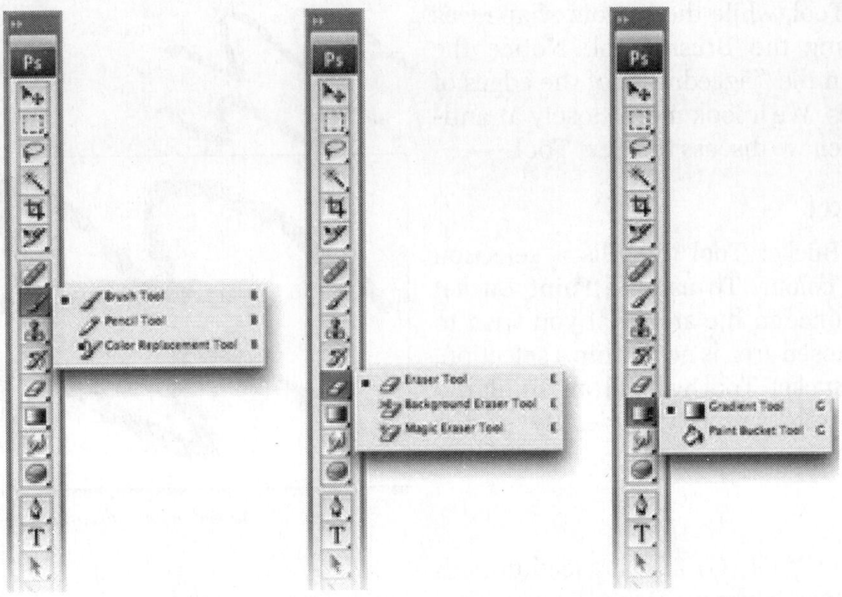

Drawing and painting tools

Brush Tool

The Brush Tool (B) is suitable for soft-edged painting or drawing. Draw strokes by clicking and dragging the mouse over the canvas. You can change the brush size and other settings in the options bar at the top of the window.

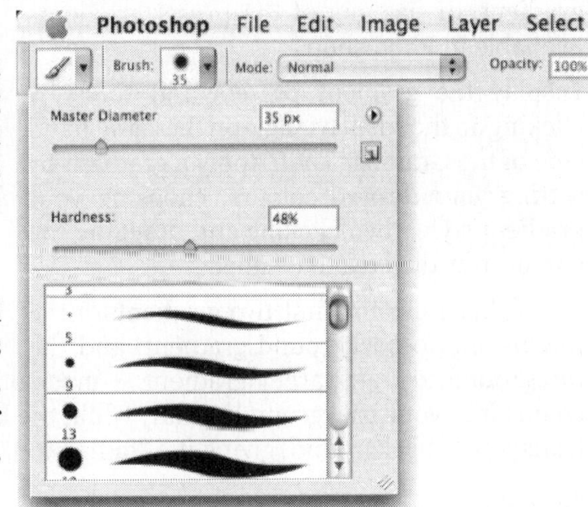

Brush tool

Pencil

The Pencil Tool (B) is suitable for hard-edged drawing or painting and has similar options to the Brush Tool for setting its size, opacity, and more. The Pencil Tool is often used for drawing on, and editing individual pixels in, zoomed-in images.

Eraser

The Eraser Tool (E) removes pixels from the canvas. You can choose between Pencil, Brush, or Block mode from the Mode drop-down menu in the options bar.

Aliased vs Anti-aliased

Unlike the Brush Tool, the Pencil Tool's edges are aliased. The term aliased refers to the edges of an object being "jagged," in contrast to an anti-aliased object, in which the edges are "smooth." In the two examples shown here, the top shape in each example was created using the Pencil Tool, while the bottom shape was created using the Brush Tool. Notice the difference in the "jaggedness" of the edges of these curves. We'll look more closely at anti-aliasing when we discuss the Text Tool.

Aliased vs anti-aliased lines

Paint Bucket

The Paint Bucket Tool (G) fills a selection with a flat colour. To use the Paint Bucket Tool, click once in the area that you wish to fill. If the chosen area is not within a selection, the Paint Bucket Tool will fill all similarly-coloured pixels within the vicinity of the clicked area.

Gradient

The Gradient Tool (G) fills a selection with a blend of two or more colours, known as a gradient. You can easily create your own gradient, or use any of the preset gradients available in Photoshop.

Gradient tool

Display the gradient presets and tools by clicking on the small triangle on the right-hand side of the Gradient Tool. Apply a gradient by setting your desired colours, choosing your gradient style, then clicking and dragging the cursor over the area to be filled.

I find that I use the first two gradients – the foreground-to-background gradient, and the foreground-to-transparent gradient – most often. The former will blend your foreground colour into your background colour, while the latter will blend your foreground colour into a transparent background, giving it a "fading out" effect.

Text Tool

The Text Tool (T), true to its name, creates text layers. This one is easy to use – just select the Text Tool, click on the canvas, and start typing! You can also click and drag to create a rectangular text area that will force text to wrap within its boundaries. You can change the font size, colour, and other text properties using the options bar along the top of the window.

When the Text Tool is active, you can move the cursor outside of the text area. The cursor will change from the "text insert" cursor to the "move" cursor, and you'll be able to move the text layer around.

It's worth noting that when the Text Tool is active, you can't use keyboard shortcuts to access other tools. This may seem like an obvious thing to point out now, but it won't always be so apparent – especially when your text mysteriously starts spurting strange characters because you've been trying to use the shortcut keys!

To finish using the Text Tool, press **Ctrl-Enter** (Command-Return on a Mac). You can then resume your regular keyboard shortcutting!

Shape Tools

You can create shapes simply by clicking and dragging Photoshop's Rectangle, Rounded Rectangle, Ellipse, Polygon, Line, and Custom Shape tools (U).

The specific options for each shape tool are displayed in the options bar, and you can access additional options by clicking on the arrow to the right of the Custom Shape button. For example, the Line Tool has options for displaying arrowheads, and for controlling the shapes and sizes of those arrowheads, as shown in the example below.

If you look at the options for each shape, you'll notice that there are three different methods you can use to create a shape:

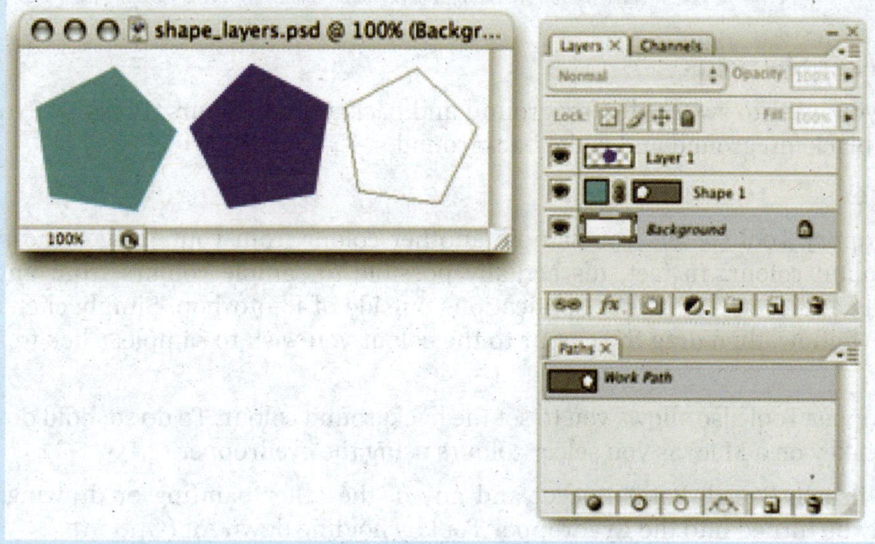

The Shape options

Different ways to create shapes

Your shape will be created as a solid-coloured layer covered with a vector shape mask. Confused? Think of the mask as a sheet of dark paper that has a hole (your shape) cut out of it so that the colour shines through the hole. To change the colour, double-click on the colour block in the Layers palette. To change the vector shape mask, use the vector editing tools.

- **As a path** – Your shape will be created as a path in the Paths palette.
- **As filled pixels** – Your shape will be created on whichever layer is currently selected.

Selecting Colours

Set foreground and background colours by clicking on the appropriate tile and choosing a colour from the Colour Picker, as demonstrated in the example below.

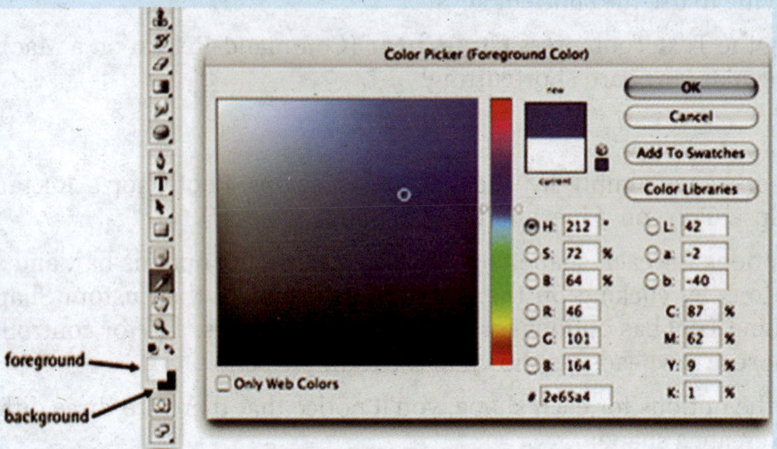

Selecting foreground and background colours using the Colour Picker

Colour Picker Shortcuts

Press X if you want to switch the foreground and background colours. Press D if you want to revert to a black foreground and white background.

Eyedropper

The Eyedropper Tool (I) lets you sample another colour from your image, and set this as the foreground colour. In fact, it's actually possible to sample colours from anywhere in your display and even from other applications outside of Photoshop. Simply click inside the document window, then drag the cursor to the colour you wish to sample. Click to select that colour.

The Eyedropper Tool also allows you to set the background colour. To do so, hold down the Alt key (Option key on a Mac) as you select colours using the eyedropper.

The Paint Brush, Pencil, Paint Bucket and any of the other painting or drawing tools can temporarily be turned into the Eyedropper Tool by holding down Alt (Option).

The Hand Tool

The Hand Tool (H) moves your canvas, which is handy (pardon the pun!) when you're zoomed in to an image, or have a very large document open.

What's even handier is the fact that you can invoke the Hand Tool while you're using any other tool (except the Text Tool) by holding down the spacebar. This is a neat way to position your image exactly where you want it without having to chop and change between tools to do so.

Useful Tasks and Shortcuts

In this chapter, we will discuss some important tasks and shortcuts which are used in photoshop.

Zooming

Zooming right into your image is the only way to make subtle changes at the pixel level. Use **Ctrl** + to zoom in and **Ctrl** – to zoom out. You can also zoom using the slider on the Navigator palette.

Making a Selection Using the Layers Palette

To select the pixels on a particular layer, press **Ctrl** (Command on a Mac) and click the thumbnail of the layer. This selection will also take into account the transparency of any pixels, so painting in the selection will recreate the transparency settings of the original layer. The example below shows a selection I made based on one of the text layers in my sunset document.

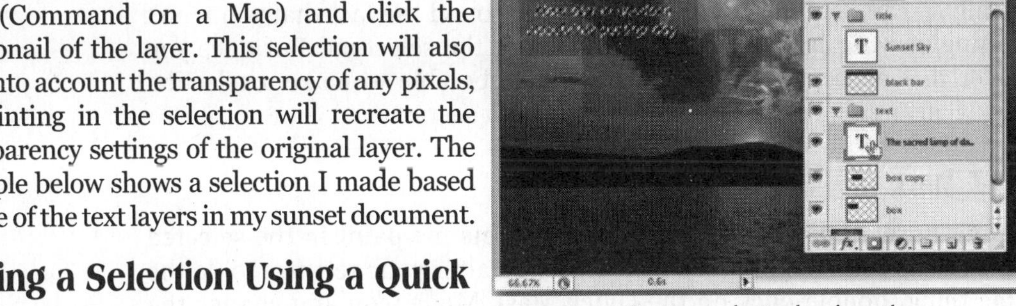

Creating a selection based on a layer

Making a Selection Using a Quick Mask

Quick Masks are one of those closely guarded trade secrets that professional designers use all the time, but beginners often are wary of trying because they seem complicated at first. Well, they're not!

A Quick Mask is an alternative way of making a selection. The usual way to use a Quick Mask is to go into Quick Mask Mode (Q) and, using a tool such as the Brush Tool, painting the things you don't want to select. This is called painting a "mask" and the resulting reverse-selection will display as the transparent red colour that you can see in the example overleaf. You can edit this red layer – honing the mask shape, for instance – using the drawing and painting tools. Those alterations won't affect your image, though: they impact only on your final selection. Switching back to Standard Mode (Q) will complete your selection.

Why would we use this technique instead of those trusty selection tools that we've all come to depend on so heavily? Well, Quick Masks have a couple of advantages over the standard selection tools:

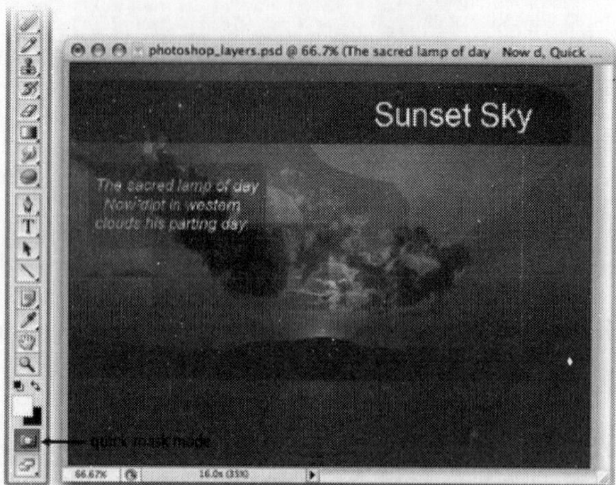

Painting a reverse selection in Quick Mask Mode

- ❑ They allow you to control the level of transparency of your selection.
- ❑ It's easier to colour an object in, than it is to carefully draw a line around it.

Initially, it can be difficult to get your head around the fact that you aren't painting on your image: you're just painting the selection. But once you master that concept, you'll feel confident to be able to make a selection quickly on any shape, no matter how difficult it seems!

Quick Mask Options

I prefer to set Quick Mask Mode so that it lets me paint in the selected areas rather than the non-selected areas. To alter your settings to do the same thing, double-click on the Quick Mask Mode icon and change the Colour Indicates: option to Selected Areas.

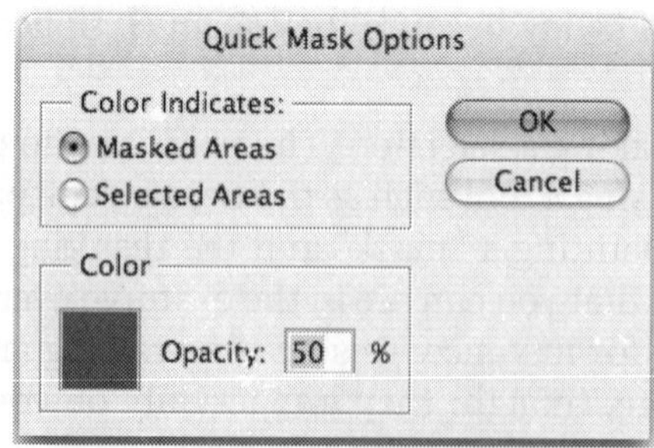

The Quick Mask Options dialog

Returning to Standard Mode

Painted areas are now selected

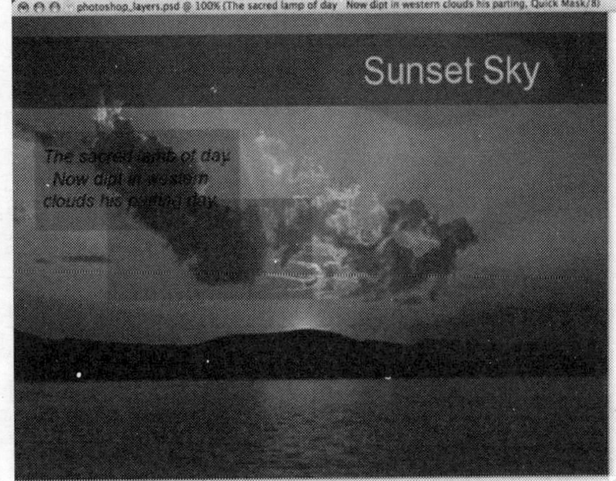

Alpha Channels and Selections

You can use alpha channels to create selections and save them for later use. If you open the Channels palette, you'll see several channels, displayed in a similar way to layers in the Layers palette. By default, you'll see the colour channels, which represent how much of each colour is represented in the document. You can click the Create New Channel icon at the bottom of the palette to create your own alpha channel.

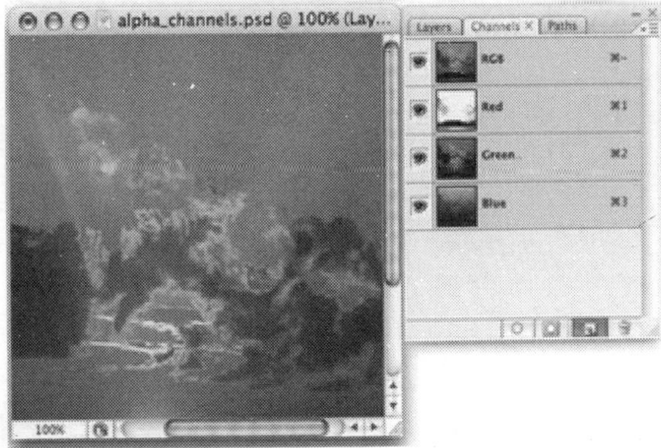

Creating a new alpha channel

You can then use any of Photoshop's painting or drawing tools to create a grayscale image that will represent your selection – white areas represent selected areas, black areas represent deselected areas, and grays represent the levels of transparency in the selection.

To turn your alpha channel masterpiece into a selection, simply hold down Ctrl and click the channel's thumbnail (hold Command and click if you're on a Mac).

To return to the normal image view, click on the Layers palette tab, and select any layer. Your selection will still be visible.

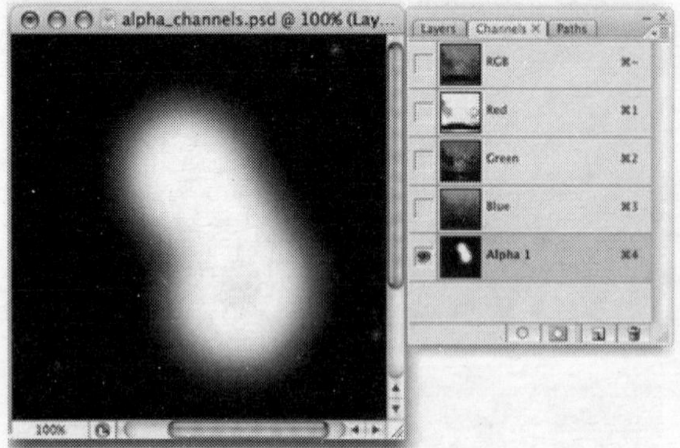

Creating a grayscale image

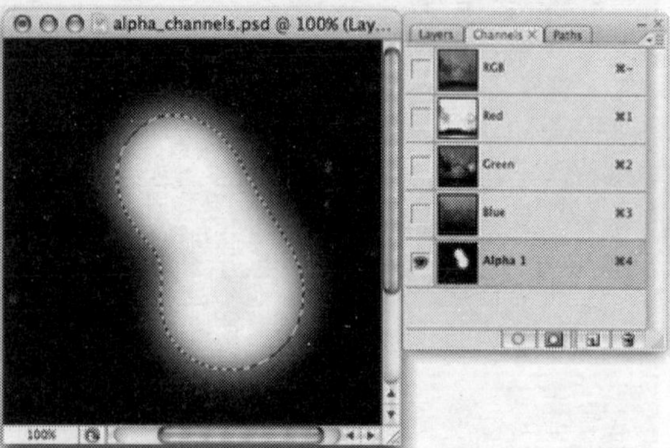

Creating a channel-based selection

You can also create your own alpha channels from existing selections – a capability that can be very useful! For example, let's say you've created a selection of an island silhouette. You have a feeling that you'll be reselecting this island pretty often, but you'd rather not recreate the selection each time. No problem! Once the selection has been made, use **Select > Save Selection.** Name your selection (in this example, Land), and click OK.

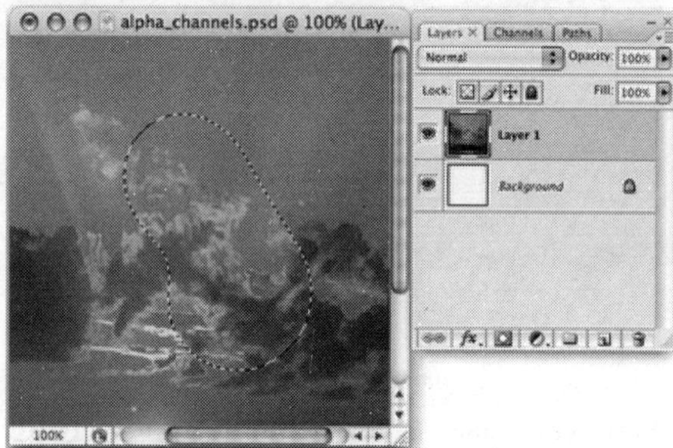

Returning to the Layers palette

Saving the selection to a channel

If you go to the Channels palette, you'll see a new selection at the bottom of the list, named Land in the following image – that's your saved selection. Now you can reload your Land selection as many times as you need to.

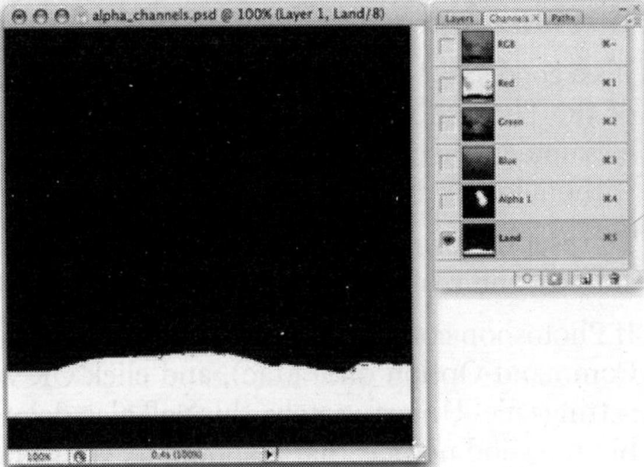
New channel in the Channels palette

The History Palette

The History palette is your key to time travel (in Photoshop, anyway). It lists the most recent steps that you've made, and allows you to undo your actions by rolling your image back to a previous state. You can set the number of steps that are stored in the memory by selecting **Edit > Preferences > Performance** (Photoshop > Preferences > Performance on a Mac) and changing the value in the History States text box.

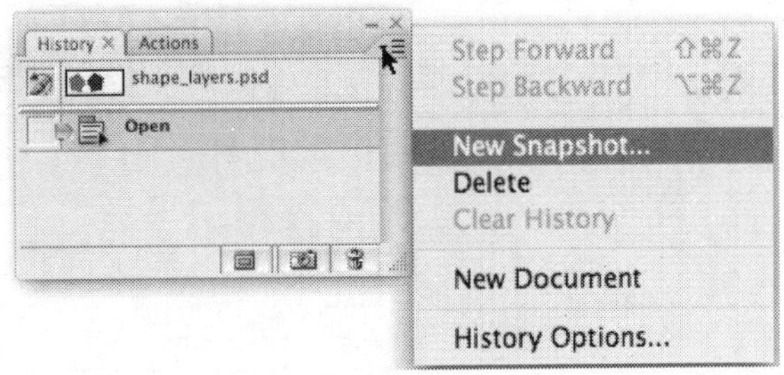

Creating a history snapshot

Like most of Photoshop's other tools, the History palette has a set of useful keyboard shortcuts for quick access:

- **Ctrl-Z** (Command-Z on a Mac) lets you undo and redo the previous step.
- **Ctrl-Alt-Z** (Command-Option-Z) steps back through the History palette.
- **Shift-Alt-Z** (Shift-Option-Z) steps forward through the History palette.

As only a limited number of history states are available, there may be cases in which you want to save a "snapshot" of your document so that you can revert back to it later if required. To do so, click on the small triangle on the top-right of the History palette and choose New Snapshot.... You can save a snapshot of the whole document, the current layer, or merged layers.

When Photoshop Stops Working

Woah! Photoshop stops working? That certainly doesn't sound too promising! Before you panic, let me explain. Given the multitude of powerful features and fantastic tools it offers, it's no wonder that, on occasion, Photoshop can exhaust itself. It may start behaving a bit erratically, and might even freeze, crash, or automatically exit during startup. If you find yourself in this situation, the first thing to do is reset the preferences file. The preferences file (which you can customize by going to **Edit > Preferences** on a PC, or Photoshop > Preferences on a Mac) holds Photoshop settings and can often become corrupted.

The location of the preferences file depends on the operating system and version of Photoshop you are using. For Photoshop CS3, the preferences file is named Adobe Photoshop CS3 Prefs. psp. The preference file for other versions of Photoshop will have a similar name.

Backing Up Your Preferences File

It's a good idea to back up your preferences file by copying and pasting it into a location outside of the Photoshop settings folder. Then, if the preferences file Photoshop is using becomes corrupted, you can copy your backup back into the settings folder to replace the corrupted file, without losing any of your settings.

To reset the preferences file, locate the current preferences file, delete it (while Photoshop is closed), and restart Photoshop – it will recreate the preferences file using default settings.

If Photoshop continues to act up, restart it while holding down the **Shift-Ctrl-Alt** keys (Shift-Command-Option on a Mac), and click OK when asked if you wish to delete the Photoshop settings file. Unfortunately, this will also delete your custom actions, tools, and other settings, but the good news is that it should fix your Photoshop problems.

User interface in Photoshop

We have talked about the Interfaces already. Now let's look over the each one in detail.

The Menu Bar

At the very top of the screen as always is the **Menu Bar**, a common feature of most programs these days. Clicking on the various menu headings brings up a list of related options and commands. For example, the **File** menu is where we find options for opening, saving and closing Photoshop documents. The **Layer** menu contains options for working with layers. Photoshop's many filters can be found under the **Filter** menu, and so on:

Photoshop File Edit Image Layer Select Filter Analysis 3D View Window Help

The Menu Bar in Photoshop CS4 (Extended)

We won't go through all the menu options here since we'd die of boredom and most of the important options and commands are covered in our other lessons. As I mentioned, I'm using the Mac version of Photoshop CS4. The **Photoshop** menu option on the far left, which is where we find Photoshop's **Preferences** on the Mac, is not found in the Windows version. You'll find the Preferences under the **Edit** menu in Windows. Also, the **Analysis** and **3D** menu headings are exclusive to the Extended version of Photoshop CS4 and not found in the Standard version.

The Tools Panel

Along the left side of the screen is Photoshop's **Tools panel**, formerly known as the Tools palette (palettes are now officially known as panels in Photoshop CS4), and also commonly referred to simply as the Toolbox. This is where we find all of the various tools we need for working on our images. In Photoshop CS4, you'll find the Tools panel displayed in a single column, but I've split it in half here just to make it easier to fit on the page.

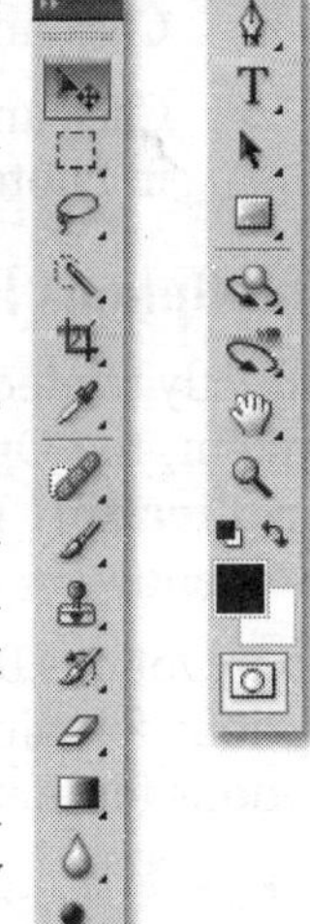

The Tools panel in Photoshop CS4

Again, there's a couple of tools shown here that are exclusive to the Extended version of Photoshop CS4 (the **3D Rotate** and **3D Orbit** tools directly above the Hand Tool), but the majority of the tools are available in both the Standard and Extended versions and most have been around in Photoshop since forever.

Single Or Double Column Layout

Photoshop CS4, like CS3 before this version, gives us a choice of how we want the Tools panel to be displayed. You can leave it in the default single column, or if you prefer, you can click on the small double-arrow icon at the top of the panel which will switch it to a double column layout, handy if you've upgraded from Photoshop CS2 or earlier and you can't get used to the new single column design. Click again on the icon to switch back to a single column:

You can switch between a single or double column layout in Photoshop CS4 ➡

Accessing The Hidden Tools

Photoshop CS4, like earlier versions, comes with so many tools that if Adobe tried to display them all at once, the Tools panel would need its own scroll bar. So instead, Adobe has grouped many related tools together, with one tool in the group visible in the Tools panel and the others hidden behind it. Whenever you see a tool in the Tools panel with a small arrow to the bottom right of the icon, it means there are additional tools behind it waiting to be selected, and if you click and hold your mouse button down on one of these tools, a fly-out menu will appear showing you the additional tools. For example, by clicking and holding on the **Rectangular Marquee Tool** at the top of the Tools panel, a fly-out menu appears giving access to the **Elliptical Marquee Tool**, the **Single Row Marquee Tool** and the **Single Column Marquee Tool**. Simply move your mouse cursor over the name of the tool you want, then release your mouse button to select it:

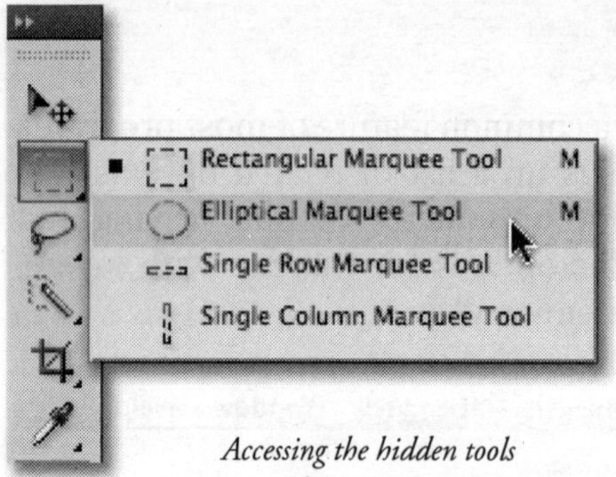

Accessing the hidden tools

- ❑ Click and hold on some tools in the Tools panel to access additional tools behind it.
- ❑ Click and hold on the other tools in the Tools panel to see all of the tools available to us in Photoshop CS4.

The Options Bar

Directly related to the Tools panel is the **Options Bar** at the top of the screen. On a Windows system, the Options Bar is located below the Menu Bar. On a Mac, it's located below the **Application Bar** which is new to Photoshop CS4. We'll look at the Application Bar in a moment.

Your Options Bar may look different from mine, and that's because it always changes to display options for whichever tool you current by have selected. Here, the Options Bar is displaying options for the **Move Tool**:

The Options Bar displays options for the currently selected tool

If I select the **Crop Tool** from the Tools panel, the Options Bar changes to display options for the Crop Tool:

The Options Bar inow displaying options for the Crop Tool

And if I select the **Type Tool**, we see options displayed for the Type Tool:

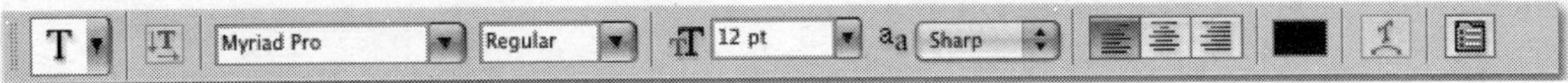

The Options Bar is now displaying options for the Type Tool

Every tool has its own set of options which will always be available in the Options Bar.

The Application Bar

New in Photoshop CS4 is the **Application Bar**. On a Windows system, you'll find the Application Bar combined with the Menu Bar at the top of the screen. On a Mac, the Application Bar is separate and located directly below the Menu Bar:

The new Application Bar in Photoshop CS4

The Application Bar itself may be new, but many of the options you'll find here are not. The bar's main purpose is not really to wow us with new features (although there are some new ones) but to give us a central location for some commonly used features, tools and options rather than having them scattered throughout Photoshop. For example, the first icon on the left (not counting the blue PS icon in the Mac version) will quickly open **Adobe Bridge**:

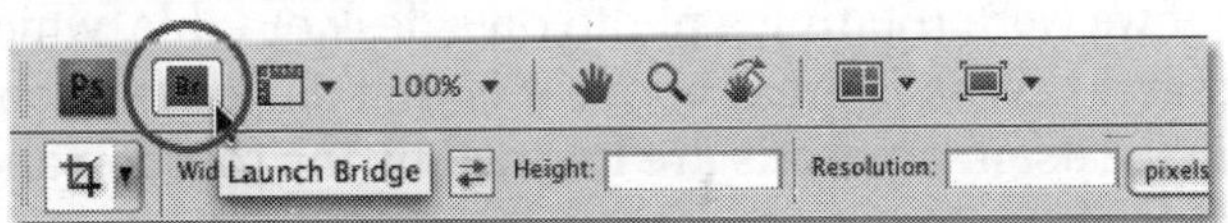

Adobe Bridge icon

We can launch Adobe Bridge directly from the new Application Bar in Photoshop CS4.

To the right of that is the **View Extras** icon, giving us easy access to Photoshop's Guides, Grid and Rulers.

View Extras icon

Use the View Extras icon to quickly turn the Guides, Grid or Rulers on or off.

Next is the **Zoom Level** icon which allows to quickly choose from four preset zoom levels – 25%, 50%, 100% or 200%. You can also type your own zoom level directly into the input box if none of the presets work for you:

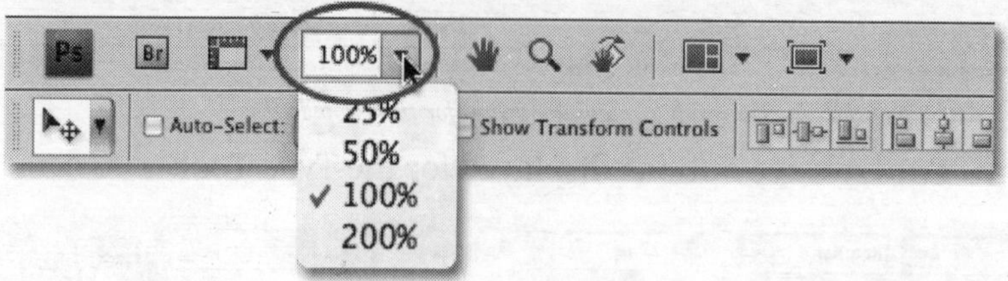

Zoom level icon

The Zoom Level icon gives us four preset zoom levels to choose from, or type your own into the input box.

Also found in the Application Bar are Photoshop's standard **Hand** and **Zoom Tools** which have traditionally been (and still are) found at the bottom of the Tools panel:

Hand & zoom tool

Both the Hand Tool and Zoom Tool from the Tools panel are now available in the Application Bar.

The New Rotate View Tool

Next, we come to a brand new feature in Photoshop CS4, the **Rotate View Tool**, which also happens to be available in the Tools panel (click and hold on the Hand Tool in the Tools panel and select the Rotate View Tool from the fly-out menu). We'll take an in-depth look at this new feature in another lesson, but essentially, the Rotate View Tool allows us to rotate our view of the image on screen as if we were rotating a photo on a desk or table, which can make it easier to paint or edit certain areas. What's great about it is that since we're only rotating our view of the image, not the image itself, no pixels are harmed by the rotation and the image will still save, print and export upright.

Rotate view tool

The new Rotate View Tool allows us to rotate our view of the image without actually rotating the image itself.

The New Multi Document Layouts

Also new in Photoshop CS4 is the **Arrange Documents** icon which gives us lots of new layouts for viewing multiple documents on screen at once. You'll also find some standard viewing options from the Window menu like Match Zoom and Match Location, but the new multi document layouts are a great new feature and we'll look at in more details later.

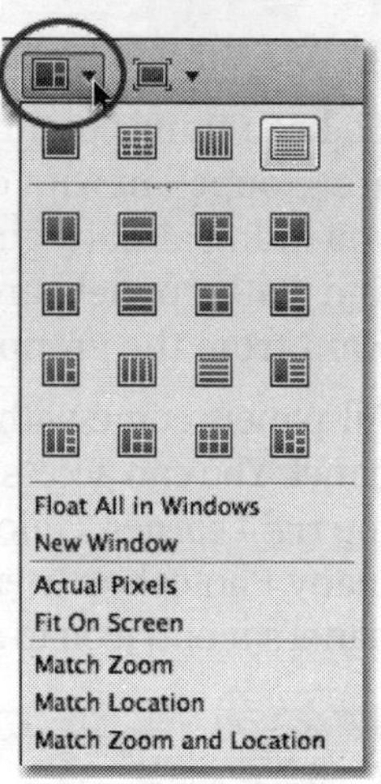

Photoshop CS4 gives us many ways to view multiple documents at once. ➡

Finally, rounding out the options in the new Application Bar is the **Screen Mode** icon, allowing us to quickly choose between Photoshop CS4's three screen modes – **Standard, Full Screen with Menu Bar** and **Full Screen Mode**:

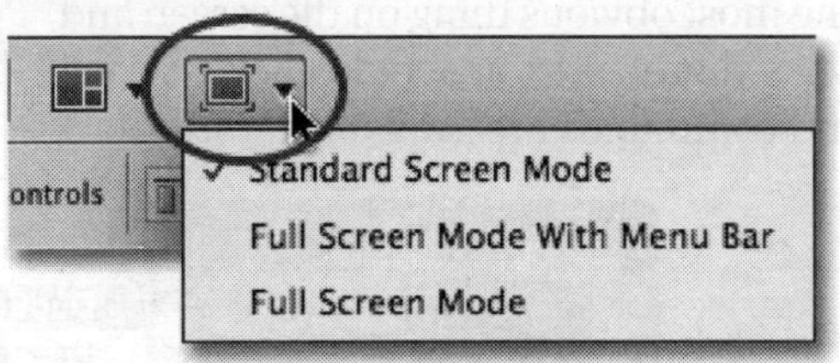

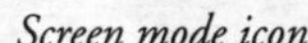

Screen mode icon

You can quickly switch between screen modes directly from the Application Bar in Photoshop CS4.

The Panels

Along the right side of the screen in Photoshop CS4 is where we find the **Panels** column (panels were known as palettes in earlier versions of Photoshop). Panels give us access to all kinds of commands and options for working on our images, from organizing layers and viewing individual colour channels to choosing colours, stepping back through history states, working with text, viewing information about our images, and so on. Most of the panels in Photoshop CS4 are the same ones that have been available in earlier versions of Photoshop, but some, like the **Adjustments Panel**, are brand new to CS4.

By default, only a handful of panels are displayed on the screen to begin with, but you can access any of Photoshop's panels at any time simply by choosing the one you want from the **Window menu** up in the Menu Bar. A checkmark beside a panel's name means it's already open on the screen. Selecting a panel that's already open will close it. A couple of the panels listed below are available only in the Extended version of Photoshop CS4, but most are available in the Standard version.

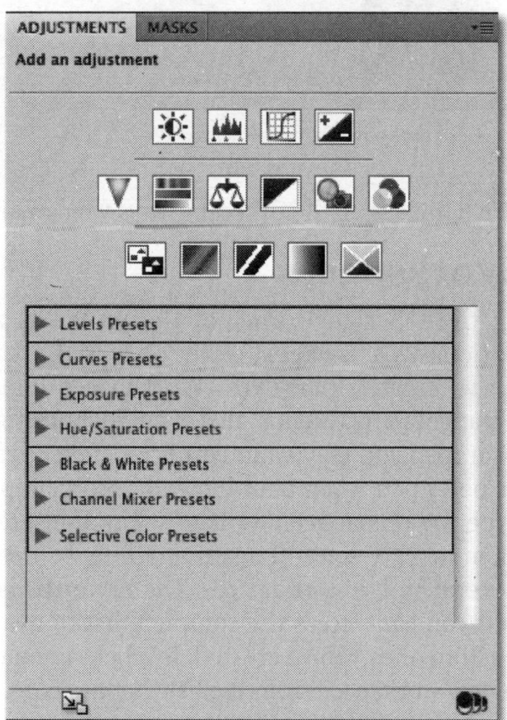

The Adjustments Panel is new to Photoshop CS4

All of Photoshop CS4's panels can be accessed from the Window menu ➡

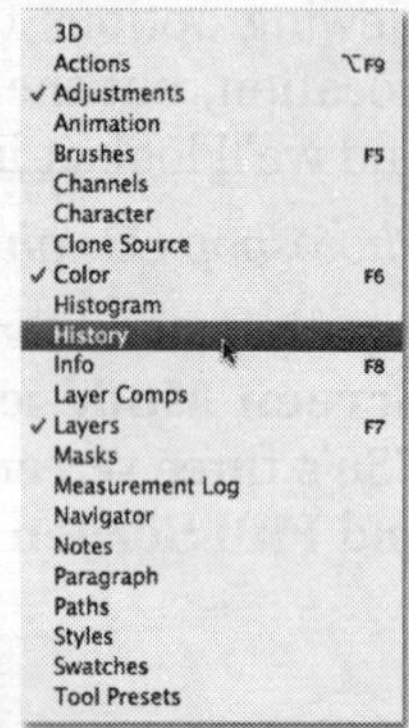

To keep things organized and save screen space, most of Photoshop's panels are grouped in with other related panels. This is known as a **panel group**, if you didn't already guess that on your own. For example, the Layers, Channels and Paths panels are grouped together by default. To select the panel you want from the group, simply click on the panel's name tab at the top.

All panels come with various options and commands that are specific to that panel. You can access these options by clicking on the panel's **menu icon** in the top right corner. Unfortunately, it's not the most obvious thing on the screen and many Photoshop users don't even know it's there, but you should click on each panel's menu icon to see what options and commands are available for it:

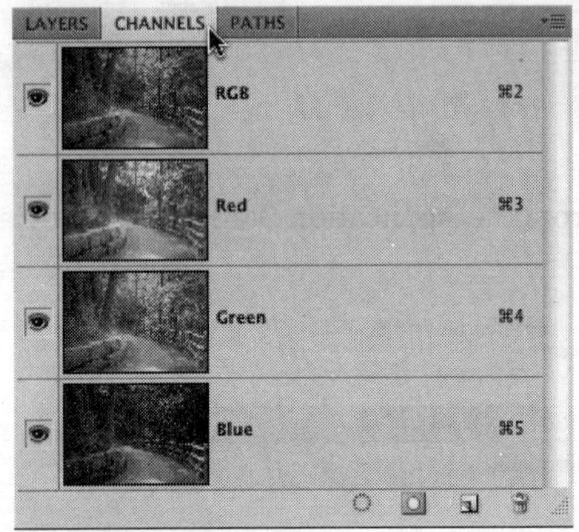

Click on a panel's name tab to select it inside the panel group

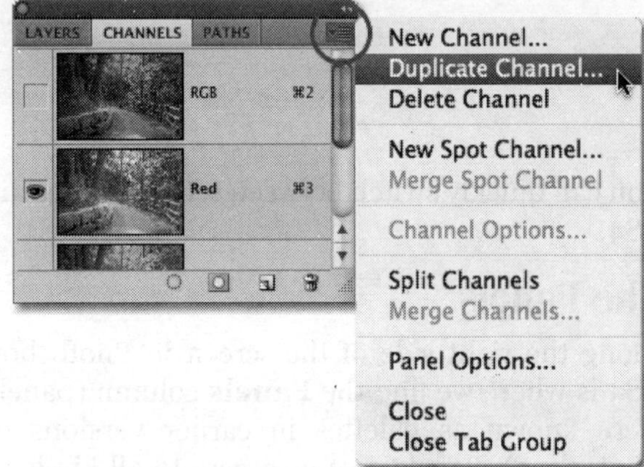

Click on a panel's menu icon to view a list of related options and commands

We'll look at all the different ways we can arrange and organize Photoshop CS4's panels later.

Workspaces

In the top right corner of the screen is an option that allows us to quickly select from various **workspaces**, either ones that are built in to Photoshop CS4 or custom workspaces we've created ourselves. Workspaces allow us to set up different panel arrangements, menus and even keyboard shortcuts for different tasks. For example, you may want certain panels open when editing images and other panels open when painting with Photoshop's brushes or when working with type. Workspaces allow us to set up the screen any way we want, save it, and then quickly select it again anytime we need it. Photoshop CS4 comes with several built in workspaces. The **Essentials** workspace is selected by default but you can access the complete list of available workspaces, including any custom ones you've created, by clicking on the word Essentials and selecting a new workspace from the list that appears. ➡

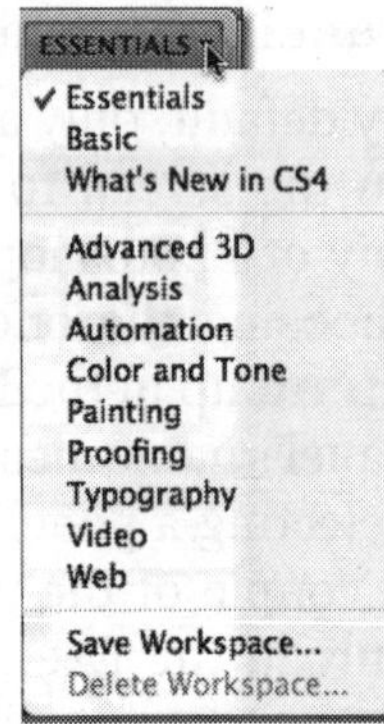

Click on the word "Essentials" in the top right corner of the screen to view all the available workspaces.

The Document Window

The largest and most obvious interface element in Photoshop is the **document window**. The document window is where we view our images and where we do all of our editing work.

Document windows in Photoshop do much more than simply display the image. They also tell us quite a few things about the image. At the top of the document window, you'll find the name of the image, followed by the current zoom level, the colour mode, and the current bit depth.

Each image appears inside its own document window

The top of the document window gives us information about the image

You'll find even more information at the bottom of the document window. In the bottom left corner is the zoom level once again, followed by the current file size of the image, which includes the size with all layers intact and the size if you were to flatten the image. If you click on the right-pointing arrow, then choose **Show**, you'll see a whole list of details about the image you can view, including the document dimensions, colour profile, and even which tool you currently have selected from the Tools panel.

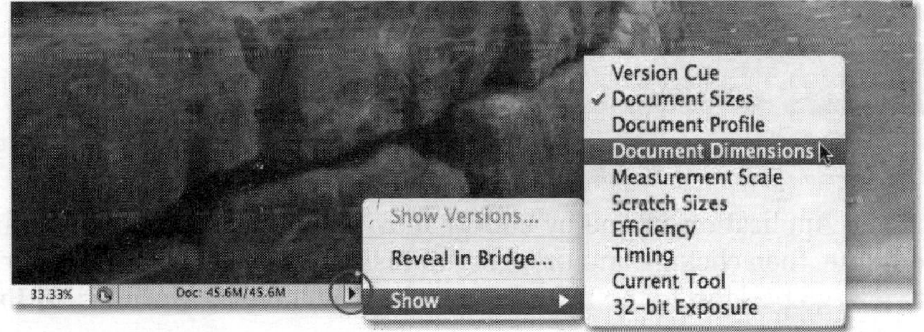

Much more information about the image is available at the bottom of the document window

The Application Frame

The last feature we need to look at in our tour of Photoshop CS4's user interface is the brand new and exclusive to the Mac version of Photoshop CS4, the **Application Frame**. Before Windows users start feeling left out and abandoned by Adobe, what the Application Frame essentially does is give Mac users the Windows experience. The Application Frame places the entire Photoshop interface inside a self-contained application window, which is how it already works in Windows and why this feature is only available in the Mac version.

Traditionally, Mac users have been used to Photoshop's interface elements floating around independently on the desktop, and if you're a Mac user and that's how you prefer to work, there's nothing you need to change. However, if you'd prefer to have Photoshop displayed entirely in its own window, similar to the interface style of Adobe Bridge and Lightroom, simply go up to the **Window** menu in the Menu Bar and choose **Application Frame** down near the bottom of the list of options: ➡

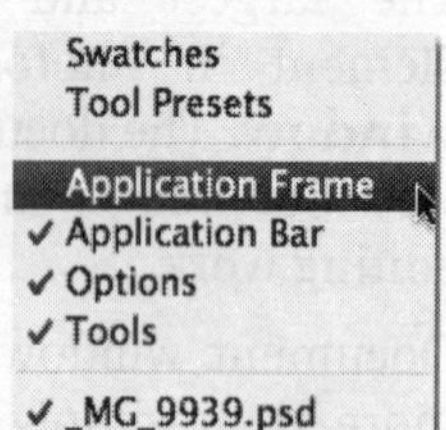

Go to **Window > Application Frame** to place Photoshop inside an independent window. The Application Frame places all interface elements inside a window, and you can move the entire application around on the screen simply by clicking anywhere on the gray bar at the top of the frame and dragging it around:

The Application Frame places all of Photoshop CS4's interface elements inside a self contained, draggable window

You can resize the Application Frame by simply moving your mouse cursor to the edges or corners of the frame, then clicking and dragging to resize it. To exit out of it and return to the Mac's default view, go back up to the **Window** menu and choose **Application Frame** once again to deselect it.

The Tool Box

Now let us learn the tool box in detail.

Anatomy of the Toolbox

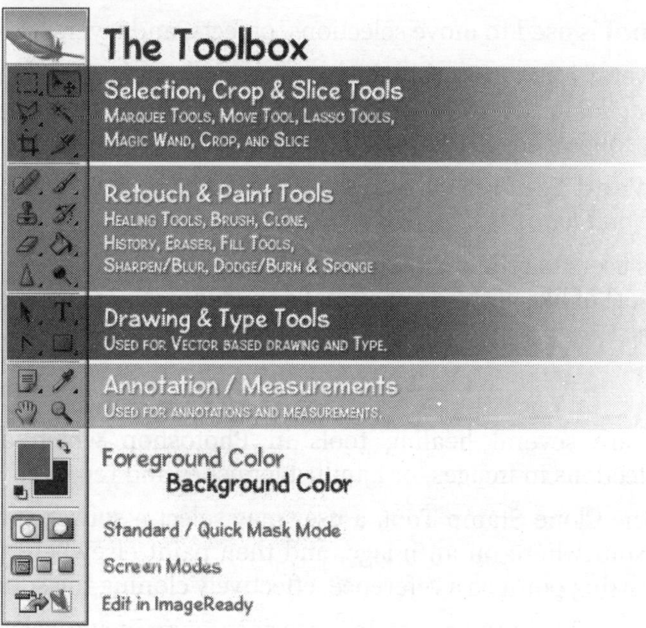

The toolbox in Photoshop is split up into 4 unique categories so that finding the right tool is never a hassle. Those categories are:

- ❑ Selection, Crop & Slice Tools
- ❑ Retouch & Paint Tools
- ❑ Drawing & Type Tools (Vector Tools)
- ❑ Annotations & Measurement Tools

In addition to these 4 sections, a few other components make up the toolbox, most notably, the Foreground and Background colours.

Now that you see how the tools are all organized, let's take a look at some of the most vital tools Photoshop has to offer. This is really just a cursory glance of the toolbox, as we'd be crazy to go into detail for EVERY SINGLE tool Photoshop has to offer in a single lesson, but you ought to now have an understanding what some of the tools are capable of. We'll go over how to use many of these tools in later lessons.

Selection Tools

- The **Marquee Tools** are used for selecting objects such as rectangles, squares, and ellipses.
- The **Move Tool** is used to move selections, objects, and layers.
- There are several **Lasso Tools** which are used to make irregular selections. There is a *polygonal lasso tool* for polygon selections, and a *magnetic lasso tool* which automatically follows edges of objects.
- The **Magic Wand Tool** selects an area of similar colours in a single click (*such as the white in the cloud logo*).

The Crop Tool allows users to redefine their active image area but not resize the ENTIRE image. It's sort of like cutting out a smaller picture from a larger photo with a pair of scissors.

Retouch Tools

There are several healing tools in Photoshop which are used to repair imperfections in images, or handle blemishes and red-eye.

With the Clone Stamp Tool, a user may select a source starting point somewhere on an image, and then paint elsewhere using that starting point as a reference, effectively cloning the source.

The Eraser Tool can be used to erase parts of an image, selection, or layer.

The Sharpen Tool is used to sharpen edges in an image, while the Blur Tool burs edges. The Smudge Tool smudges an image, similar to using fingerpaint.

The Dodge Tool lightens parts of an image while the Burn Tool darkens. The Sponge Tool is used to saturate, or desaturate parts of an image.

Painting Tools

The Brush and Pencil tools are used to paint strokes in graphics. These tools can be highly customized for very effective painting.

The Fill Tools are used to fill entire layers, selections and areas with a solid colour, or gradient.

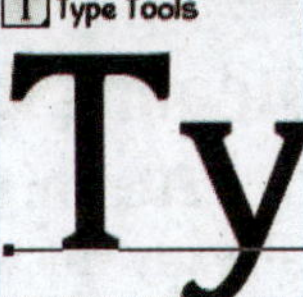

Vector Drawing & Type Tools

The **Type Tools** are used for creating and setting type in an image. Both vertical and horizontal type can be created.

The **Pen Tools** are used to create clear shapes and paths which can be used as vector objects that can be scaled to any size.

Cutom Shapes are vector objects that can be created on the fly from a list of presets (including user created shapes).

Foreground / Background Colour

A foreground colour and background colour can be set to be used to paint with, colour text, and fill objects among other things. This view provides an easy way to see what colours are currently selected, and allows for easy switching between two different colours.

Using Tools

To actually use a tool varies from case to case (again, we'll be covering nearly everything you'd want to know in the future lessons). To Select a Tool from the toolbox, simply click it once. If the tool displayed has a black arrow in the bottom right corner, that means that there are more tools of that type hidden underneath it. To select one of these hidden tools, *hold down the mouse button while over it*, and then release once you're over the tool you'd like to select.

Retouch & Healing Tools

Photoshop offers a large selection of tools and features for retouching photographs and images. In this discussion, you'll learn how to use the common touch-up tools.

Spot Healing Brush Tool

The **Spot Healing Brush** is primarily used to quickly remove blemishes, imperfections or other unwanted elements from an image. To use it, *paint* over an imperfection you'd like to get rid of

Spot Healing Brush tool

using a suitable brush (*brushes can be selected and modified in the options bar*). The Spot Healing Brush Tool will automatically try to repair the imperfection by sampling the surrounding area.

Careful! Although the Spot Healing brush can be a great tool for quick fixes, it's not always guaranteed to work if the area surrounding the imperfection is busy. Generally speaking, the surrounding area should be an approximate match in colour and texture to what you want to take place of the unwanted element in your image.

Healing Brush Tool

The **Healing Brush Tool** performs a similar function to the spot healing brush tool mentioned already. Instead of automatically trying to determine the lighting, shading, and texture from the surrounding area, the healing brush tool lets you manually select a source, and then paint over an imperfection. To select a source, hold Alt and click the desired part of the image. Then paint over the area you wish to replace. As with the Spot Healing Brush Tool, settings such as brush size can be controlled in the *options bar*.

Healing Brush tool

Patch Tool

With the **Patch Tool**, an entire area can be repaired with pixels from another area. Just like the healing brush tool, the patch tool will try to correct lighting, shading, and texture. To use the patch tool, first **draw a selection** with any of the selection tools (or the patch tool, which will function as a lasso tool). Then, using the **patch tool**, **drag that selection** over the destination you want to use to repair that area.

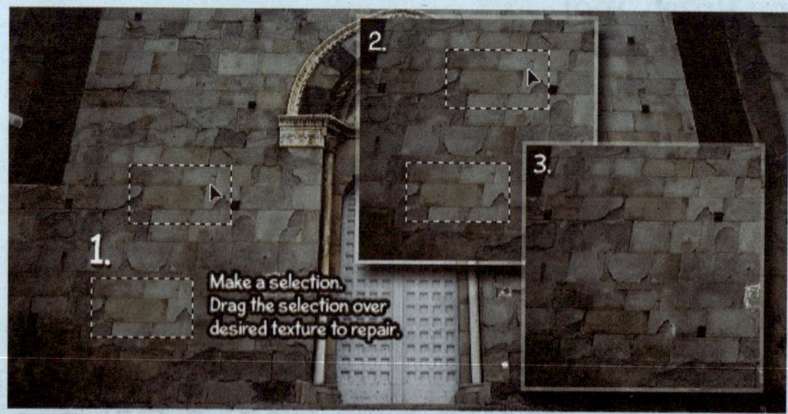

Patch tool

Clone Stamp Tool

The final tool we'll cover in this lesson is called the **Clone Stamp Tool**. The Clone stamp tool allows you to paint with a sample of an image.

Clone Stamp tool

Keep in mind that you are not healing/repairing an image when you use the Clone Stamp Tool. Therefore, **lighting and shading will not be maintained** when you paint over an area. What you see is literally what you get when you paint from a given source, making it very useful in certain situations.

Blur & Sharpen Tools

The **Blur** and **Sharpen Tools** allow us to manipulate edges by making them softer or harder. They do exactly what you would expect them to do – blur and sharpen.

Both tools have similar attributes such as *Strength* (increase or decrease the strength of the tool, or how much it will blur) and the *brush*, all of which can be adjusted in the *Options Bar* for each tool. To use the blur or sharpen tool, simply set up the brush to your specification, hold down the mouse button, and hover over the areas you'd like to alter in your image.

Blur & Sharpen tool

You should have a pretty good feel of the basic retouching tools by now. The next step in mastering Photoshop is usually learning how to use the painting tools to compliment your photo re-mastering abilities!

Pen Tools

Click on the canvas to create paths with straight segments, click and drag to create paths with Bezier curves.

Freehand Pen tool: Click on the canvas and drag to draw paths freely, as though using a brush.

Add Anchor Point tool: Click on a path segment to add anchor point.

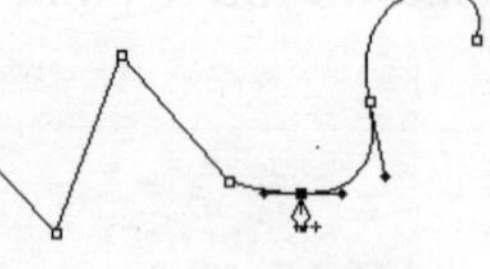

Delete Anchor Point tool: Click on anchor point to remove from path.

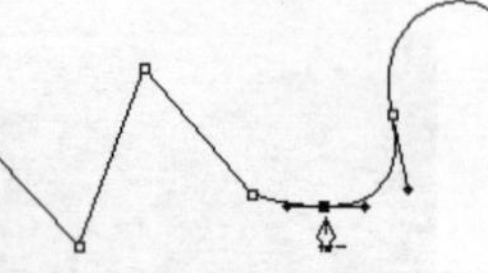

Convert Point tool: Click on an anchor point and drag to create bezier handles, where there were none, click on an anchor point with handles to remove them.

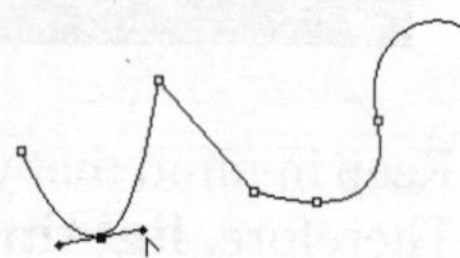

Let's Acquaint ourselves with The Cursors

The Pen tool takes on different forms depending on what you're doing when you're using it. Each one intuitively makes you aware of the action you are about to perform.

(*Caps Lock* to toggle between pointer and cross hair in some cases)

❑		Prepared to begin path
❑		While midway through creating or editing a path
❑		When mouse is pressed
❑		Add an anchor point to path
❑		Remove anchor point from path
❑		When hovered over begin point of path; to close path
❑		When hovered over endpoint of existing path; to continue path, or (if path is active) to edit that point
❑		Prepared to convert existing anchor point
❑		Freehand Pen Tool
❑		Magnetic Freehand Pen Tool
❑		Direct Selection Tool; Pen Tool with *Command* pressed
❑		Path Selection Tool; Pen Tool with *Command* + *Alt* pressed
❑		When hovered over canvas with *Ctrl* pressed; prepared for options menu

Learn Secondary Mouse Controls (with path selected and Auto Add/Delete checked)

- ❑ *Pen tool hover over anchor point*: changes to Delete anchor point tool
- ❑ *Pen tool hover over path segment*: changes to Add anchor point tool

Keyboard Controls used while using Pen Tool

- ❑ Hold *Ctrl* and click on canvas. Opens up options menu.
- ❑ Hold *Shift* to constrain movements to 45°, 90°, 135° or 180° while creating or editing anchor points and handles.
- ❑ Select anchor point with Direct selection tool and click *Delete*. Anchor and adjoining path segments are deleted leaving two paths.
- ❑ Pen tool + *Option (Alt)*: changes to Convert anchor point tool.
- ❑ Pen tool + *Option (Alt)* while editing bezier curve: splits curve (unhinges handles).
- ❑ Pen tool + *Command* whilst creating path: changes to Direct Selection tool allowing repositioning of previously drawn anchor points.

Options

The Options Bar (*Window > Options*), usually located at the top of your screen, provides the most important options for whichever tool is selected. This is also true of the Pen Tools and their options are outlined below:

- ❑ **Presets:** Allows presets to be saved for whichever tool is selected. Define the options as discussed below and save as a Preset to quickly come back to those settings later.

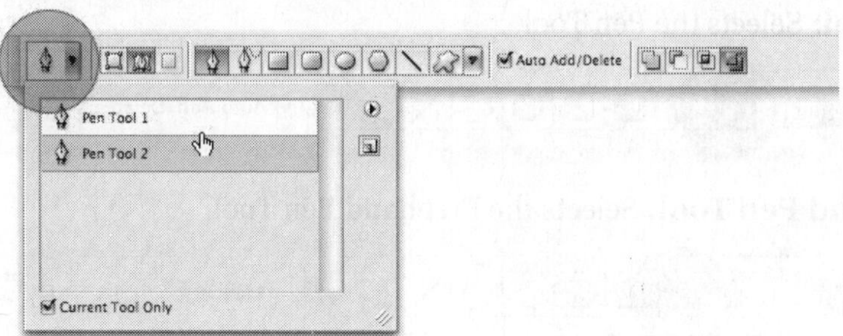

- ❑ **Shape Layers:** While this is selected, paths created will contribute to a shape, visible within the *Paths* palette and within the *Layers* palette as a vector mask.

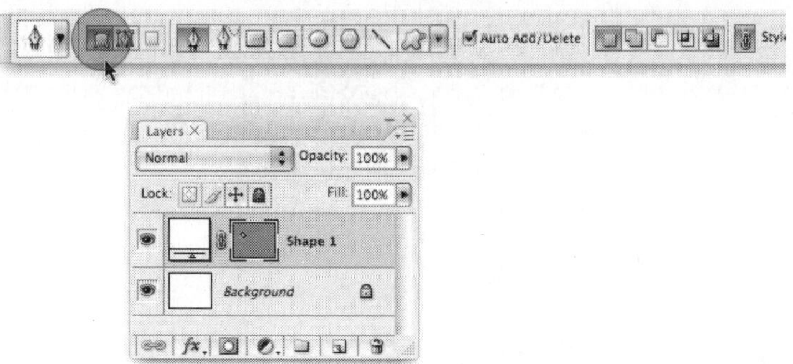

- **Paths:** While this is selected, paths created will contribute to a path, visible within the *Paths* palette.

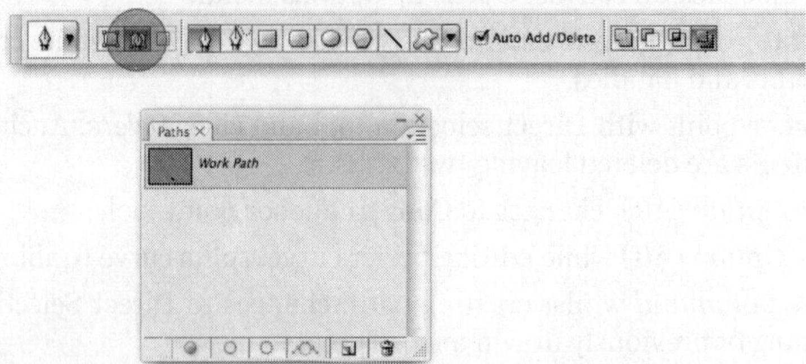

- **Fill Pixels**: The third path type option, available while one of the shape tools is selected. While this is selected, paths created will become filled areas.

- **Pen Tool:** Selects the Pen Tool.

- **Freehand Pen Tool:** Selects the Freehand Pen Tool.

- **Rubber Band:** Available from within the Pen Options dropdown while the Pen Tool is selected. Rubber Band gives a visual of the path you're about to create, without you having the cursor pressed on the canvas.

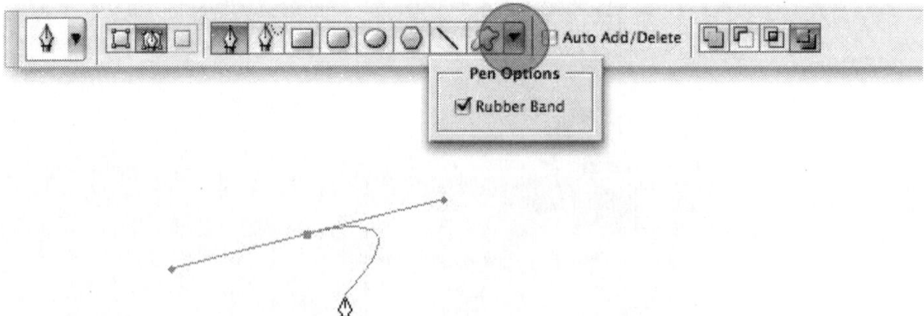

- **Curve fit:** Available from within the Freehand Pen Options dropdown while the Freehand Pen Tool is selected. Value entered determines the accuracy to which bezier handles will be added to your freely drawn path. The higher the value, the more accurate your result will be. A value of between 0.5 and 10 pixels is required.

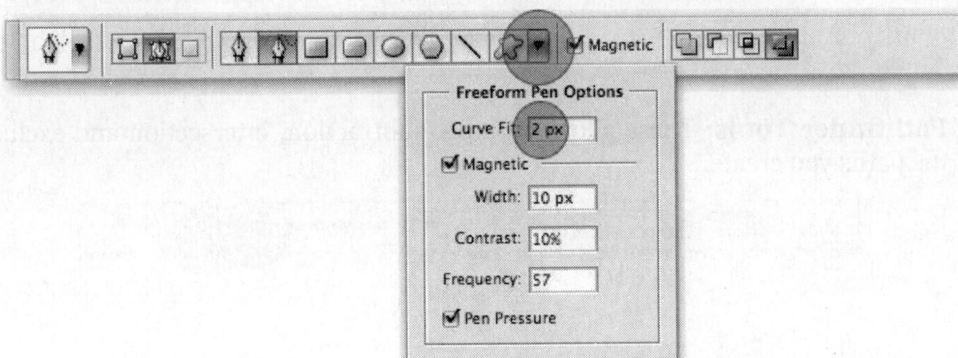

- **Magnetic:** Available from the Options bar and within the Freehand Pen Options dropdown while the Freehand Pen Tool is selected. When selected, paths drawn will *magnetize* to pixels. The Magnetic settings determine the width of the area the path is prepared to jump across, the contrast of the pixels necessary to attract the path and the frequency of anchor points added to the path.

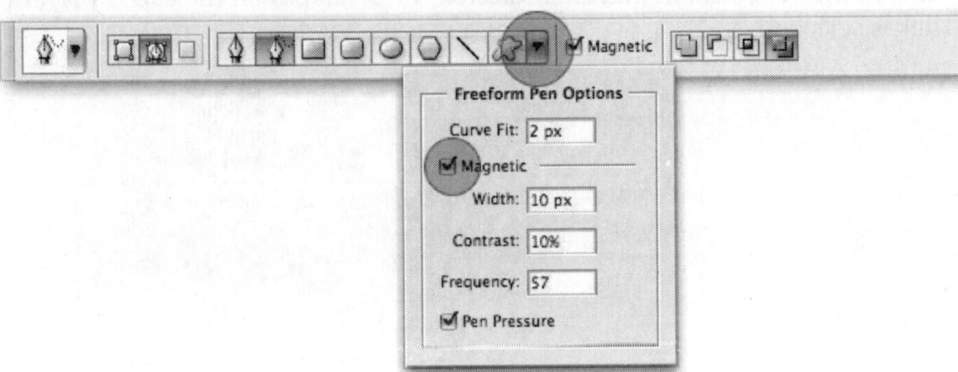

- **Pen Pressure:** Available from within the Freehand Pen Options dropdown while the Freehand Pen Tool is selected. When selected, the pressure applied to a graphics tablet (if you're using one) influences the pen width.

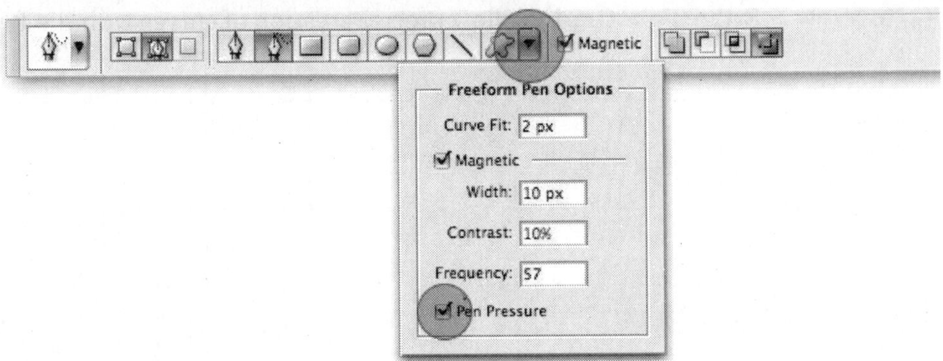

- ❑ **Auto Add/Delete:** Available when the Pen Tool is selected; allows adding and removing of anchor points with the normal Pen Tool *(see Secondary Mouse Controls)*.

- ❑ **Pathfinder Tools:** These allow addition, subtraction, intersection and exclusion of the paths you create.

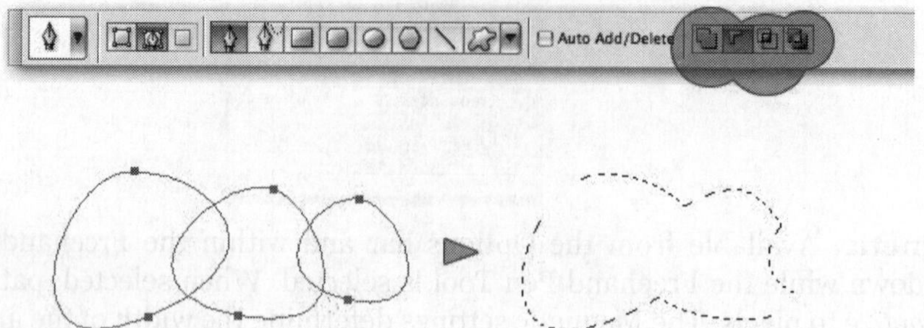

- ❑ **Layer Style:** Available when Shape Layer is selected; this applies layer styles to shapes on a new layer (if chain link is unselected) or to shapes on the current layer (if chain link is selected).

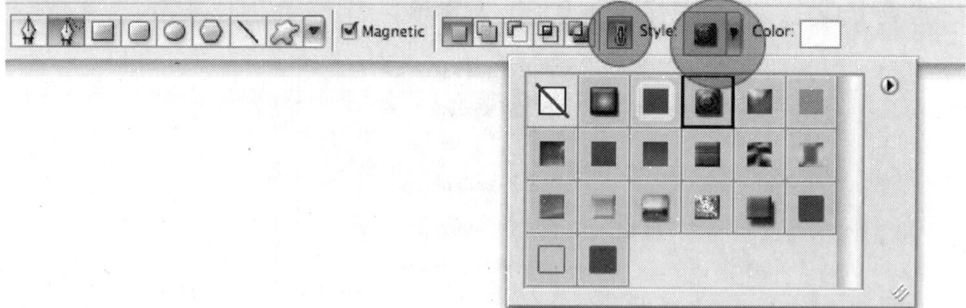

Other Shortcuts and Tips

- ❑ (With path selected) *Spacebar* to give you access to the Hand tool. Move your screen without deselecting the path or changing tools.
- ❑ Go to **View > Snap To > Grid** to allow precise creation of curves with the Pen Tool.

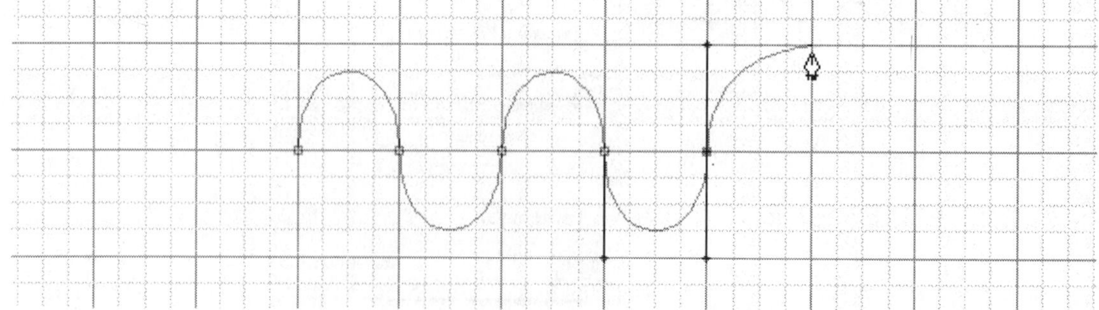

Best Practice Suggestions

- ❏ Drag handles from the first anchor point when beginning a curved path.
- ❏ Drag your handles around just one third of the curve you're creating for a smooth path.

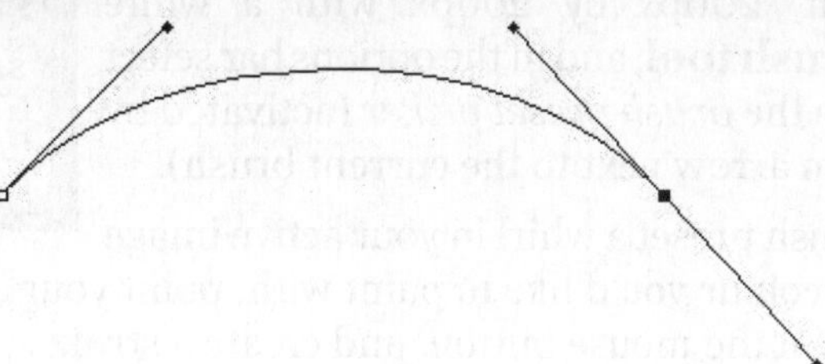

- ❏ Position anchor points on a curve where the paths begin to change direction, not in the middle of its curve.

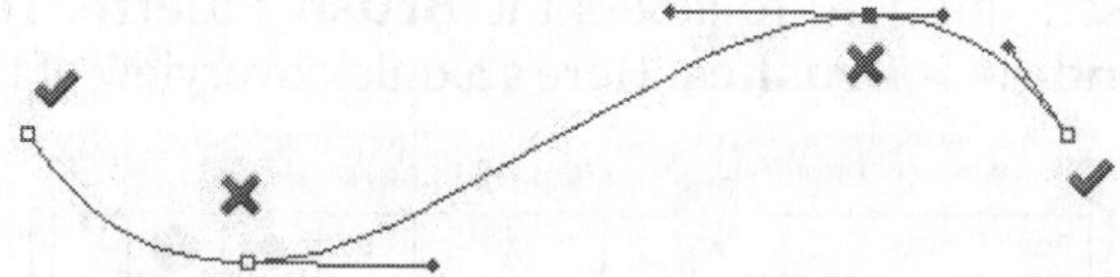

- ❏ Be sparing with your use of anchor points, fewer points = neater path.

Photoshop Painting Tools

In Photoshop, the painting tools are used to paint strokes, and fill areas with colour or with colours that blend together. Knowing how to use the paint tools is a must for any artist who wishes to use Photoshop. We have already discussed a bit about it earlier, let's discuss it in detail.

The Brush Tool

A predefined brush tip.

Creates a perfect match!

In order to use the **brush tool** to its full extent, it's important to understand *what* exactly a brush is in Adobe Photoshop. A **brush** uses **brush presets** that are predefined (or user defined). A **brush preset** is any brush tip with defined characteristics (such as size and shape).

Think of brushes in Photoshop as a large collection of different paintbrushes, each with a different shaped tip. Imagine when you press the tip of one of these paintbrushes against a canvas, the shape of the tip is imprinted immediately. It's a rough explanation, but it gets the *basic idea* across.

Brushes in Photoshop have plenty of other characteristics which make them entirely unlike a real world paint brush. By manipulating these attributes, we can create entirely new brushes that act in unique ways. You could create a brush that changes in shape and size as you are painting, a brush that scatters itself in random directions, and even a brush that becomes more and less transparent while creating strokes. *The possibilities are literally endless.*

Let's Create a Quick Brush for demonstration purposes

Create a new document, 200px by 200px with a white background. Select the **Brush tool**, and in the options bar select the first brush preset from the *brush preset picker* (activated by clicking on the small down arrow next to the current brush).

Go ahead and give this brush preset a whirl in your active image area. Select a foreground colour you'd like to paint with, point your cursor to where you'd like to start painting, hold down the mouse button, and create a stroke.

Modifying Brushes

This brush preset creates a 1px *hard* stroke. We can modify some of the characteristics of this brush to create something entirely different.

To modify a brush preset, you need to access the **Brush Palette**. To open the brush palette, go to **Window > Brushes**. Here's a quick overview of the palette.

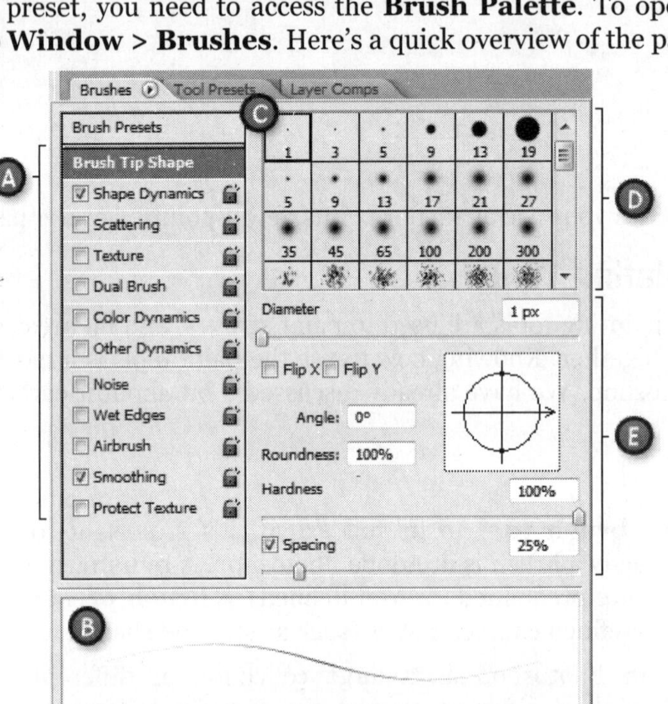

Modifying Brushes

A. Brush Settings – Various settings for the selected brush tip.

B. Brush Stroke Preview – A preview of the current brush stroke will look when used.

C. Selected Brush Tip – The currently selected brush tip.

D. Brush Tip Shapes – A list of all brush tip shapes available.

E. Brush Options – Options for modifying the currently selected brush tip. Changes will not be permanent unless a new brush preset is saved.

From the **Brush Tip Shape** settings, a user can select a brush tip shape from a list of available shapes (predefined or user defined).

By clicking any of the various **brush settings** on the left, a panel of *options* will be displayed that can be adjusted to your own preference.

In the **Brush Tip Shape** area, set the diameter of your brush to 20px. By changing the diameter, you affect the size of the brush.

Now go to **Shape Dynamics** and set the *size jitter* option to 100%. By changing shape dynamics, you're adjusting how a brush mark changes during a stroke.

Finally, go to **Scattering**, and set *scatter* to 300% with a *count* of 1. Scattering will affect placement and number of brush marks.

Try painting with your brush now, and you ought to see a huge difference from when you first started. Modifying brushes is really that simple!

Eraser Tool

We're not going to go into too much detail with the eraser tool, simply because you should already have a pretty good understanding of how it works. *How so?*

Well, like many other tools in Photoshop, the **Eraser Tool** uses brushes which effect the size, shape, and hardness of the tool. Essentially, the eraser tool is controlled in the exact same way as the brush tool, only it erases rather than paints. **Watch Out!** If you're erasing directly on the **"Background"** layer, you'll leave the currently selected **background colour** wherever you erase. Always be sure to set your background colour before erasing from the Background layer.

Paint Bucket Tool

The **Paint Bucket Tool** is used for filling areas with solid colours. It can be used to fill selections with a selected foreground colour, or fill areas that are similar in colour to the part of an image that is clicked. To use the paint bucket tool, select a foreground colour you'd like to paint with, and click anywhere in the active image area you'd like to fill.

Paint Bucket tool

Gradient Tool

The **Gradient Tool** is very similar to the paint bucket tool, in that it fills entire areas or selections with colours. However, rather than filling an area with a solid colour, the Gradient Tool creates a series of colours than blend into one another.

When the gradient tool is selected, a preset gradient can be selected from the **gradient picker** in the options bar. A gradient can then be created in the active image area by clicking and holding the mouse button, and dragging in the direction you'd like the gradient to go. Release where you'd like the gradient to stop.

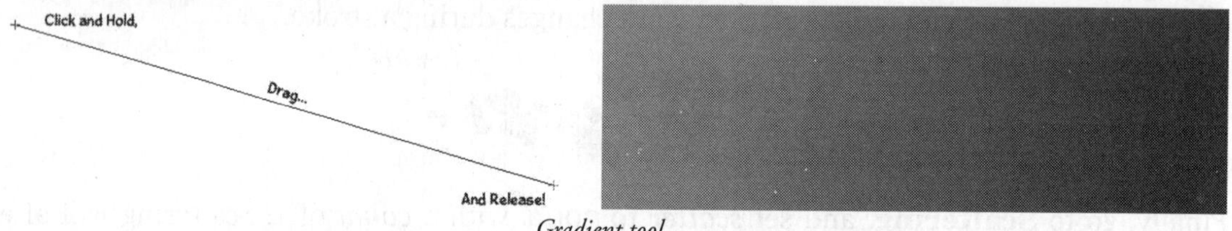

Gradient tool

There are 5 different **gradient styles** which can be selected to create different effects. You can set them from the Options Bar.

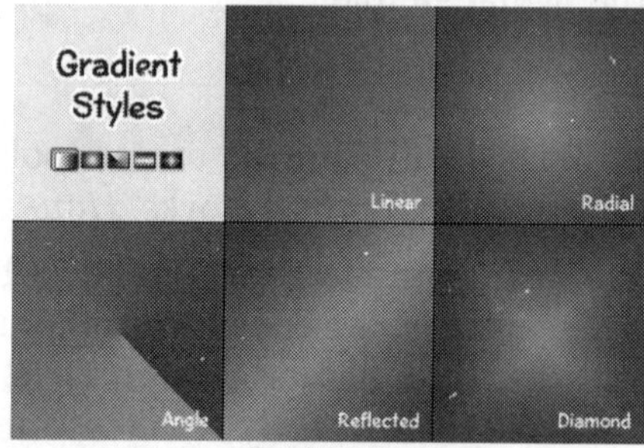

Gradient Style

Photoshop Colour Replacement Tool

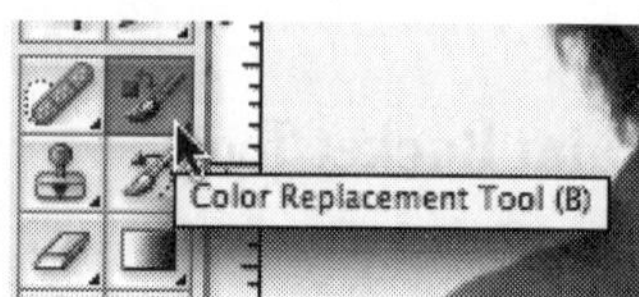

Some tools don't get enough attention, this tool might be one of them. You could compare it somehow with the Healing Brush, although there is a difference. This tool **works like a regular paint brush**, it manipulates the colour on your image while the underlying texture stays unaffected. Because of this, you can apply a colour change in a preciser way.

If you select the tool in the Toolbox, you'll get to see the various options in the Options bar like different Modes to work with in which the **Replace Colour Tool** can be applied – Hue, Saturation, Colour and Luminosity. The Hue will apply the replacement in the most subtle way, while the Colour mode might result in a far too vibrant effect.

Sampling determines the source for the colour replacement. "**Continuous**" means you will be continuously sampling as you go. "**Background Swatch**" uses the background swatch as a pre-defined sample colour. Only areas containing the current background colour will be replaced. "**Once**" will replace the targeted colour only in areas containing the colour that you've first clicked.

You also have **Limits** options. "**Contiguous**" will replace colours that are contiguous with the colour immediately under the pointer. "**Discontinuous**" will replace the sample colour under the pointer wherever you go. "**Find Edges**" will replace connected areas containing the sampled colour while preserving the sharpness of the shape edges.

The **Tolerance** is a bit like with other tools, the higher the percentage the broader the range and the more colours will be replaced. Check the anti-aliasing option to get softer edges, although it could give you a less precise result. You can use the "**Find Edges**" options to limit the anti-aliasing.

The foreground colour will be used as your new colour that will replace the unwanted colour.

Before and after

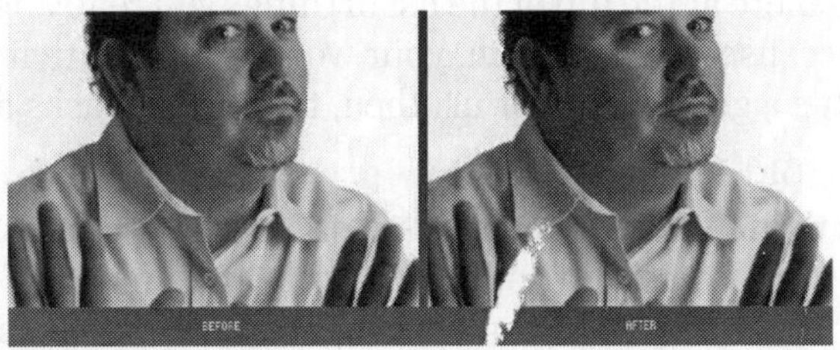

This is what needed to be done:

- Choose the "Once" option for the more dangerous areas and the "Continuous" for the safer areas
- Used the "Hue" mode for a more subtle replacement (the others will create pretty drastic results)
- Used the "Colour" mode in combination with a less vibrant colour to enhance the pink colour of the shirt
- Used the "Background Swatch" sampling option to resolve the grey areas

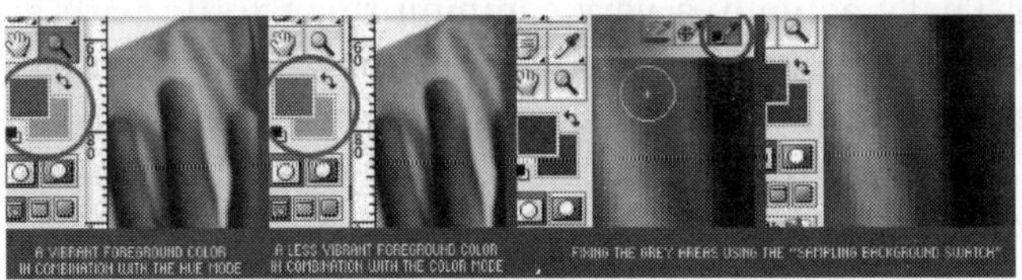

Understanding Layer Masks in Photoshop

In this discussion, we're going to look at one of the most essential features in all of Photoshop – **layer masks**. We'll cover exactly what layer masks are, how they work, and why you want to use them. If you've been staying away from using layer masks with your Photoshop work because you thought they were somehow beyond your skill level, well, if you know the difference between black and white and can paint with Photoshop's Brush Tool, you already have all the skills you need!

Layer masks are right up there at the top of the list of things you really need to know about when working in Photoshop because without them, your work, your creativity and your flexibility all suffer. It's that simple. It's a good thing for us, then, that layer masks are so incredibly simple and easy to understand!

So what are layer masks then? Well, if the term "mask" is what's confusing you (and who could blame you), replace the word "mask" in your mind with "transparency", because that's exactly what a layer mask does. It allows you to control a layer's level of transparency. That's it, that's all. There's nothing more to them than that. Now, you may be thinking, "But... I can already control the transparency level with the Opacity option, can't I?", and yes, you certainly can. The Opacity option in the top right corner of the Layers palette also allows you to control a layer's transparency.

But here's the difference. The Opacity option changes the transparency level for the entire layer at once. If you lower the Opacity level down to, say, 50%, the entire layer becomes 50% transparent. That may be fine for some situations, but what if you want only *part* of a layer to be transparent? What if you want the left side of the layer to be completely transparent, the right side to be completely visible, with a gradual transition between the two through the middle of the layer? That's actually a very common thing to do with a layer in Photoshop, allowing you to fade from one image to another. But you can't do that with the Opacity option since as I said, it's limited to controlling the transparency of the entire layer at once. What you would need is some way to control the transparency of different areas of the layer separately. What you would need is a layer mask.

Let's look at an example. Here I have a couple of wedding photos that I think would work well blended together. Here's the first one:

And here's the second one:

In order to blend them together, whether I'll be using a layer mask or not, I need to have both photos inside the same Photoshop document so with each photo open in its own separate document window, I'm simply going to press V on the keyboard to select the Move Tool and then click inside one of the documents and drag that photo into the document containing the other photo:

Dragging one photo into the same Photoshop document as the other photo with the Move Tool

Now both photos are in the same Photoshop document, and if we look in the Layers palette, we can see that each one is on its own separate layer, with the photo of the couple facing towards the camera on top and the photo of the couple walking away from us into the woods below it:

Photoshop's Layers palette showing each photo on its own separate layer ➡

So far, so good. Now, how am I going to blend these two photos together? Well, let's see what happens if I simply try lowering the opacity of the top layer. I'm going to lower it to about 70% just to see what sort of effect I end up with:

Lowering the opacity of the top layer to blend it with the layer below it ➡

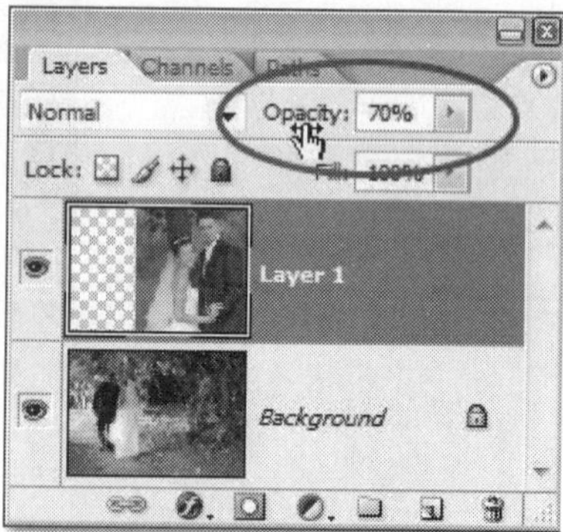

Here's my result:

The image on the bottom is now showing through the image on the top layer.

After lowering the opacity of the top layer (which again contains the image of the couple facing towards the camera on the right), the image on the bottom layer of the couple walking in the woods is now showing through the image above it. This effect may work if I was trying to turn the wedding couple into a couple of ghosts, but it's not really what I was hoping for, so I'm going to raise the opacity of the top layer back to 100% to make the top image fully visible once again. Let's try something else.

So far in our quest to blend our two photos together, we've tried lowering the opacity of the top layer with disappointing results, since all that basically did was fade the entire image. What I really want is for the couple in both images to remain fully visible, with the blending of the two images happening in the area between the bride walking away from us on the left and her looking towards us on the right. I know, why don't I just use Photoshop's Eraser Tool! That's what I'll do. I'll use the Eraser Tool with nice, soft edges to erase the part of the image on the right that I don't need. Yep, this should work.

I'll press E on my keyboard to quickly select the Eraser Tool. As I said, I want soft edges for my Eraser, so I'm going to hold down my Shift key and press the left bracket key a few times, which softens the edges. I can also increase or decrease the size of the Eraser as needed using the left bracket key on its own to make the Eraser smaller and the right bracket key to make it larger (the same keyboard shortcut works with any of Photoshop's brush tools). And now that I have my Eraser at the right size and with soft edges, I'll go ahead and erase away parts of the left side of the top image so that it blends in with the image below it:

Erasing parts of the left side of the top image so it blends seamlessly with the image below it

After finishing up with my Eraser, here's my result:

After erasing away part of the top image, both images now seem to blend together well.

Things definitely look much better now than they did when we tried lowering the opacity of the top layer. The couple is still visible in both images with a nice transition area in the middle, which is what I wanted. The Eraser Tool worked great! Who needs layer masks! I'm happy with this. But when I asked experts to comment, they said they like the image overall, but they think I've removed too much of the bride's veil from the photo on the right and they'd like me to bring some of it back into the image. I said "No problem!" and head back to my computer, open my Photoshop document back up, and all I need to do now is bring back some of the bride's veil on the right. Uh oh. How do I do that when I've gone and erased that part of the image?

Simple answer? I can't. Not without doing the whole thing over again, anyway, which would be my only option in this case. There's nothing else I can do here because I've erased that part of the image and when you erase something in Photoshop, it's gone for good. If I look in the top layer's preview thumbnail in the Layers palette, I can see that I have in fact erased that part of the image.

The preview thumbnail of the top layer shows the left part of the top image now missing.

And if I click on the eyeball icon to the left of the bottom layer to temporarily turn it off, leaving only the top layer visible in my document, it's very easy to see that the section I erased from the left of the top image is now completely gone:

The checkerboard pattern in the image above is how Photoshop represents transparency in an image, as in there's nothing there anymore. As in I've messed up and now I have to do the work all over again from the beginning. Stupid Eraser Tool.

So now what? I've tried lowering the opacity of the top layer and that didn't really work. I've tried erasing parts of the top image away with the Eraser Tool and while that *did* work, I ended up permanently deleting that part of the image and now if I need to bring some of it back, I can't. I guess all I can really do then is set the number of undo's in Photoshop's Preferences to 100 and never close out of my Photoshop documents.

Or... What about these layer masks I keep hearing so much about? Would they work out any better? Let's find out!

The Opacity option left us disappointed. The Eraser Tool did the job but also caused permanent damage to our image. Wouldn't it be great if we could get the same results we saw with the Eraser Tool but without the "permanent damage to our image" part? Well guess what? We can! Say hello to Photoshop's layer masks.

As I mentioned at the beginning of this discussion, layer masks allow us to control the transparency of a layer, but unlike the Opacity option which controls overall transparency, layer masks allow us to set different levels of transparency for different areas of the layer (although technically, you *could* use them to control the overall opacity as well, but the Opacity option already handles that very well and layer masks are capable of so much more).

How do layer masks work? Well rather than talking about it, let's just go ahead and use one to see it in action. Before we can use a layer mask though, we first need to add one, since layers don't automatically come with layer masks. To add a layer mask, you first want to make sure that the layer you're adding it to is selected in the Layers palette, otherwise you'll end up adding it to the wrong layer. I want to add a layer mask to the top layer, which is already selected, so I'm good to go. You could add a layer mask by going up to the Layer menu at the top of the screen, choosing Layer Mask, and then choosing Reveal All. You could also add a layer mask by simply clicking on the Layer Mask icon at the bottom of the Layers palette (it's the icon that looks like a filled rectangle with a round hole in the centre of it).

Add a layer mask to a layer by selecting the layer in the Layers palette and then clicking on the "Layer Mask" icon

Once you've clicked on the icon, nothing will seem to have happened in your document, and that's because by default, layer masks are hidden from view. After all, the whole point of them is to show and hide different parts of the layer and it would be pretty difficult to do that if the mask itself was blocking our view of the image. So how do we know, then, that we've added a layer mask if we can't see it? Easy. Look back over in the Layers palette, to the right of the preview thumbnail on the layer you added the mask to, and you'll see a brand new thumbnail. *This is your layer mask thumbnail, and it's how we know that a layer mask has been added to the layer:* ➡

Layer mask appearing in white

Notice that the layer mask thumbnail is filled with solid white. That's not just some random, meaningless colour that Photoshop uses to display layer mask thumbnails in. The reason why the thumbnail is filled with white is because the mask itself is currently filled with white, even though the mask is currently hidden from view. If you want proof that the mask really is there in your document and really is filled with white, simply hold down Alt (Win) / Option (Mac) and click directly on the layer mask thumbnail in the Layers palette.

Doing this tells Photoshop to show us the layer mask in our document, and sure enough, there it is, filled with white:

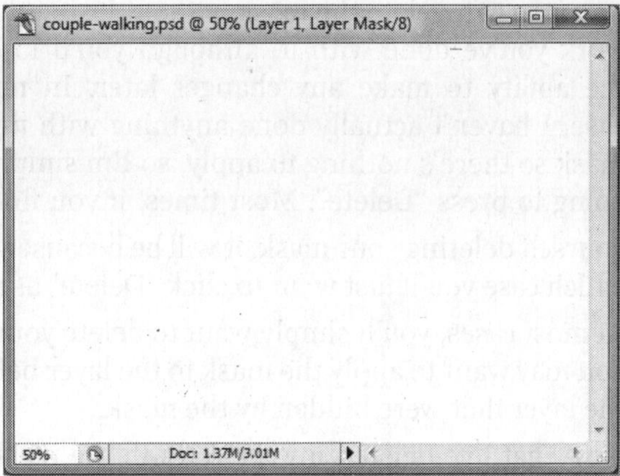

The layer mask, filled with solid white, appears in the document window

The layer mask is now blocking our image from view though, so once again hold down Alt (Win) / Option (Mac) and click on the layer mask thumbnail to hide the mask.

So, why is the layer mask (and its thumbnail in the Layers palette) filled with white? Why not red, or green, or yellow? It's because of how layer masks work in Photoshop. Layer masks use only white, black, and all the shades of gray in between, and they use these three colours (white, black and gray) to control the transparency of a layer. White in a layer mask means 100% visible, Black in a layer mask means 100% transparent, and Gray in a layer mask means some level of transparency depending on how light or dark the shade of gray is. 50% gray will give us 50% transparency. The lighter the shade of gray, the closer it is to white and the less transparent that area of the layer will be. The darker the shade of gray, the closer it is to black and the more transparent that area will be.

The reason layer masks are filled with white by default is because usually, you want to see everything on your layer when you first add the mask, and white in a layer mask means 100% visible. What if instead, you wanted to *hide* everything on the layer when you add the mask, so that as soon as the mask is added, everything on that layer disappears from view? Well, we just learned that black on a layer mask means 100% transparent, so we would need a way to tell Photoshop that instead of filling the new layer mask with white, we want it to be filled with black. You'll most likely come across situations where it makes more sense to hide everything on the layer when you add the mask rather than leaving everything visible, and fortunately, Photoshop gives us a couple of easy ways to do that. First of all, I'm going to delete my layer mask by simply clicking on its thumbnail and dragging it down onto the trash bin icon at the bottom of the Layers palette.

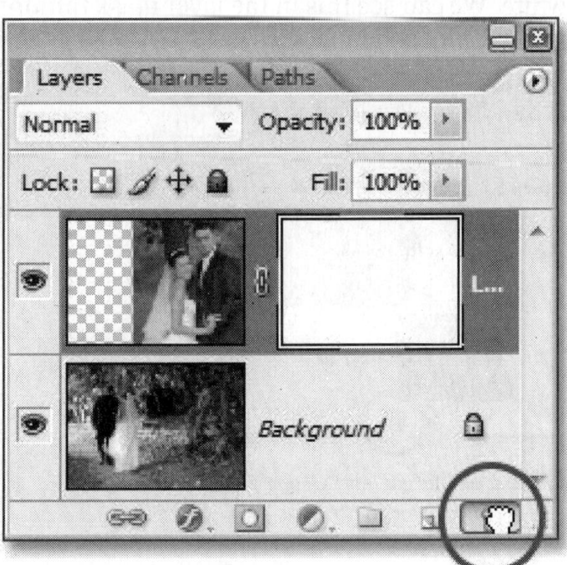

Photoshop will pop up a message asking if you want to apply the mask to the layer before you delete it. "Applying" the mask basically means telling Photoshop to erase all the pixels on the layer that were hidden from view by the layer mask, as if you had erased them yourself with the Eraser Tool. This way, you can delete the mask without losing the work you've done with it, although you'll lose the ability to make any changes later. In my case, I haven't actually done anything with my mask so there's nothing to apply, so I'm simply going to press "Delete". Most times, if you find yourself deleting your mask, it will be because you're unhappy with it and want to start over, in which case you'll just want to click "Delete" as well.

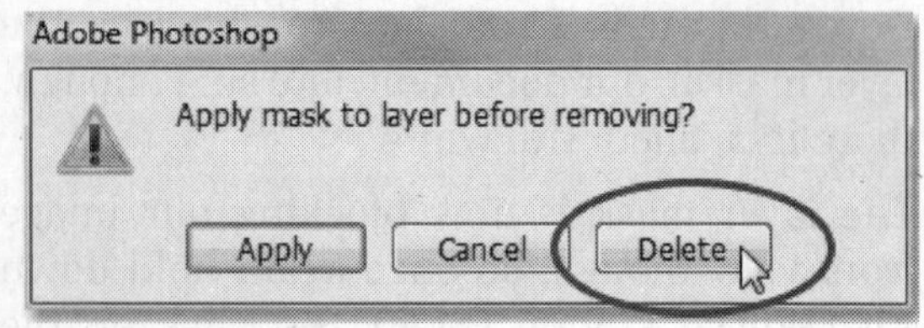

In most cases, you'll simply want to delete your mask and start over, but there are times when you may want to apply the mask to the layer before deleting it, which will erase all the pixels on the layer that were hidden by the mask.

Now that I've deleted my mask, both the mask itself and its thumbnail in the Layers palette are gone.

When you delete a layer mask, its thumbnail in the Layers palette also disappears

This time, I want to add a mask to the top layer and have Photoshop hide everything on the layer as soon as the mask is added, which means the mask will need to be filled with black instead of white. One way to accomplish this would be to go up to the Layer menu at the top of the screen, choose Layer Mask, and then choose Hide All (remember last time, we chose "Reveal All"). The faster and easier way though is to hold down your Alt (Win) / Option (Mac) key and click on the Layer Mask icon at the bottom of the Layers palette.

Either way you choose to do it, Photoshop adds a new layer mask to the currently selected layer, just as it did before, but this time, it fills the mask with black instead of white. We can see this in the layer mask thumbnail which is filled with solid black:

Hold down "Alt" (Win) / "Option" (Mac) and click on the "Layer Mask" icon

The new layer mask thumbnail is filled with black

And, unlike the first time we added a layer mask where nothing seemed to have happened to our image, this time the top layer (the photo of the couple facing the camera) is completely hidden from view, leaving only the image visible.

The photo on the top layer is now 100% transparent, leaving only the photo visible in the document

Once again, the layer mask itself is hidden from view, but if you want to see it in your document, hold down Alt (Win) / Option (Mac) and click directly on the layer mask's thumbnail in the Layers palette, which will tell Photoshop to show you the mask in the document window. This time, the mask is filled with black.

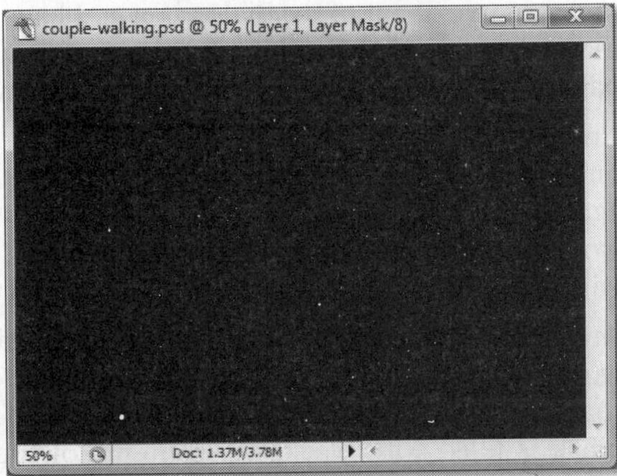

Hold down "Alt" (Win) / "Option" (Mac) and click on the layer mask thumbnail in the Layers palette to view the mask in the document, which is filled with solid black.

Hold "Alt/Option" and click again on the layer mask thumbnail to hide the mask in the document when you're done.

This is where the important difference between the Eraser Tool and layer masks comes in. Remember when we used the Easer Tool to blend the images together by erasing away part of the left side of the top image? The Eraser Tool physically deleted that part of the image and it was forever gone at that point, and if we looked in the top layer's preview thumbnail, we could see that large chunk of the image missing on the left. This time though, we've used a layer mask to hide not just part of the left side of the image but rather the entire image, yet if we look in the layer's preview thumbnail, the image is still there, completely intact.

⬅The image on the top layer is still intact on the layer, as shown in the layer's preview thumbnail, even though it's hidden from view in the document.

Where the Eraser Tool deleted the contents of the layer, the layer mask simply hides it from view! To prove that the photo on the top layer is still there, I'm going to fill the layer mask with white. To fill a layer mask with white, or do anything at all with a layer mask, you first need to select the mask so that you're working on the mask itself and not the actual layer, and to select it, all you need to do is click directly on the mask's thumbnail in the Layers palette.

Select a layer mask by clicking on its thumbnail in the Layer's palette

You can switch between selecting the layer itself and its layer mask by clicking on the corresponding thumbnail. You can tell which one is currently selected by which thumbnail has the white highlight border around it, as we can see around the layer mask thumbnail in the image.

To fill the mask with white, I'll go up to the Edit menu at the top of the screen and choose Fill, which brings up Photoshop's Fill command dialog box. For contents I'll choose white.

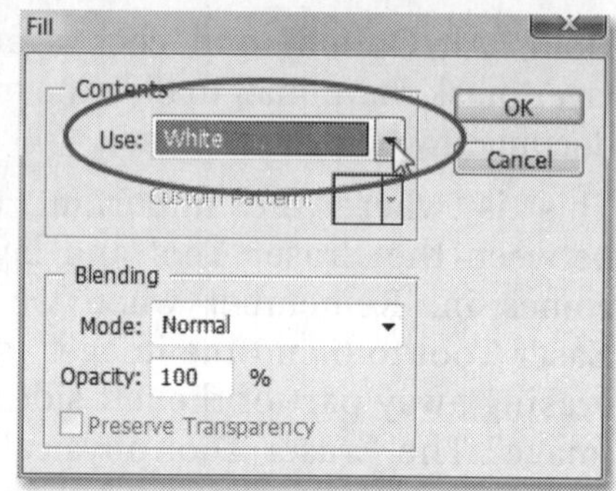

Photoshop's "Fill" dialog box

With white chosen as my fill contents, I'll click OK in the top right to exit out of the dialog box and have Photoshop fill my layer mask with white. I can now see in the Layers palette that the mask thumbnail is filled with white.

And with the mask now filled with solid white, my photo on the top layer is completely visible in the document once again, proving that even though the image was hidden from view a moment ago when we filled the layer mask with black, it was always there, untouched and unharmed.

And that's the basics of how Photoshop's layer masks work. When the mask is filled with white, the contents of that layer are 100% visible in the document, and when the mask is filled with black, the contents of the layer are 100% transparent – hidden from view but not deleted as was the case with the Eraser Tool. Layer masks don't physically alter or affect the contents of the layer in any way. All they do is

The layer mask thumbnail in the Layers palette is now filled with white

After filling the layer mask with white, the photo on the top layer becomes fully visible once again

control which parts are visible and which are not. The contents of the layer are always there, even when we can't see them.

We've seen how we can hide a layer completely by adding a layer mask to it and filling it with black, and we've seen how we can show the layer completely once again by simply filling the layer mask with white. And we know that whether the contents on the layer are visible or not, they're still always there. The Eraser Tool deletes parts of the image but layer masks simply hide them. That's all great. But is this all we can do with a layer mask, either show the entire layer or hide it? How do we use a layer mask to blend these two images together like we did with the Eraser Tool?

To blend the two images together using the layer mask, we don't use the Eraser Tool. In fact, while the Eraser Tool still has its place, you'll find yourself using it less and less as you become more comfortable with layer masks. Instead, we use Photoshop's Brush Tool, and with our layer mask filled with white as it currently is, which is making the entire layer visible, all we need to do is paint with black on the layer mask over any areas we want to hide. It's that simple!

To show you what I mean, I'm going to select my Brush Tool from the Tools palette:

Selecting Photoshop's Brush Tool from the Tools palette ➡

I could also press B on my keyboard to quickly select it. Then, since we want to paint with black, we need to have black as our Foreground colour, and by default, whenever you have a layer mask selected, Photoshop sets white as your Foreground colour, with black as your Background colour. To swap them so black becomes your Foreground colour, simply press X on your keyboard. If I look in the colour swatches near the bottom of my Tools palette, I can see now that black is my Foreground colour:

Photoshop's Tools palette showing black as the Foreground colour ➡

I'm going to resize my brush to the same general size I used with the Eraser Tool by once again using the left and right bracket keys, and I want my brush to have nice, soft edges so that I get smooth transitions between the areas of the layer that are visible and the areas that are hidden, and I can soften my brush edges by holding down Shift and pressing the left bracket key a few times. Then, with my layer mask selected (I know it's selected because the layer mask thumbnail has the white highlight border around it), I'm going to do basically the same thing I did with the Eraser Tool, except this time I'm painting with black on the layer mask over the areas I want to hide rather than erasing anything.

Paint with black over areas that you want to hide

After spending a few more seconds painting away the areas I want to hide, here's my result, which looks pretty much the same as it did after I used the Eraser Tool:

The image after painting away the left part of the top image to blend it with the image below

If we look at the layer mask thumbnail in the Layers palette, we can see where I've painted with black, which are now the areas of the top image that are hidden from view.

The layer mask thumbnail now shows the areas I've painted with black

Let's say I'm happy with this and again asked the experts to comment. They said that they like it but they want some of the bride's veil on the right brought back in. When I faced this situation after using the Eraser Tool, I was out of luck because I had deleted that part of the image and had no choice but to start all over again. This time though, I was smarter! I used a layer mask, which means that the entire image on the top layer is still there and all I need to do is make more of it visible!

I was able to hide parts of the layer initially by painting on the layer mask with black, so to bring back some of the image that's now hidden, all I need to do is press X on my keyboard to swap my Foreground and Background colours, which makes white my Foreground colour, and then I can simply paint with white over the areas I want to bring back into view, again making sure that my layer mask, not the layer itself, is selected. I think I'll use a smaller brush this time with harder edges so there isn't such a large transition area between the two images, and I'll use the bride's veil, along with the tree trunk above her, as the dividing point between the two images, which will

look more natural. As I paint with white on the layer mask, the areas I paint over that were hidden become visible once again.

🡄 *Painting with white on the layer mask with white to bring back some of the image I had hidden originally by painting with black.*

If I make a mistake as I'm painting and accidentally show or hide the wrong area, all I need to do is press X to swap my Foreground and Background colours, paint over the mistake to undo it, then swap my Foreground and Background colours once again with X and continue on. And here, after a couple of minutes worth of work painting the veil and the tree trunk back into the image, is my final result:

The final result

Thanks to the layer mask, I didn't have to redo everything from scratch because nothing was deleted! The mask allowed me to hide parts of the layer without harming a single pixel. Not only does this give you a lot more flexibility, it also gives you a lot more confidence when working in Photoshop because nothing you do with a layer mask is permanent.

And there we have it! That's the basics of how layer masks work in Photoshop!

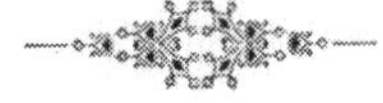

Layer Styles in Photoshop

Effects can be added to individual layers in Photoshop that automatically change as a layer is modified. The combination of effects on any given layer is called its Layer Style. We'll discuss how to use and make your own layer styles in this lesson.

What are Layer Styles?

Layer styles are special effects that can be quickly and easily applied to individual layers in Photoshop to drastically change the appearance of something in very little time. They can be preset, customized, or even saved and used for later.

One of the useful properties of Layer Styles is their relationship to the layer contents. Since the style is actually a separate entity that is just linked to the layer, it will continually update itself as a layer's contents are edited or moved. Furthermore, the effects can easily be adjusted after applying them, making them non-destructive in nature.

Some shapes and text with and without layer styles applied

Using Layer Style Presets

Photoshop comes packed with a good number of **Layer Style Presets**, all which are accessible through the **Styles Palette** (*Window > Styles*). To apply a **Layer Style**, select the Layer you'd like to work with in your document from the ***Layers Palette***, and then select the *Layer Style* which you would like to apply.

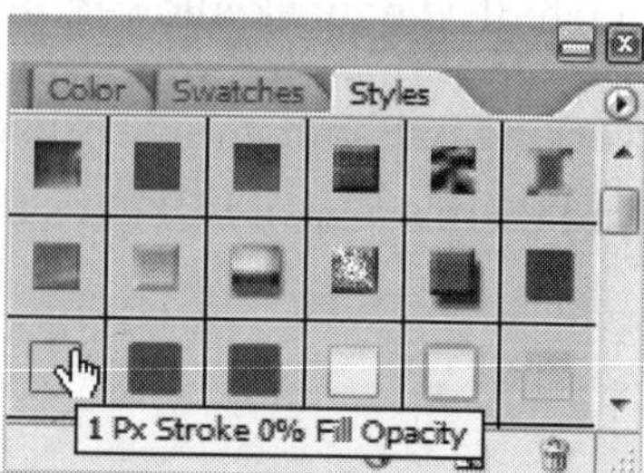

Layer Style

Some Text Some Text

A Text Layer before and after a Layer Style Preset is applied to it

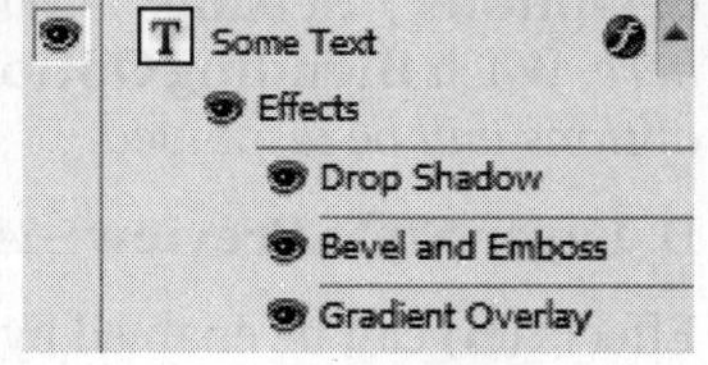

After applying a *Layer Style*, the effects in the layer can be seen, adjusted, disabled or re-enabled from the *Layers Palette*. Layers with effects applied to them will have a small round icon with an '*f*' in it. To expand or collapse the effects applied to a layer, click the arrow to the right of this icon.

When a layer's effects have been expanded, you can quickly disable specific effects within the layer style by clicking the *eye* icon next to the effect. Just like a layer, these effects can become visible again by clicking the blank area (*where the eye would reside*) when an effect is disabled.

Making Quick Changes

You can make quick changes to a layer's style by double clicking the '**f**' icon to pull up the **Layer Style Options**. From here, you can completely customize your layers style.

Creating your own Effects and Styles

To add your own layer effects, and create your own styles, go to **Layer > Layer Style > Blending Options**, or **Right Click your Layer,** and **select Blending Options**. This will bring up the **Layer Style Options**.

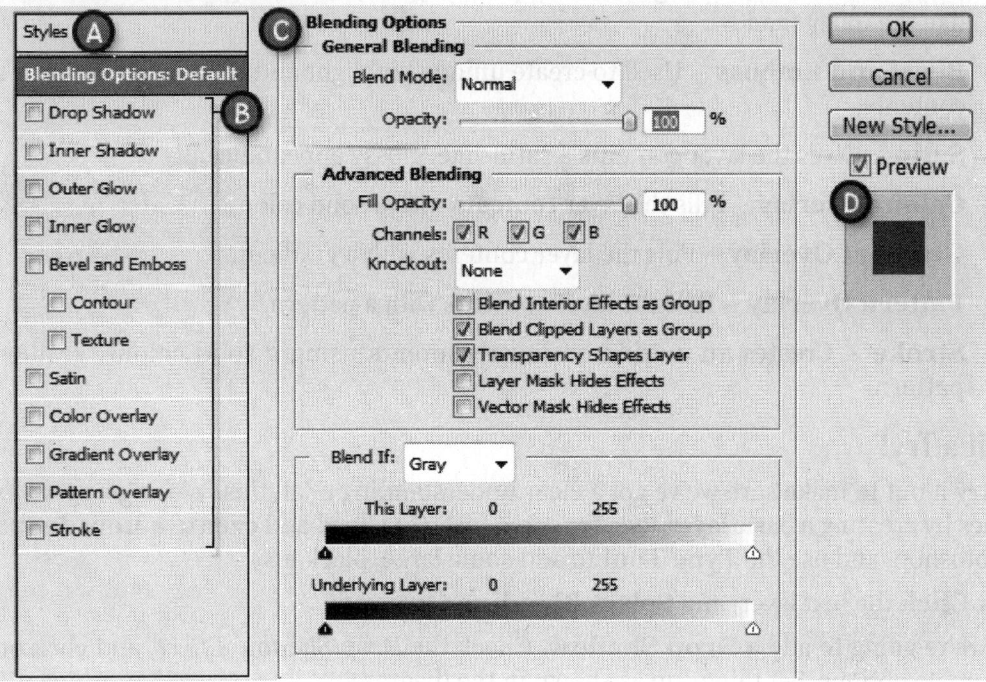

A. **Style Presets** – *List of the Style Presets.*

B. **Effects** – *The various effects that can be used in a layer style. It's important to note that by clicking on the name of any of the effects will enable that effect, and display the options for the individual effect.*

C. **Options / Settings** – *When the name for an effect is checked, its options will be shown here. When* **Blending Options** *is selected, settings such as Opacity, Fill, and other advanced options will be displayed.*

D. **Layer Style Preview** – *A preview of the Layer Style.*

Effects (**B**) can be enabled by checking them, and likewise, disabled by un-checking them. To edit an effect, you need to **click the name** (*rather than checkbox*). The effects settings will be displayed in the **Options** area (**C**), where they can be easily adjusted. To apply a set of effects and options, simply press **OK.**

Layer Effects

Styles can be built with the following effects:

- ❑ **Drop Shadow** – Creates a shadow behind the layers contents.
- ❑ **Inner Shadow** – Creates a shadow on top of the layers contents.
- ❑ **Outer Glow** – Creates a glow behind the layers contents. Cannot be distanced like the drop shadow.
- ❑ **Inner Glow** – Creates a glow on top of the layers contents. Again, cannot be distanced like the inner shadow.
- ❑ **Bevel and Emboss** – Used to create unique highlight and shadow effects on a layers contents.
- ❑ **Satin** – Gives the layer contents a satin-like, glossy appearance.
- ❑ **Colour Overlay** – Fills the layer contents with a solid colour.
- ❑ **Gradient Overlay** – Fills the layer contents with a gradient.
- ❑ **Pattern Overlay** – Fills the layer contents with a pattern.
- ❑ **Stroke** – Creates an outline on layer contents using a solid colour, gradient, or pattern.

Give it a Try!

Let's try it out to make sure we've got a clear understanding of all this. We're going to test our abilities by creating a basic layer style for some text. Go ahead and **create a new document** in Photoshop, and use the **Type Tool** to add some large, black text.

Right Click the text layer, and **Select Blending Options**.

First we're going to add a **Drop Shadow**. Check the *Drop Shadow Effect*, and click on it to bring up its options. Set things up as shown in the diagram:

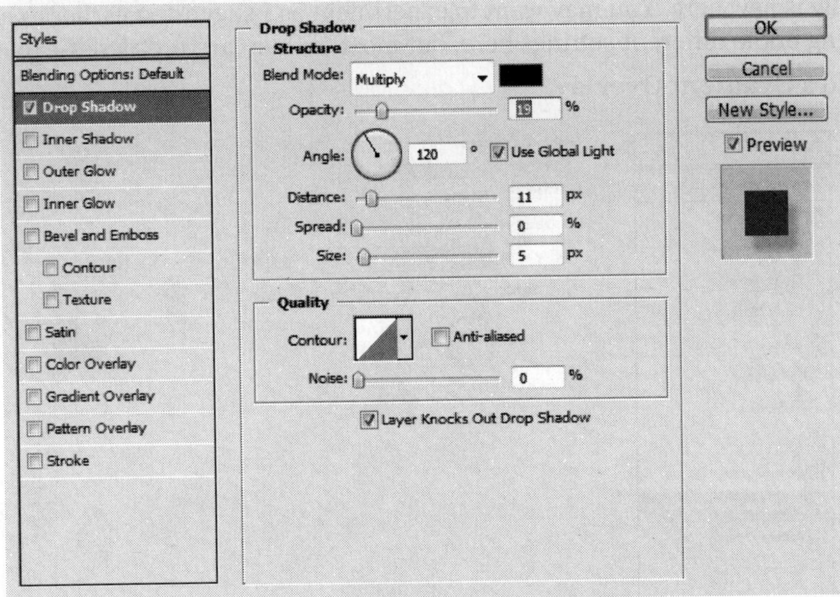

As you're making adjustments, you should be able to see changes being made in your actual document. Keeping an eye on your document while adding effects will allow you to better determine how to adjust settings.

Now let's add a **Bevel and Emboss**. We're going to create a bevel that is subtle, so that it doesn't draw too much attention, but at the same time pops our text a bit. Again, mimic the settings shown in the diagram below.

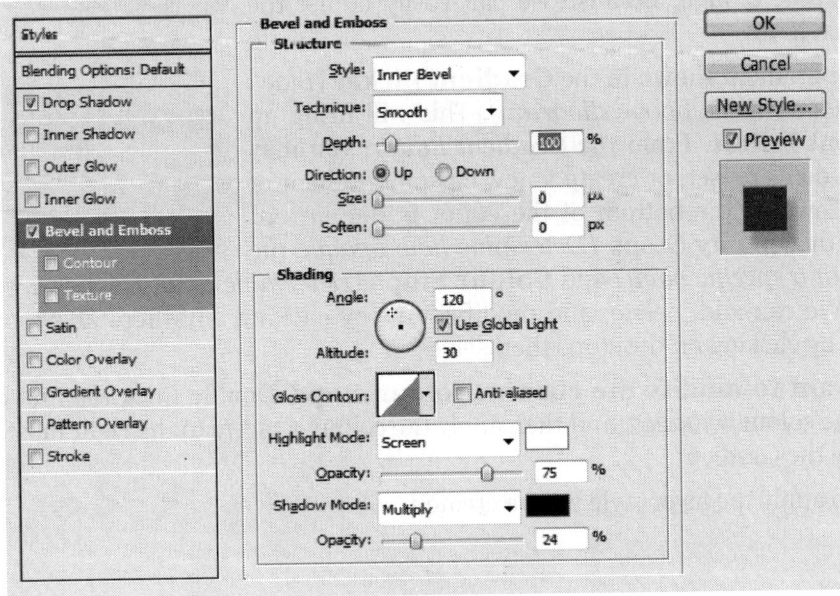

Nothing really is new here. You may want to experiment as I suggested earlier to have a better understanding of the different settings here, but most of them are pretty self-explanatory.

Now let's add a **Gradient Overlay**.

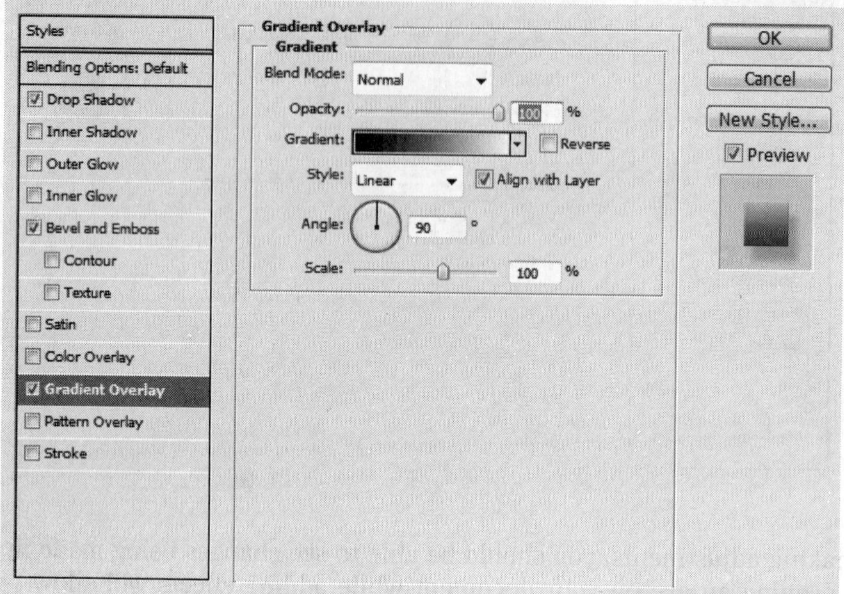

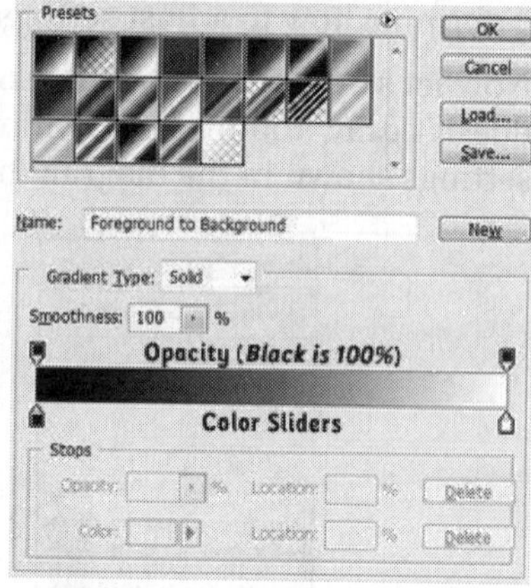

By default, the Gradient Overlay will probably use a *Foreground to Background* gradient, which is not exactly what we are looking for (unless we've setup the Foreground and Background Colours in Photoshop specifically for this step). That's OK though, because we can easily adjust the gradient from here.

Click on the gradient shown in the **Gradient Picker** (*Black fading to White in the above diagram*). This will bring up the **Gradient Editor**. From the *Gradient Editor*, you may choose a gradient preset, or create a new custom gradient of your own. Towards the bottom of the editor is the current gradient, with **Opacity Stops** (*Determine how opaque the gradient is at a specific point*) and **Colour Stops** (*Determine what colours are used in the Gradient*). We can add, delete, and modify stops by clicking anywhere above or below the gradient, or by clicking on the stops themselves.

We only want to modify the current colour stops. Double Click the first colour stop, and apply the colour *#50a2e7*, and then apply the colour *#75cefc* to the right most stop. **Click OK** to Apply the Gradient.

Click OK to apply the layer style you've created.

Chapter 10

Working with Layer styles – Understanding Bevel and Emboss

The versatile effect of bevel and emboss helps create a feeling of depth by adding highlight and shadow to layer shapes. Depending on where these highlights and shadows are placed, a 3D effect can be quickly generated.

The **bevel effect** makes an object look as though it has been chiselled away, and is great for giving hard, sharp edges. The **emboss** options are a bit softer and make objects seem to rise out of the document or look as though they have been stamped into the page. In addition to deciding on a **bevel or emboss**, you also have control over the size of the effect, the direction of light and shadows and the shape of the edges. The option to apply a texture is also worth investigating and opens up even more options.

With the **Layer Style** window open and the **Bevel and Emboss** checkbox checked, go to the **Style** drop-down menu in the middle section to pick whether you go for a bevel or an emboss.

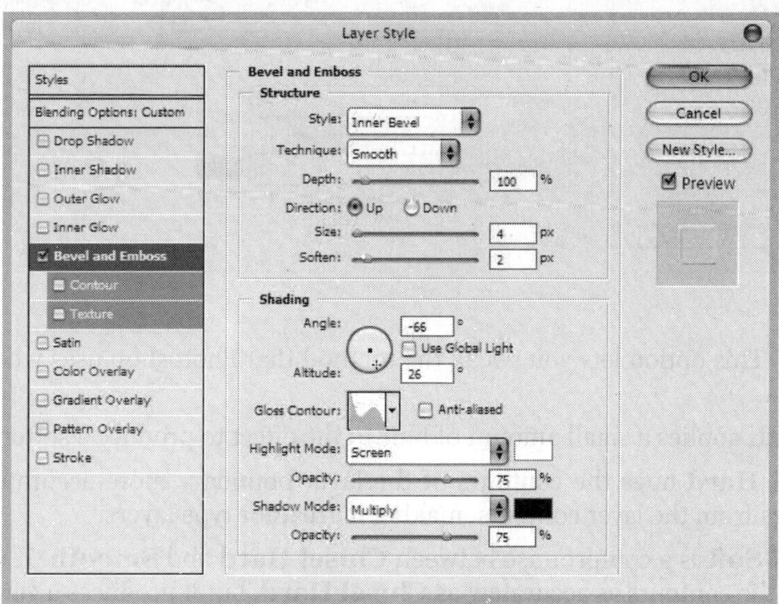

Opening Layer style window

Bevel and Emboss options

Style – This is where you choose the type of bevelling that you want to apply.

- ❑ **Outer Bevel** adds a bevel outside the layer boundary, giving the impression of the layer being raised from its background.
- ❑ **Inner Bevel** adds the bevel inside the layer boundary instead, making the layer itself look bevelled and 3D.
- ❑ **Emboss** adds a bevel across the layer boundary, giving the impression of the layer being stamped on the underlying layers.
- ❑ **Pillow Emboss** adds shading to both the inside and outside of the layer boundary to make the layer look like it's embedded in the underlying layers.
- ❑ **Stroke Emboss** adds embossing to the layer's Stroke effect only.

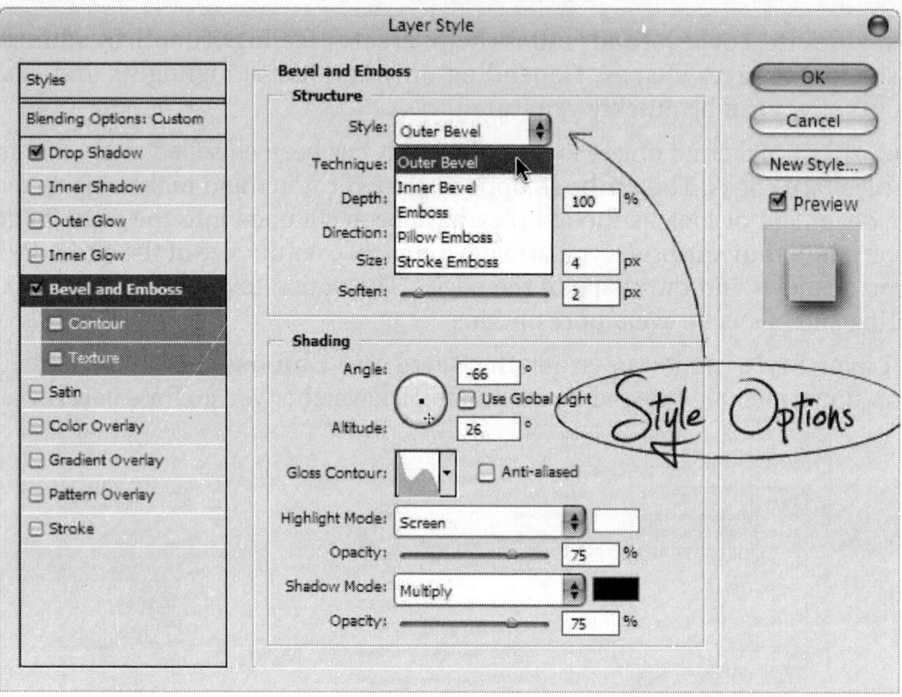

Technique – This option lets you tweak the method that Photoshop uses when forming the bevelling effect.

- ❑ **Smooth** applies a small amount of blur to the effect to produce a softer result.
- ❑ **Chisel Hard** hugs the contours of the layer boundary more accurately, preserving features from the layer contents, making it great for type layers.
- ❑ **Chisel Soft** is a compromise between **Chisel Hard** and **Smooth**. It usually doesn't follow the contours as accurately as **Chisel Hard**, but it produces a gentler effect.

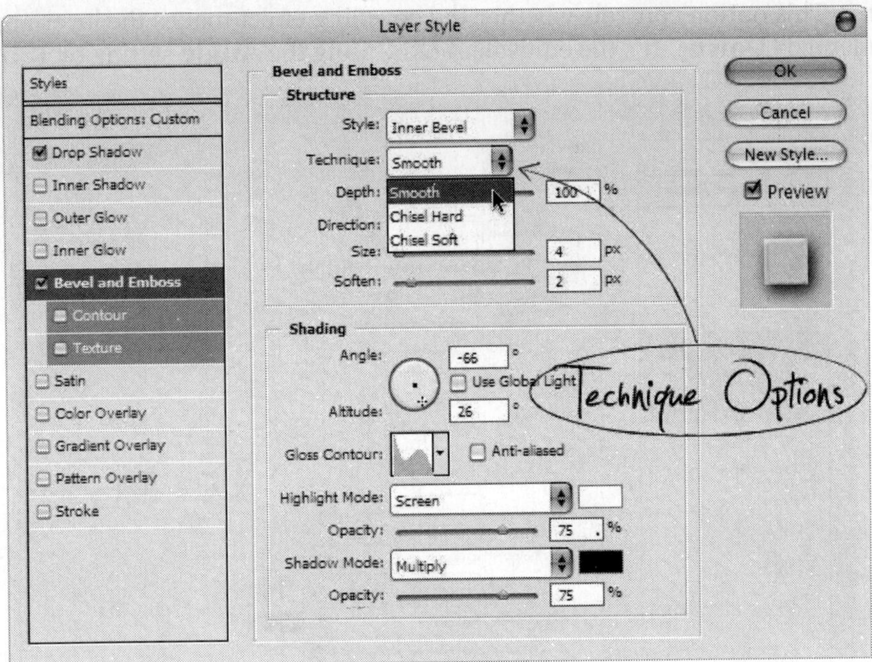

Depth – This option specifies the contrast of the shading used for the effect.

A high value results in a high level of contrast, producing a pronounced, or deep, bevel. A low value produces low-contrast shading, giving the impression of a shallow bevel.

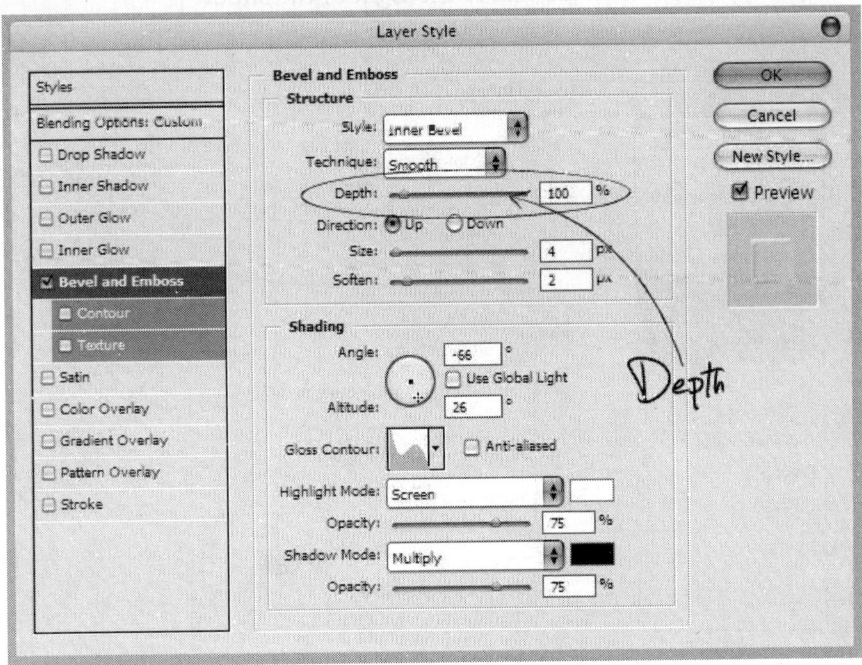

Direction – This option controls whether the bevelling effect makes the layer appear raised (**Up**) or indented (**Down**). It's the equivalent of rotating the **Angle** setting by **180 degrees**.

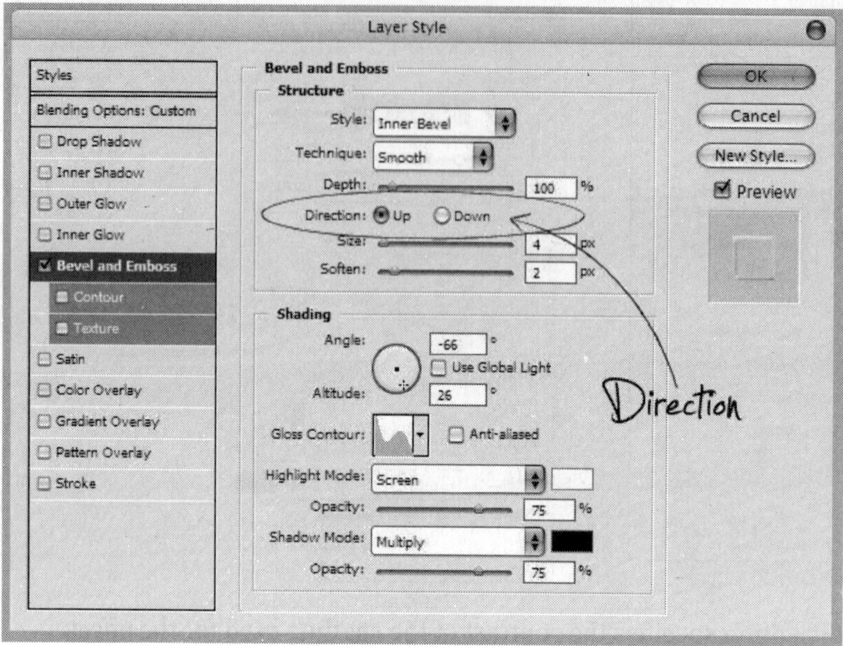

Size – Use this option to control the size of the bevel in pixels. Click and drag the slider to change the size, or type a value in the box to the right of the slider.

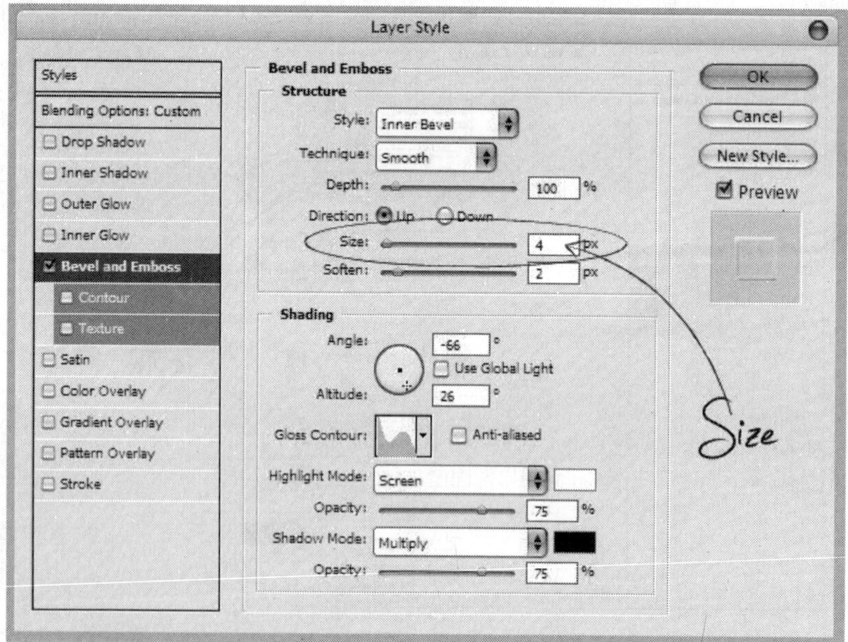

Soften – This option is great for smoothing over artifacts caused by using either of the **Chisel** techniques. It adds a touch of blurring to the effect to help smooth things out.

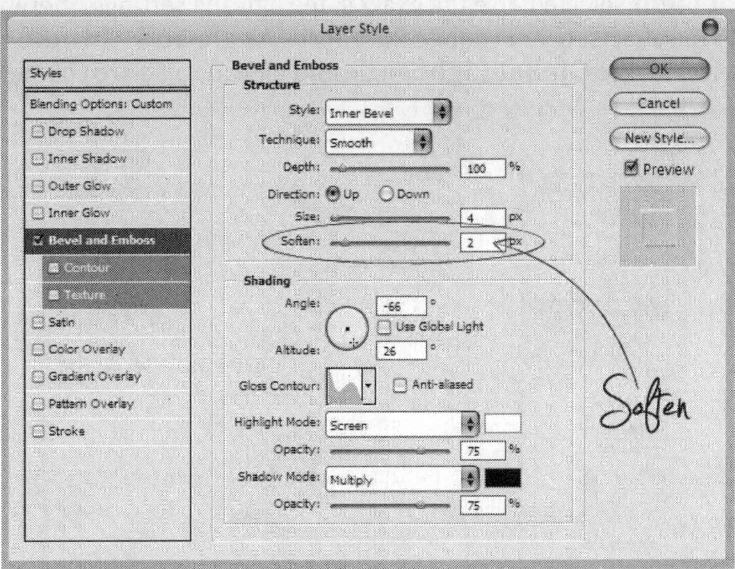

Angle and Altitude – Use the **Angle** option to adjust the direction of the light source used for the bevel effect. Click and drag the little crosshair in the circle, or type a value in the **Angle box** to the right. You can also adjust the **altitude** of the light source. Drag the crosshair toward the centre to move the light source directly overhead and high up. Drag it toward the edge to move the source more toward the horizon. You can also type a value for the light source **altitude**, in degrees, in the **Altitude box**, **0 degrees** – puts the light source on the horizon, while **90 degrees** – puts it directly overhead.

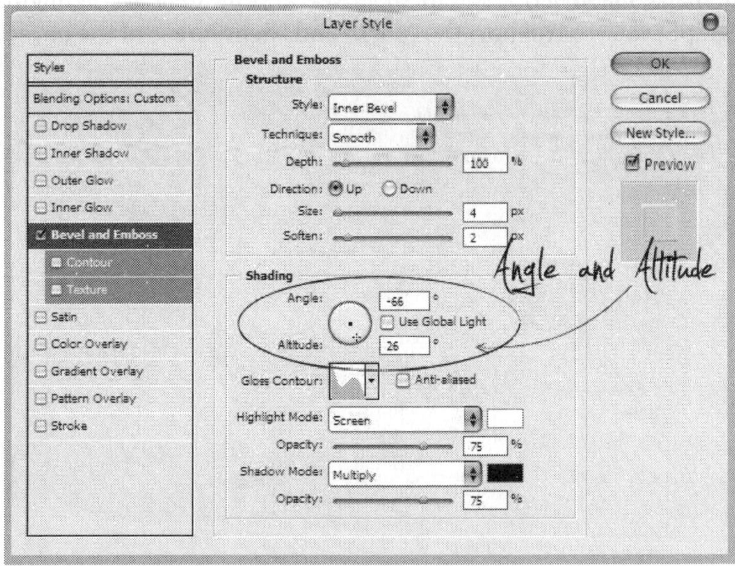

Use Global Light – This option locks the effect's **Angle and Altitude** settings to the **Global Light** settings. This means that this effect, and all other effects in your document that have **Use Global Light** selected, use the exact same lighting settings, thereby guaranteeing a consistent look to the effects. If you change the effect's **Angle and Altitude** settings with **Use Global Light** selected, the **Global Light** angle and altitude also are changed.

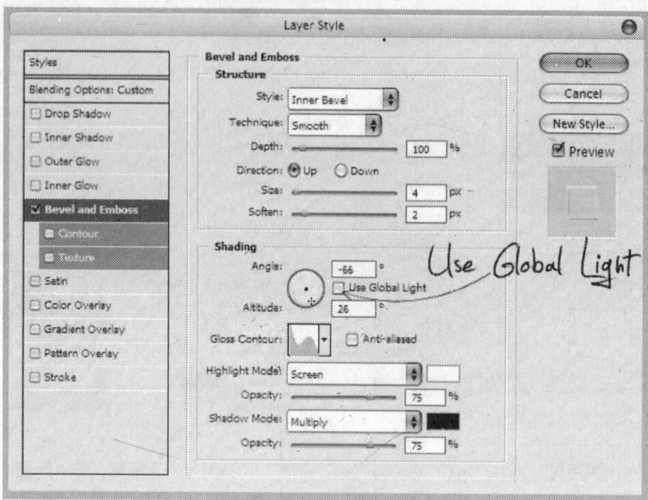

Gloss Contour – This option controls how the highlights and shadows that make up the effect are mapped across the range of the effect. Choose a preset contour by clicking the downward-pointing arrow next to the box, or create your own contour by clicking the graph in the box. The **Input values** along the bottom of the graph represent the areas in shadow in the effect (on the left) to the areas in the light (on the right). The **Output values** up the side of the graph represent the amount of shadow (at the bottom) or highlight (at the top) to apply. So the default **Linear gradient** exactly maps shadowed areas to shadows, and lit areas to highlights. By varying the curve within the graph, you control how the "dark" and "light" areas of the bevel are shaded.

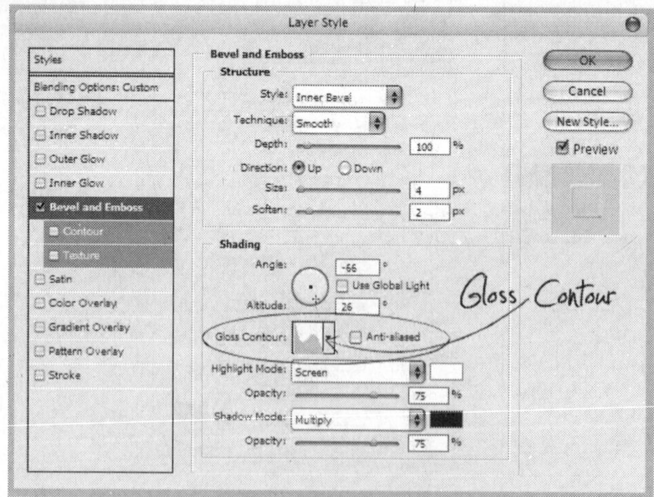

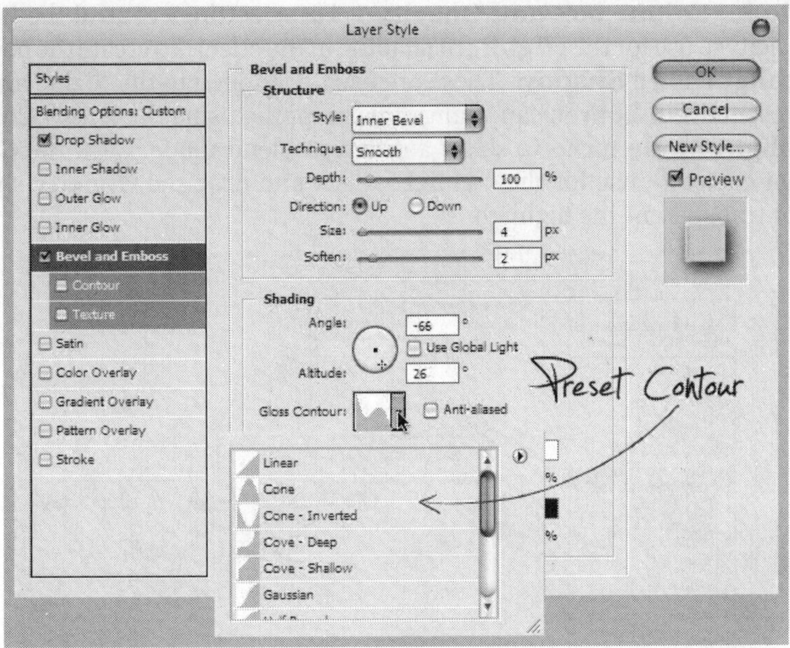

Anti-Aliased – If you use a fairly complex **Gloss Contour** graph, with lots of spikes, then you'll probably notice that the glossy effects appear jagged in the image, particularly if your original layer is quite small or detailed. By selecting the **Anti-Aliased** option, you can smooth out these transitions, resulting in a less jagged effect.

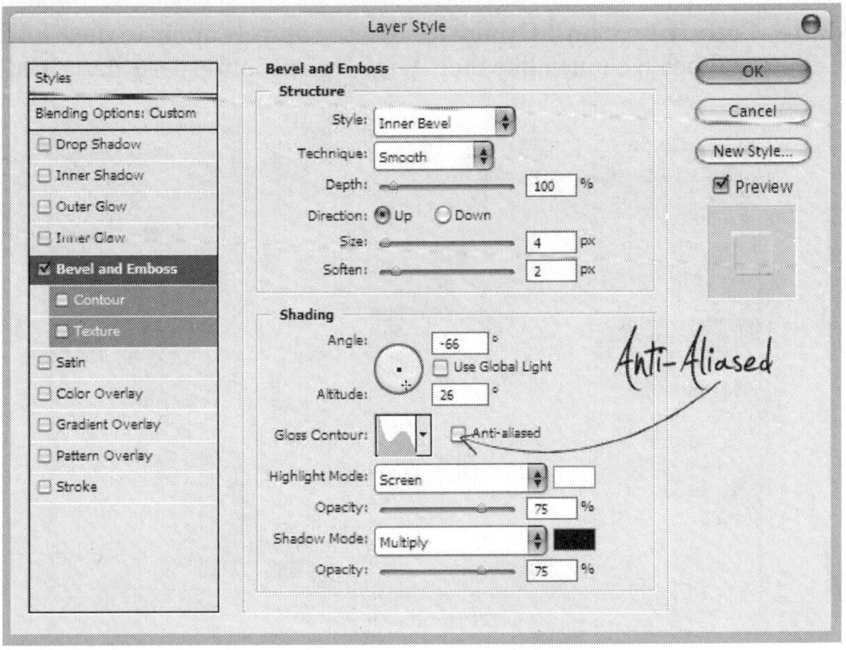

Highlight Mode, Colour box and Opacity – These settings control the blending mode, colour, and opacity to use for the **Highlight** shading in the effect. To create the bevel, Photoshop applies a **Highlight** and a **Shadow**. These are usually applied to the "light" and "dark" areas of the effect, respectively, but you can change this mapping using the **Gloss Contour** option. Use the **Highlight Mode** menu to select a different blend mode. Click the **Colour box** to pick a different colour to use for the highlight. Click and drag the **Opacity** slider to control how opaque or transparent the highlight is.

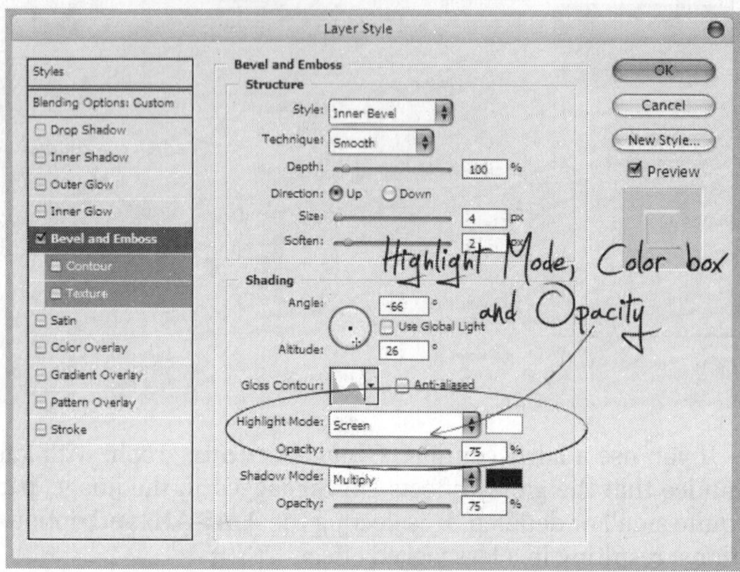

Shadow Mode, Colour box and Opacity – These controls apply to the **Shadow** shading used for the effect and behave much like their **Highlight** counterparts described previously.

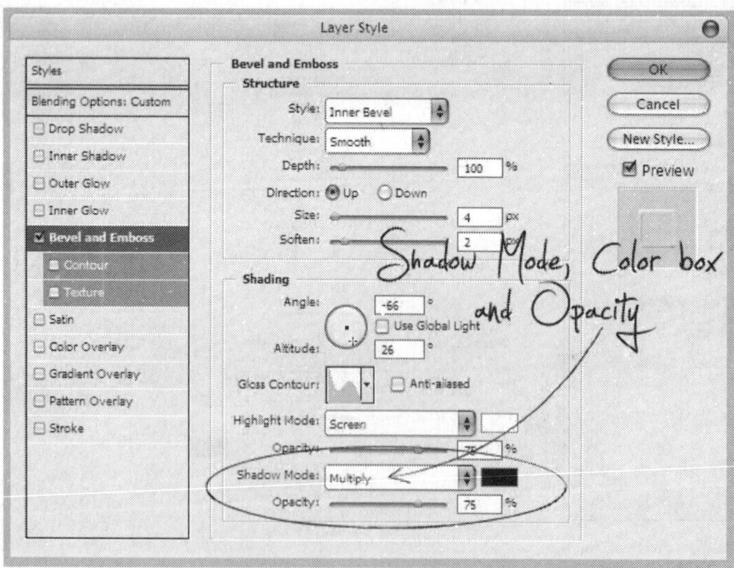

By adding an **Inner Bevel** to text, we've managed to create a pretty realistic 3D effect. Examples of **Bevel and Emboss** in action (**text colour – white, Fill – %**):

Outer Bevel

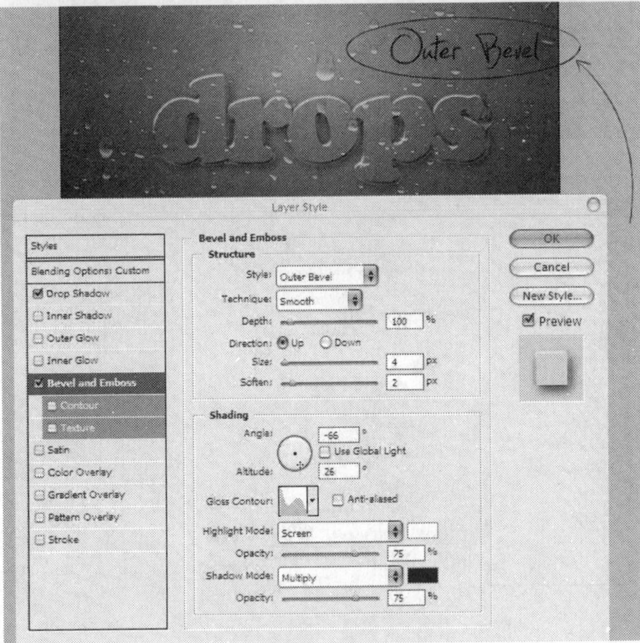

Inner Bevel

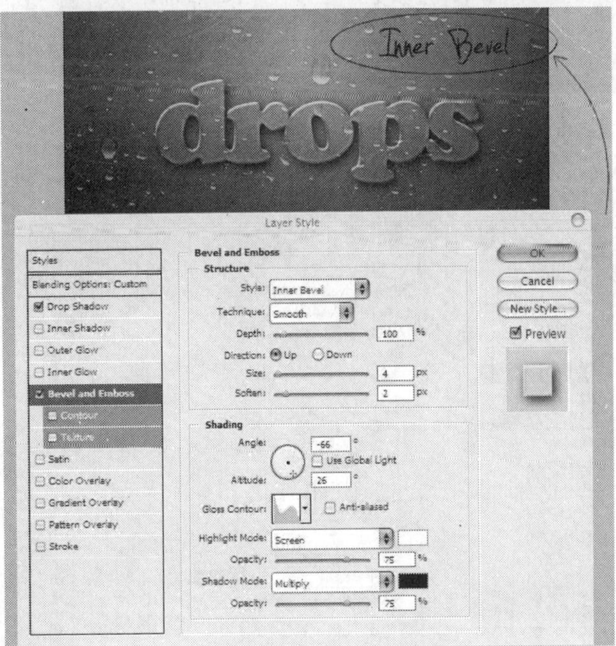

Emboss

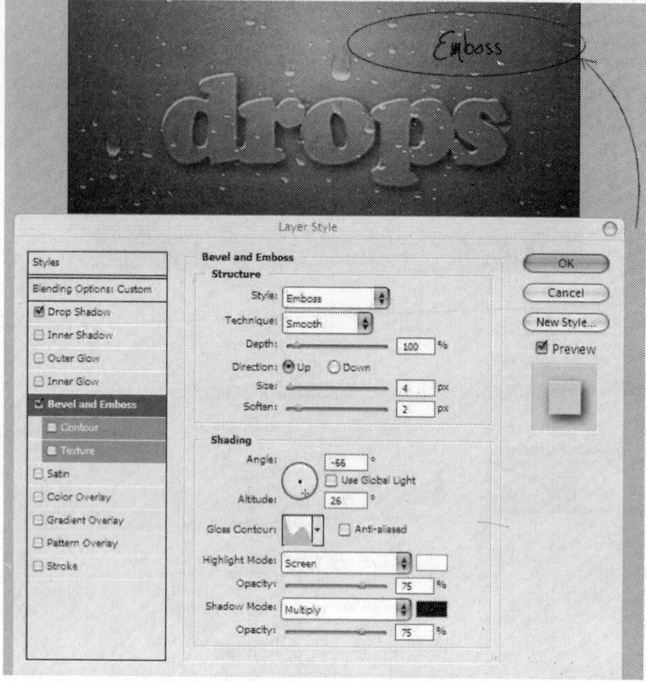

Pillow Emboss

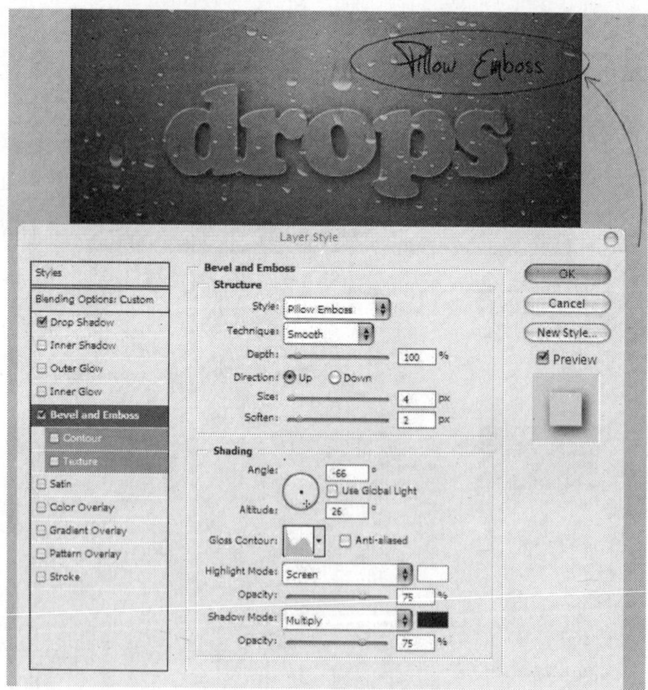

Stroke Emboss

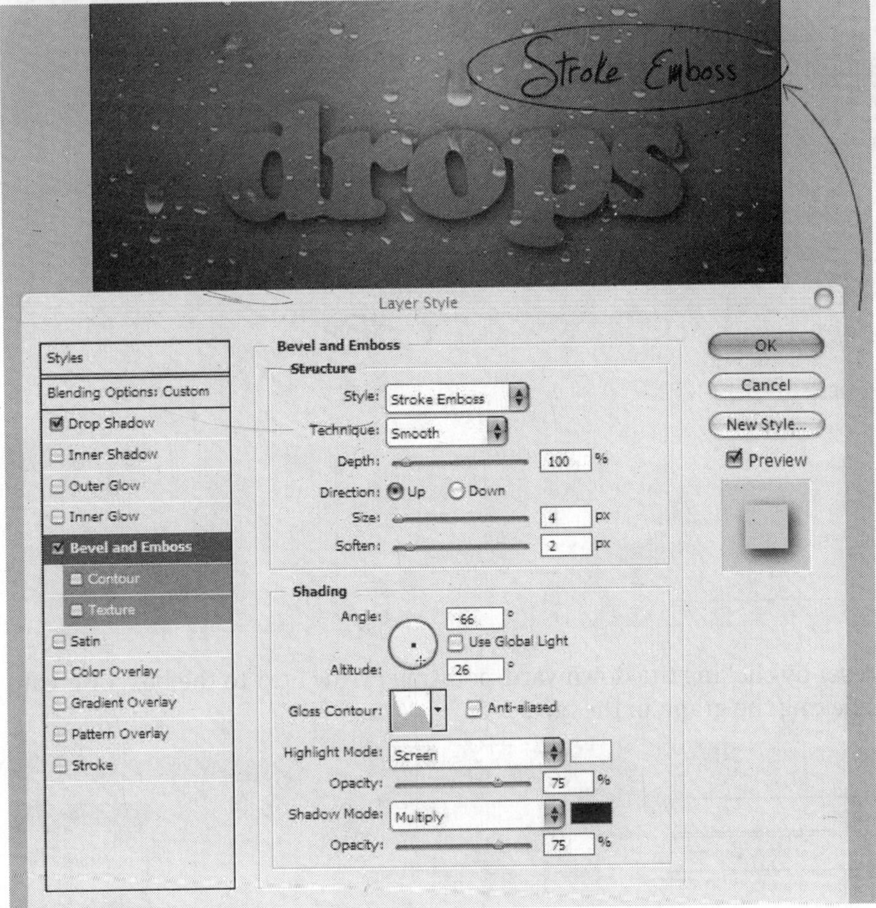

The **Bevel and Emboss** effect has two sub-effects: **Contour** and **Texture**.

Contour allows you to sculpt the shape of the bevel itself, while **Texture** lets you apply a pattern as a bumpy texture to the layer contents.

Select the check box to the left of **Contour** or **Texture** to enable the sub-effect, or click the sub-effect name itself to both enable the sub-effect and edit its options.

The Contour options

Contour – The contour you choose here affects the shape of the raised and lowered parts of the bevel effect around the edge of the layer contents. Think of the bevel as a 3D shape viewed from above, with the contour being a cross-section of that shape as viewed from the side; if you could cut through the bevel at any point with a saw, you'd see your selected contour shape. The default contour, **Linear**, produces a standard, 45 degree sloping bevel which is the same as not enabling the **Contour** sub-effect at all – but you can get some great effects with the other presets.

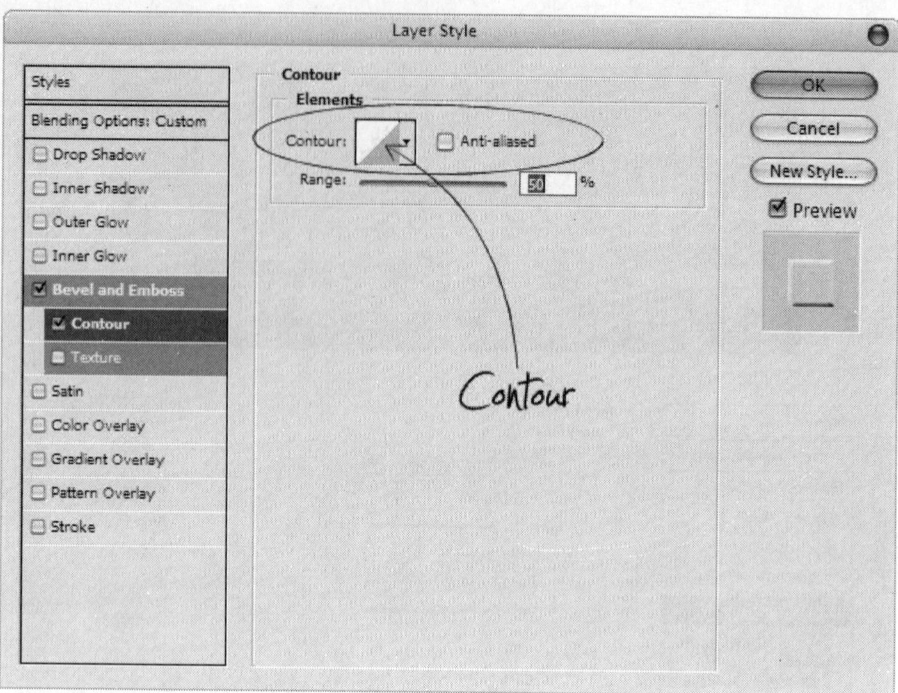

Choose a preset by clicking the downward-pointing arrow next to the box, or create your own contour by clicking the graph in the box.

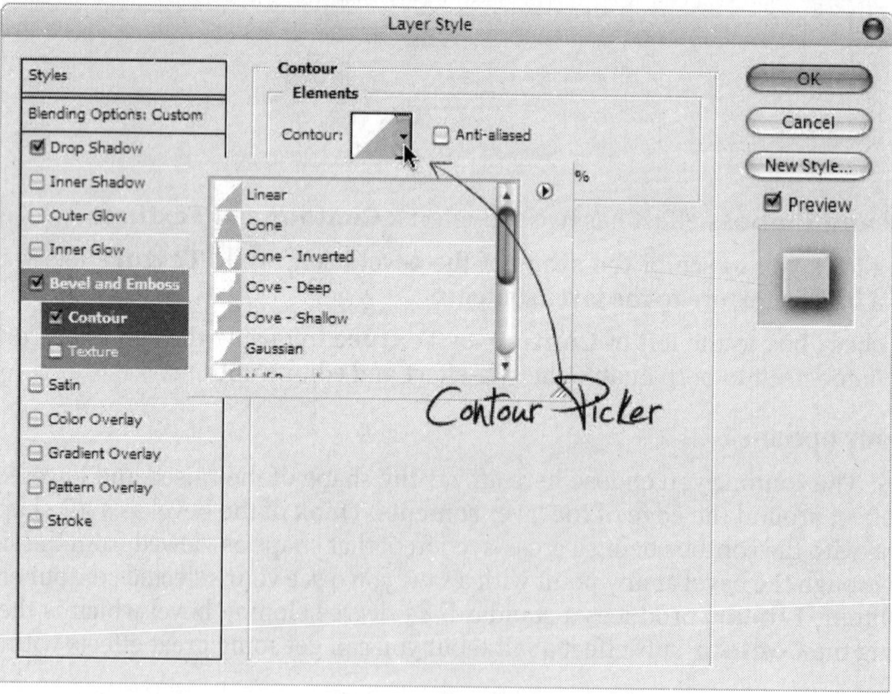

Anti-Aliased – The **Anti-Aliased** option is particularly useful for this effect, because it's very easy to produce quite jagged-looking bevels, especially with some of the spikier contours. Simply select this option to smooth out all those nasty jagged bits, and create a nice smooth bevelling effect.

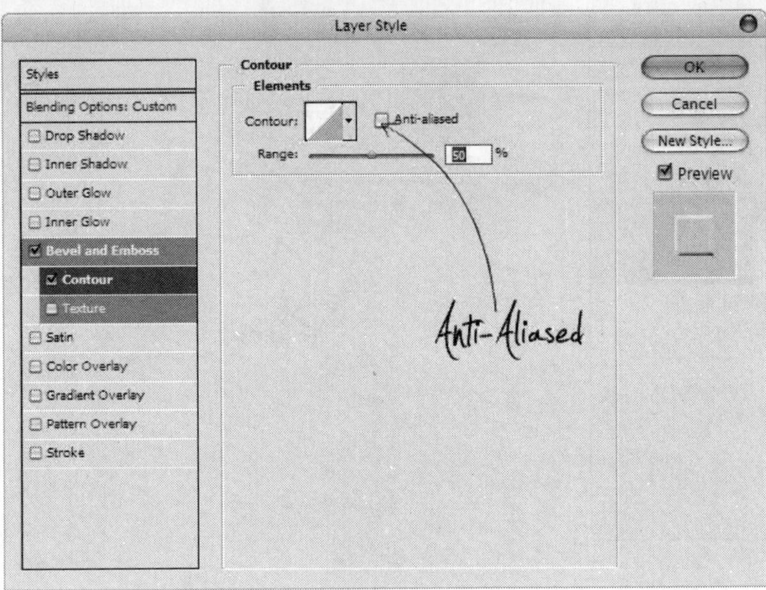

Range – Use this option to adjust the position and size of the contour within the bevel's cross-section. For value of 0, the contour is pushed to one edge of the bevel and only takes up a tiny proportion of the bevel, for value of 100 percent, the contour stretches to fill out twice the width of the bevel.

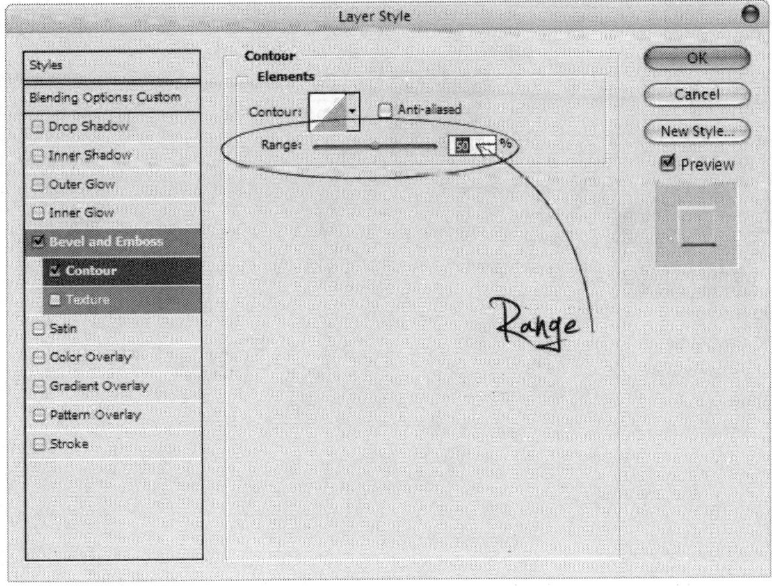

The Texture options

Pattern – This option lets you choose a pattern to use for the texture.

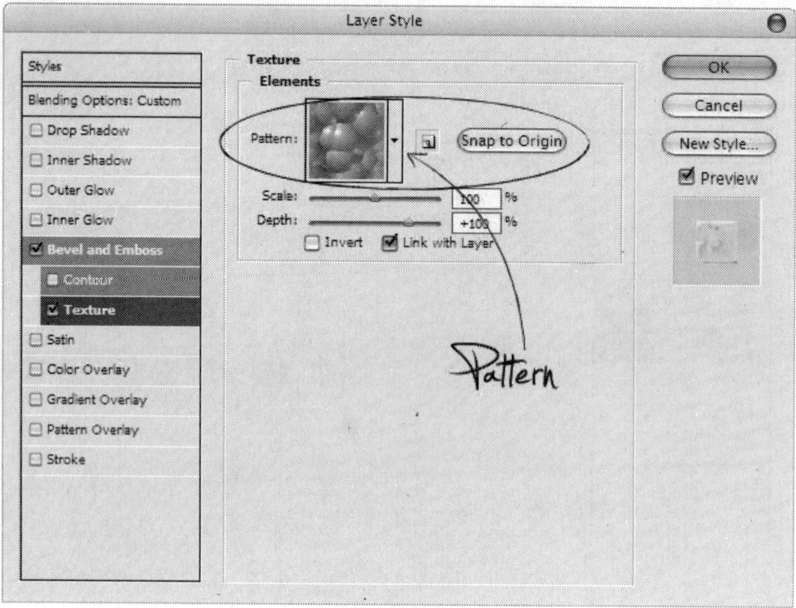

Click the pattern to display the pop-up **Pattern picker**, then click the pattern you want to use. You can also click the triangle in the top right of the **Pattern picker** to bring up the palette menu — this lets you create and delete patterns, change the appearance of patterns in the palette, load and save patterns and pick from a range of pattern presets.

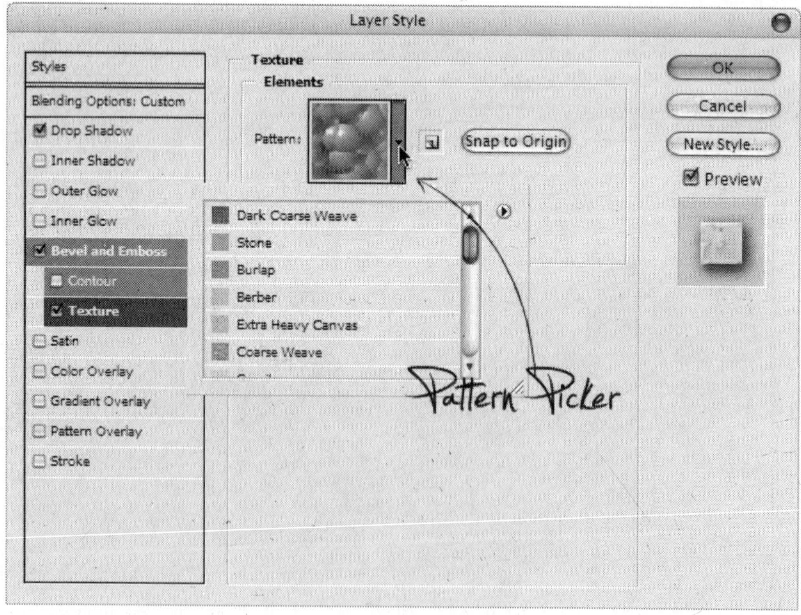

Snap to Origin – If you have moved the texture from its original position by clicking and dragging it in the document window, you can move the texture back to its default position by clicking this button.

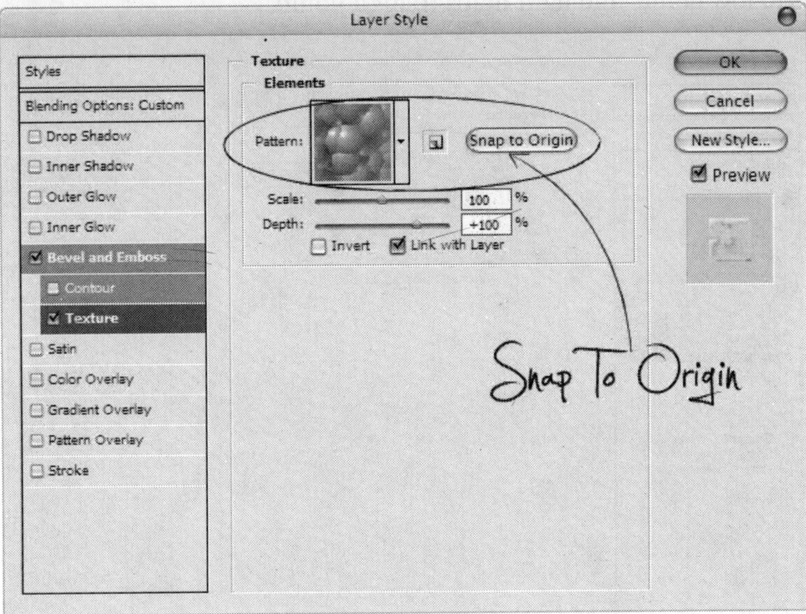

Scale – By clicking and dragging this slider you can control the size of the texture as it appears in the effect. This is useful because the resolution of the pattern probably won't match the resolution of your document.

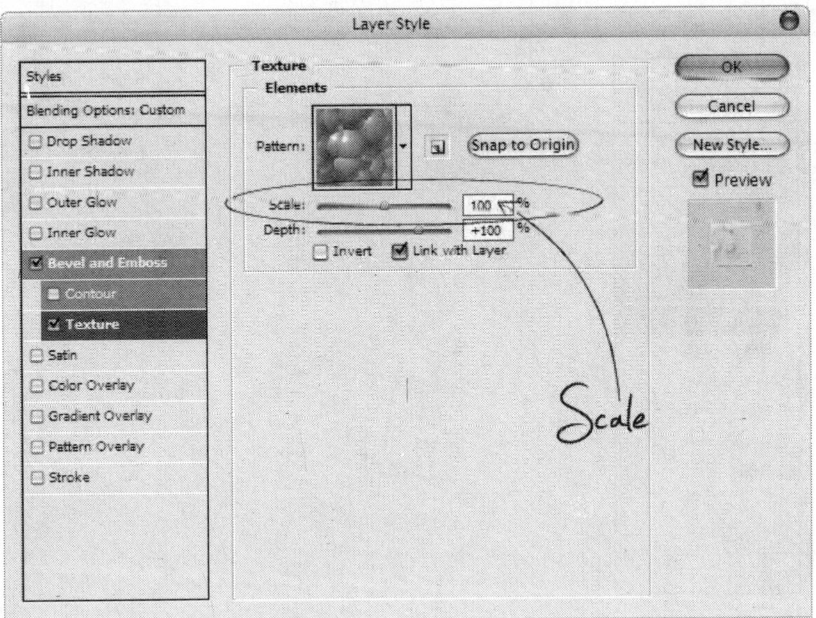

Depth – This option lets you control how much the texture is "raised" or "lowered." Positive values raise the texture, so that dark pixels in the pattern correspond to high points in the texture and light pixels correspond to dark points; negative values reverse this mapping, so that dark maps to low points and light maps to high points.

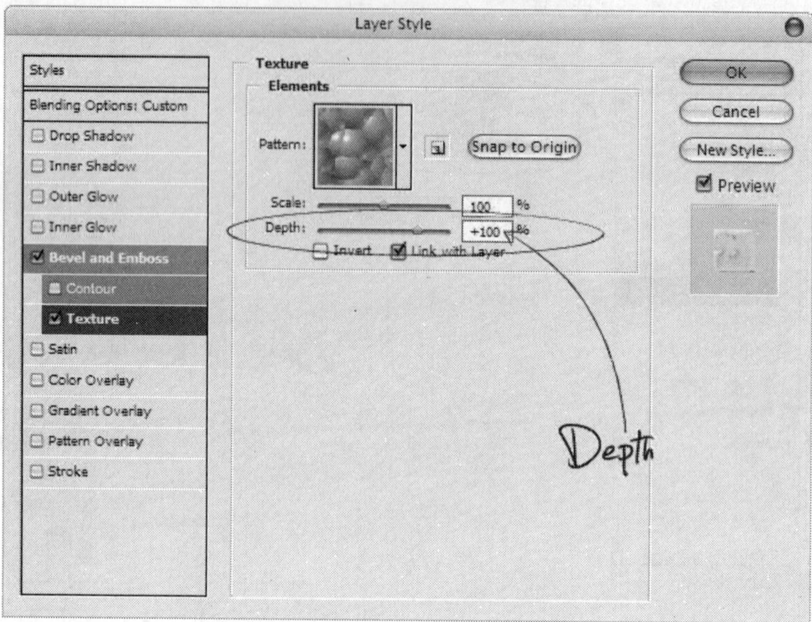

Invert – This option simply inverts the high and low points of the texture, so that dark pixels of the pattern map to low points in the texture and light pixels map to high points.

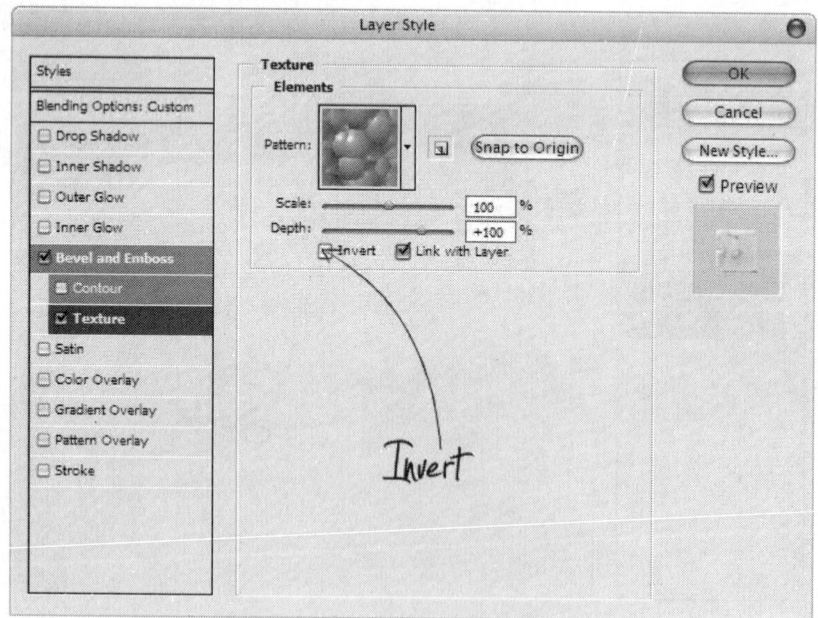

Link with Layer – Selecting this option causes the texture to move with the layer contents when using the **Move tool**, which is usually what you want to happen. Disable this option, and the texture remains fixed relative to the document window.

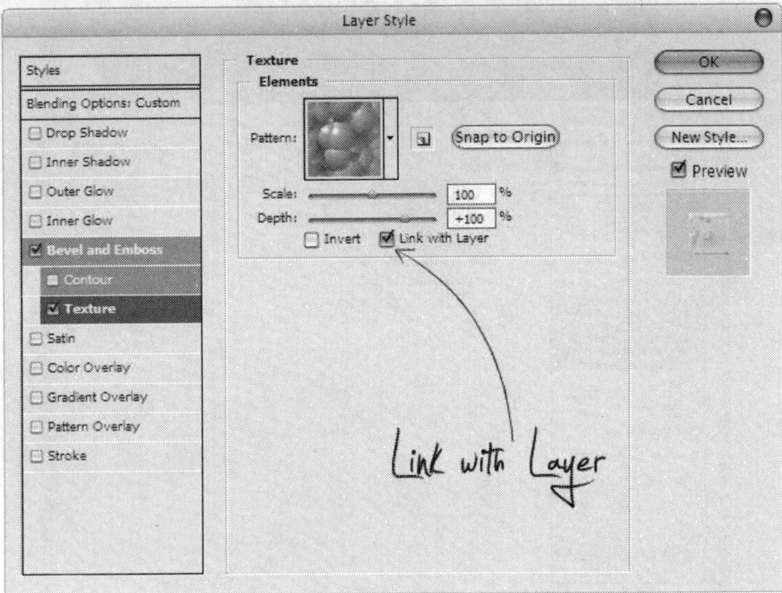

Examples of **Contour** and **Texture** in action:

In the first example, the **Rounded Steps** contour is applied to the text using the **Contour** sub-effect, while the second example uses the **Texture** sub-effect to apply the **Bubbles pattern** as a texture to the text.

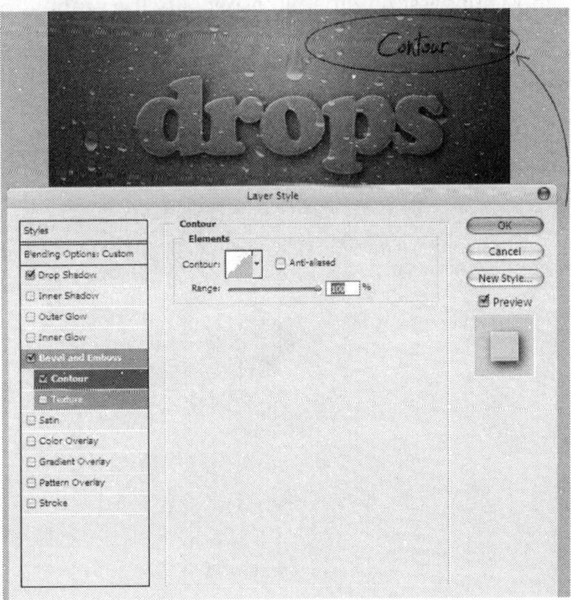

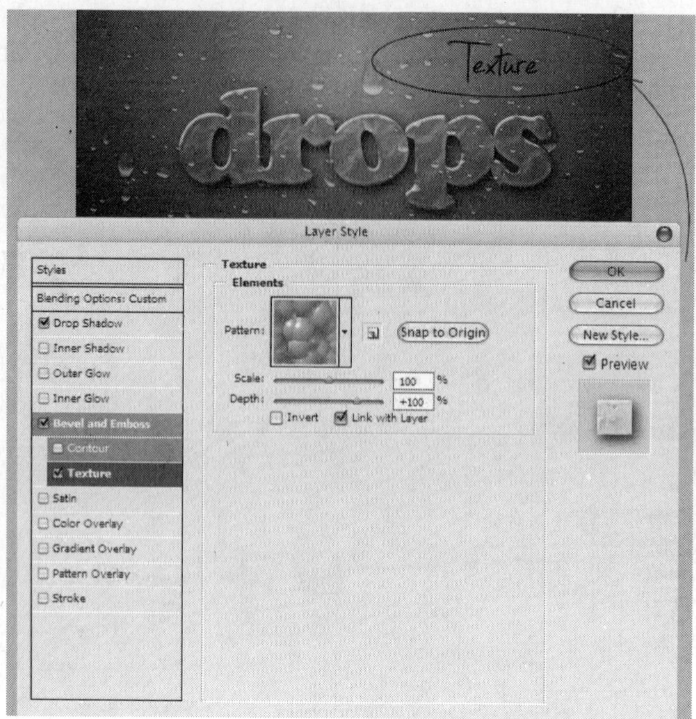

TIPS

- You can apply **Bevel and Emboss** effects to text layers as well as shape layers. In fact, the effect is probably most successful with text, especially the emboss options.
- The shape of the **Bevel**, as defined by the chosen **Contour**, is most obvious when using the **Chisel Hard** technique.
- When you're applying a **Texture** to a **Bevel and Emboss**, you can select the **Link with Layer** checkbox. This allows you to move the **Texture** and layer in complete unison.

Ps

Understanding Drop Shadows

Adobe Photoshop includes Layer Styles, a number of automated effects that you can apply to layers, including drop shadows, glows, bevelling, and embossing, as well as a colour fill effect. Layer styles allow you to edit applied effects dynamically without having to create a smart object version of the image layer first. This means that you can apply editable effects to a selected image, shape, or type layer without permanently altering any pixels.

Each layer style contains its own settings; however, many of the controls are available for more than one effect and they operate in the same way. The best way to become familiar with them is to experiment. Apply a **Layer style**, play around with the control settings, and use the **Preview** option to decide whether you like what you see. You'll notice as you experiment that many of the controls are self-explanatory and the dialog is very intuitive.

Applying effects to layers is easy. Either double-click on a layer to open the **Layer Style** dialog, or go to menu **Layer>Layer Style**. Alternatively, you can click **Add Layer Style** button at the bottom of the Layers palette (the one with the *fx* icon), and choose an effect from the list.

Some things to take note of when working with layer style effects and the **Layer Style** dialog:

- ❑ **Layer styles** cannot be applied to the **Background layer**.
- ❑ **Layer styles** can be applied to only a single selected layer at a time – not to multiple selected layers or to layer groups.
- ❑ **Layer styles** are attached to the layer. Therefore, when you move the layer in the **Layers palette**, the effects tag along.
- ❑ Type layers remain editable even after a layer style effect is applied.
- ❑ **Layer styles** can be copied from one layer to another.
- ❑ Adobe Photoshop displays applied **Layer style** effects as items in the **Layers palette**.

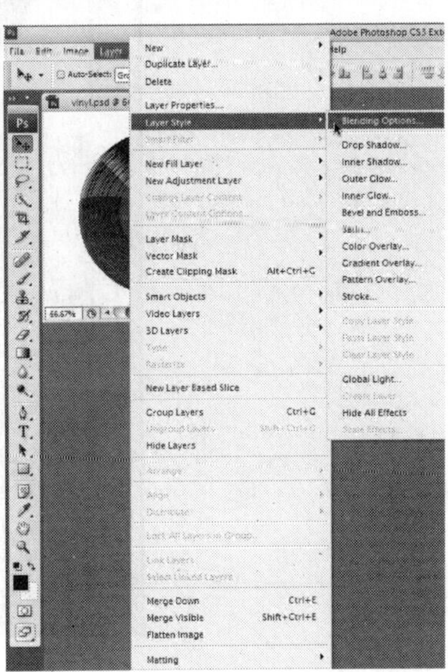

Layer stlye dialog

- Clicking the eye icon next to each effect's name in the **Layers palette** temporarily disables the layer style. Click the eye next to the word **Effects** to temporarily disable all the applied layer styles for that layer.
- Lowering the **Fill** percentage in the **Layers palette** reduces the **Opacity** of the layer, but not the applied **Layer styles**.
- **The Global Light** option in the **Layer Style** dialog box tells Adobe Photoshop to apply the same angle to all direction-dependent effects, such as **Drop Shadow**, **Inner Shadow**, and **Bevel and Emboss**. The idea here is to simulate consistent real-world lighting.
- Combinations of layer style effects can be saved for later use in the **Styles palette**.

How Drop Shadows work

Drop Shadow applies a basic drop shadow—not a perspective drop shadow—to the images, type, or shapes that are contained within the layer. Adobe Photoshop allows you to specify the colour, opacity, blend mode, position, size, and contour of the effect.

Applying effects to layers is easy. Either double-click on a layer to open the **Layer Style** dialog, or go to menu **Layer>Layer Style**.

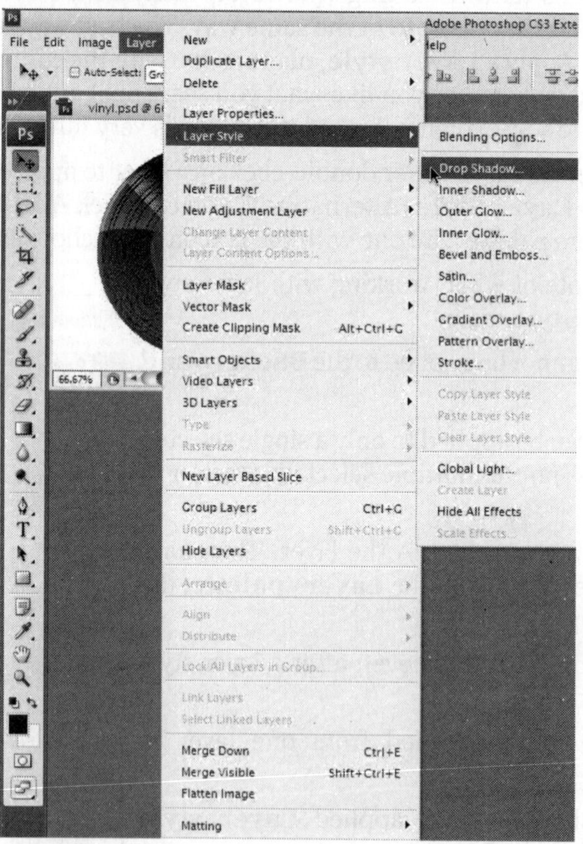

Opening Layer style dialog

Alternatively, you can click **Add Layer Style** button at the bottom of the **Layers palette** (the one with the ***fx*** icon), and choose an effect from the list.

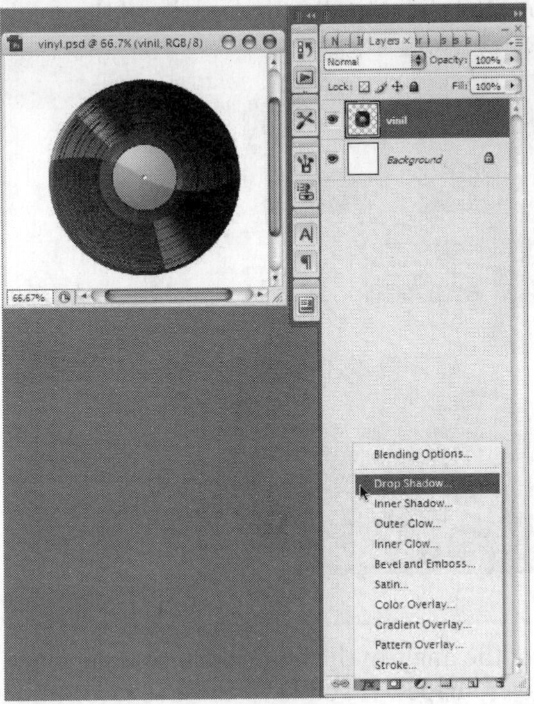

Once the **Layer Style** window opens, pick the **Drop Shadow**, apply settings and click **OK**.

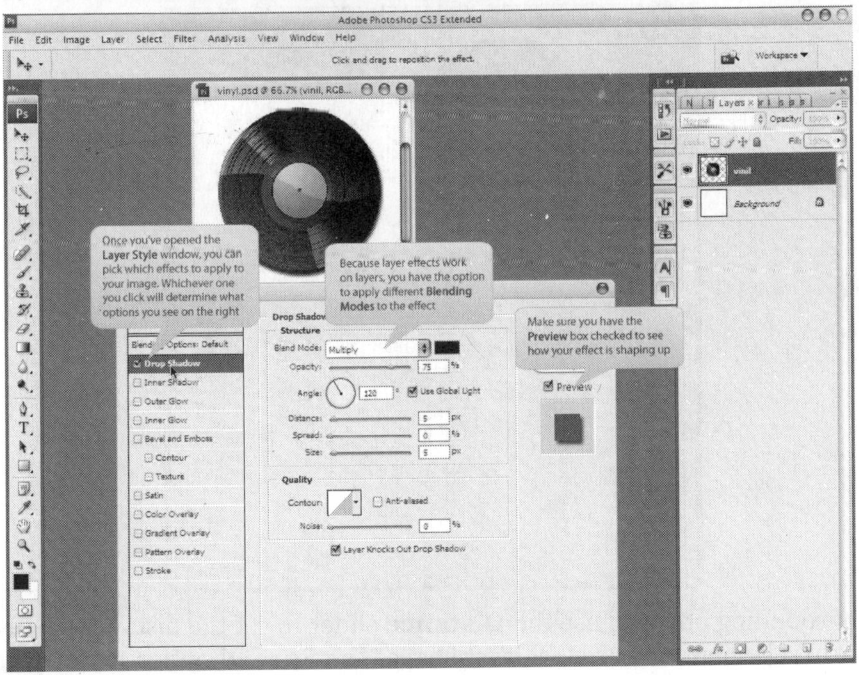

The top part of the **Drop Shadow** settings allows you to set a blending mode for the effect as well as the colour of the shadow. Just double-click the black rectangle to bring up the **Colour Picker**. You can also move the slider to alter the opacity of the shadow.

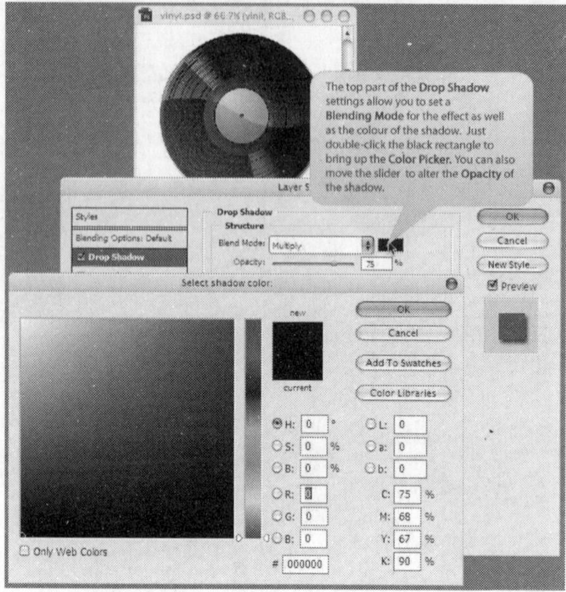

Use the **Angle** circle to set the angle of the light source. Whatever angle you choose will be in relation to the original layer shapes. If you keep the Use **Global Light** option checked, the effect will use the current angle setting from **Layer>Layer Style>Global Light**.

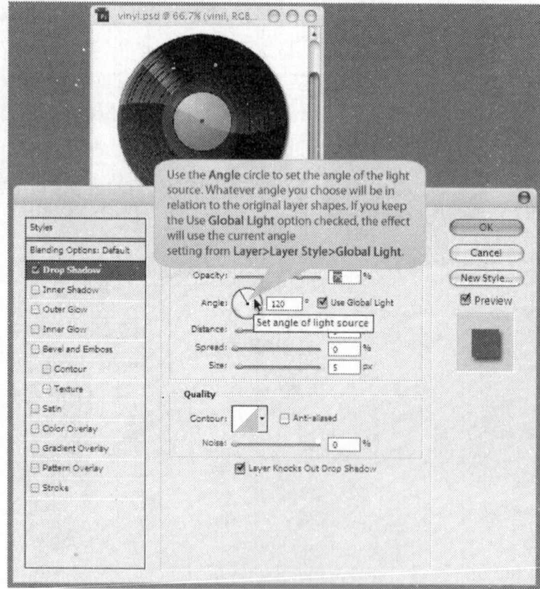

At the risk of sounding obvious, use the **Distance** slider to set the distance (in pixels) of the drop shadow in relation to the original layer shape. The **Spread** option allows you to control where the shadow starts to fade, while the Size slider controls the size of the shadow, again in pixels.

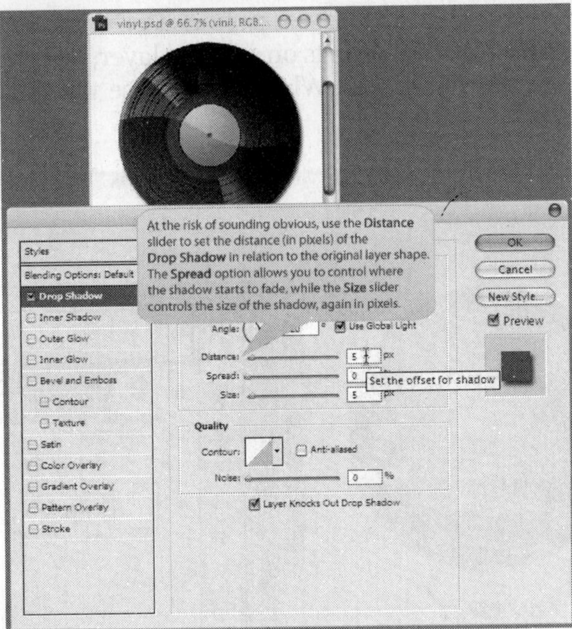

The **Quality** area of the dialog allows you to set different contours. These beauties control the edge shape of the shadow and can dramatically alter the effect. Keep the **Anti-aliased box** checked to soften the edges between the shadow and other parts of the image, and also experiment with the **Noise** slider.

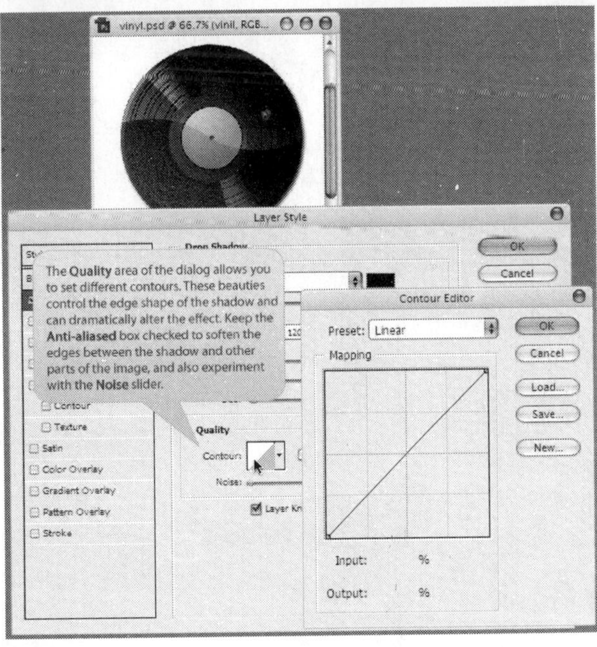

When working with **Drop Shadows**, it's worth keeping the **Layer Knocks Out Drop Shadow** option checked. This will prevent the shadow from showing through layer pixels that have a low **Fill** opacity.

Tip: To use the same **Drop Shadow** settings on another layer, drag the **Drop Shadow** layer in the **Layers palette** to the other layer. When you release the mouse button, the shadow attributes are applied.

Chapter 12

Photoshop Filters

Filters are used to change the appearance of an image, layer or selection in Photoshop. In this lesson, I'll introduce you to some common filters, and show you how to use them.

For me, filters in Photoshop are sort of like those special effects you can add to home videos with those consumer handheld video cameras – easy to use, but they certainly have their place in design. That said, there are plenty of ways to get creative using filters, so they are definitely worth understanding in Photoshop.

Using Filters from the Filter Gallery

Photoshop's **Filter Gallery** is basically a one-stop place for working with filters in your documents. In the Filter Gallery, you can browse through many different types of filters, apply them individually to your image, or even stack them on top of one another like you would with layers. You can get to the Filter Gallery by going to **Filter > Filter Gallery**.

Here's a quick overview of the Filter Gallery:

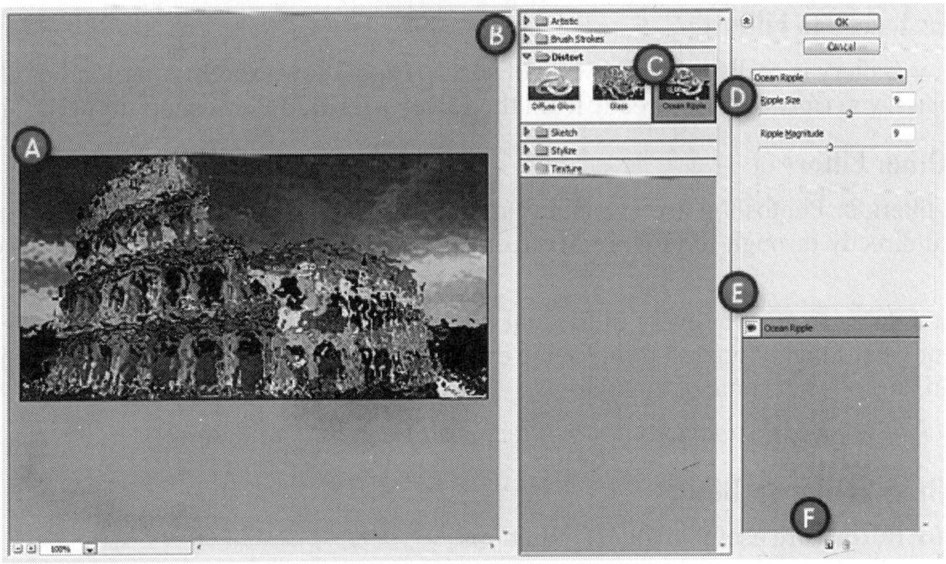

Filter Gallery

Filter Gallery Interface

A. Filter Preview

B. Filter List (*Note: You can show or hide this list by clicking the arrow icon to the top right of it*)

C. Currently Selected Filter

D. Filter Options

E. Effect Layers

F. New / Delete Effect Layer

The Filter Effect Layers work just like ordinary filters in Photoshop, and can be dragged and dropped on top of one another for desired results.

Applying a filter from the gallery is very easy to do. Simply **click on a filter**, adjust its options to your liking, and click **OK** to apply. To stack multiple filters on top of one another, just hit the **New Effect Layer**, and select another filter. You can expand filter types by clicking the folders in the filter list.

The Cutout Filter quickly transforms a photograph into an abstract piece of art

Quicker Access to Filters

The Filter Gallery is really just a browser of sorts. If you know exactly what kind of filter you want to use, you can access it directly from the **Filter menu** in Photoshop to speed things up.

Using Other Filters

Not all filters in Photoshop are available through the Filter Gallery. Many of them must be accessed directly through the **Filter Menu**, and have unique interfaces and options of their own.

We're not going to go over every individual filter in this lesson (*doing so would take a very long time*), but I highly suggest doing some experimentation on your part with different filters to get an idea of what some of them do.

Let's look at some of the more common filters used frequently in design.

Blur Filters (Filter > Blur)

The **Blur Filters** are useful in lots of situations.

*The **Lens Blur Filter** makes it very easy to create a realistic lens blur effect in Photoshop*

Noise Filters (Filter > Noise)

Noise Filters are great for adding, or reducing noise and grain in photographs. You may find filters such as the **Reduce Noise Filter** extremely useful if you work with old, damaged, or dusty photographs that need repair work done to them. The **Add Noise Filter** can also come in handy, and has some creative applications of its own.

*Noise can easily be reduced with the **Reduce Noise Filter** in Photoshop*

Sharpen Filters (Filter > Sharpen)

The **Sharpen Filters** are also great for correcting imperfections in photographs, as well as putting emphasis on important elements in a design. When working with blurred images, a sharpen filter can be used to clarify and better define edges by increasing contrast between pixels.

*The **Smart Sharpen Filter** used to sharpen a photograph of a statue*

Filters Disabled?

While all filters are available to be used on 8-bit RGB images, many will be unavailable if working with other colour spaces, 16-bit, or 32-bit documents. Filters will also be unavailable for use in Bitmap and Indexed-colour documents.

If you're not able to use filters, you may need to go to **Image > Mode**, and make sure you're set to **RGB**, and **8 Bits/Channel**.

Chapter 13

Applications of Clone Stamp Tool

Maybe the Clone Stamp Tool is one of the most known tools in Photoshop, but have you ever wondered: what else can I do with the cloning stamp than duplicating pixels and hiding objects? Now I will show you some new uses of this wonderful tool.

Cloning a "Baby" Car

Before we get started, let's take a look at the image we'll be creating.

The Basics

The Clone Stamp Tool is an awesome feature of Photoshop. It has been a part of the application for quite some time. Using this tool is really simple. First, select the brush type, choose the area you want to duplicate. Next press and hold only the Option key, and then click one time over the area that we call the *Clone Source*. Finally, just paint anywhere you want it.

You can clone from only one layer or several layers selecting the sample combo box. Also, you can paint the clone source on the original layer or into a new one. This tool is well known as the *object remover*, see the image next page for a sample of the tool in action, which shows us how to

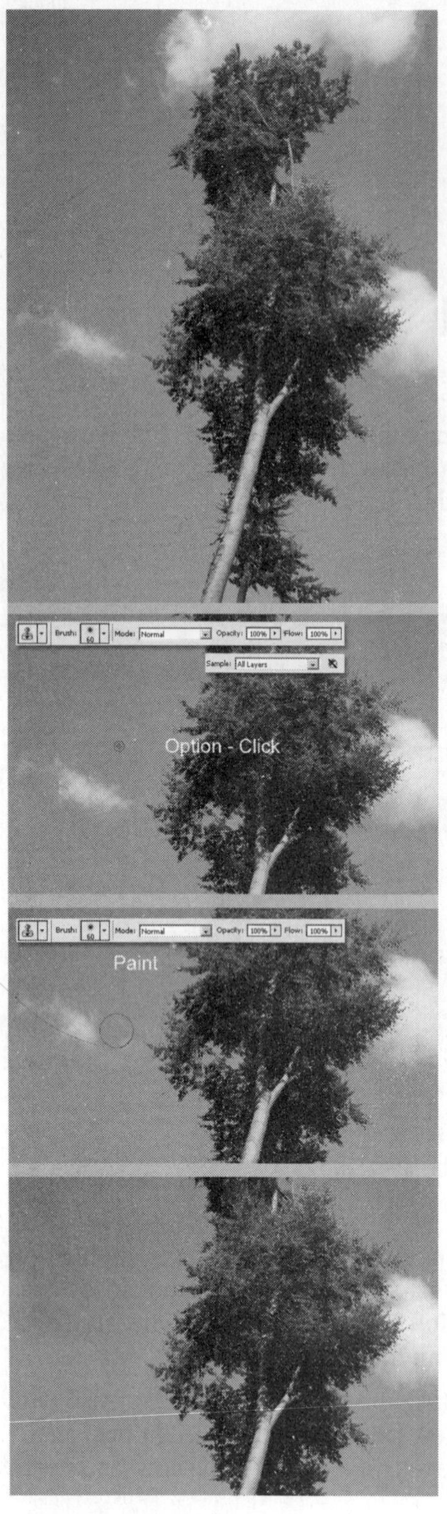

remove a small cloud from a picture. Simple right? Let's go to something a little bit more complicated next.

Step 1

First, open your original picture. I'm using this one of an old white truck, then go to **File > Save as...** and save it somewhere as a PSD. I pasted the image into a new document at 1422 pixels by 1024 pixels, but you can work in the original file size.

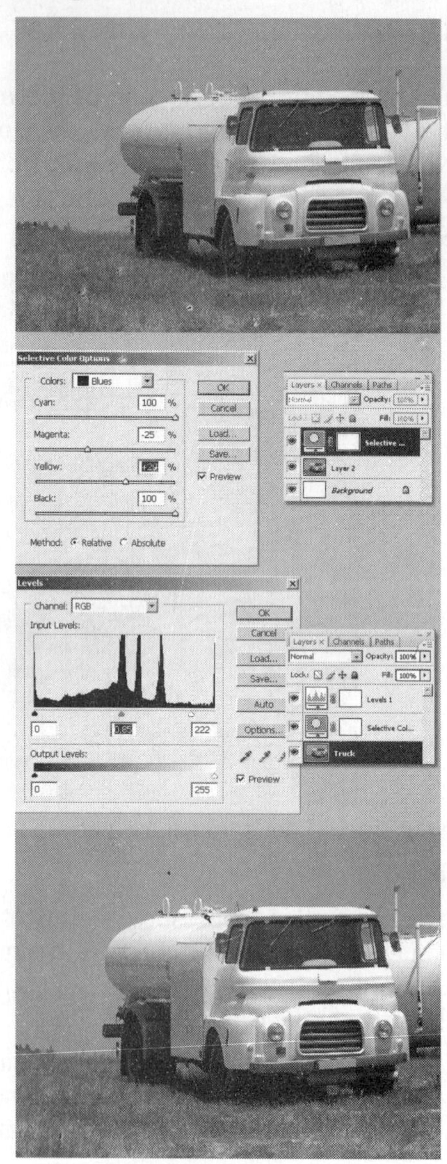

Actually, my picture looks a little bit purple, so I'll fix this by using two Adjustment Layers, a Selective colour adjustment, only the blue colour, and a Level Adjustment layer. Why adjustment layers? Well this way all the adjustments will be applied to any other layer on the document, but without distorting your original image. Name the image layer "Truck."

Step 2

Now select the "Truck" layer in the Layers Palette and select the Clone Stamp Tool. Set the brush at around 50px and set the Hardness to 0%. Now to select the cloning source Alt-Click somewhere on your image, a good point is just at the top left of the truck. Also, go to **Window > Clone source** to show the advanced options.

Step 3

When you have selected your clone source, create a new layer above the "Truck" layer and name it "Mini truck." Go to the Clone Source window and mark the Show Overlay checkbox. This way you'll have a transparent copy of your clone source. Try moving your brush here and there to see how it works.

Now in the Clone source window, change these values W: 30% and H: 30%, this way you'll be resizing your clone source to 30% of the original size. Next, place the clone transparent overlay on a proper place and start painting until you duplicate the entire truck. Remember, you'll be painting on the "Mini truck" layer.

Step 4

Now very carefully, using the Eraser Tool, delete all the dirt areas cloned around the "Mini Truck".

Step 5

Now using the Burn tool, burn some areas of the "Mini truck" layer.

Step 6

I'm adding two more Adjustments layers: a Exposure adjustment and a Gradient map (Blending Mode set to Linear Burn).

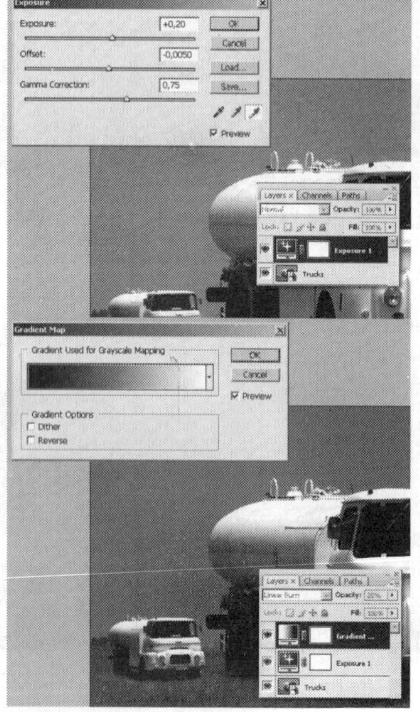

And that's it, just to improve the distance sensation, blur the "Mini tuck" layer just a little bit by going to **Filter > Blur > Blur**.

Getting To Grips With Vanishing Point Filter

Adding Floors to a Building

Step 1

The Vanishing Point filter is all about perspective. When you're editing photography, perspective is one of the most important issues to consider; the Vanishing Point filter helps us to make it easy. This time I've got two short lessons to help you to understand this amazing filter.

The first one is about adding realistic floors to a building. Before getting started you'll need an image to edit, I choose this picture because the perspective is very clean and easy to follow. As a first step, paste the image into a new document, a lot bigger than the original picture, then add a new colour fill layer using the sky colour as a sample (you can use the Eyedropper tool to get a similar colour).

Add a layer mask to the picture layer and paint with a huge brush on it. Delete the sky over the buildings. Finally, merge the blue background of the sky with the original picture and name the resulting layer "Buildings."

Step 2

Now, go to **Filters > Vanishing point**, remember when you're working with the Vanishing point filter, all the editing (paste, select, clone) must be done into the Vanishing Point Filter window and nowhere else. At this point, you'll only need to draw a reference plane, do this by selecting the Create Plane Tool (C) in Vanishing Point Filter window. You can use the windows as a guide.

Step 3

Select the Edit Plane tool (V) and resize your plane, make it wider and taller as you'll need. Hit OK to save the Vanishing Point plane. Then create a new layer above the original picture and name it something like "Edited picture." We're going to add all the painting in this layer to keep the original file handy. Select the new layer and go to the Vanishing Point window again.

Step 4

Now the fun! First, we're going to clone the pipes to get a higher clean area to select in the next step. Select the Clone Tool within the vanishing point window, it works just like the standard clone tool, but this one keeps the perspective when you're cloning. Hold the Alt key and click to select the cloning source, try to click over the area of one of the pipes, then just paint up. Without changing the clone source, clone the other two pipes of our picture. Hit OK if you want to see the result.

Step 5

Let's add some floors next. In the Vanishing Point window, click on the Marquee Tool, and make a selection using two or three buildings, try to make a selection as clear as possible. Next, hold the Alt key and click + drag the selection some pixels up. Do it as many times as floors you want to add, never mind if there's some bad areas for now.

Step 6

As you'll see duplicating the selection isn't always a perfect process, so as there are a lot of tiny imperfections, use the Clone tool to fix them.

Step 7

Finally, crop the image. Also if you want, add more details, like cloning the windows to create some variants between them, use the Blur tool to blur the hard line between building and sky, and whatnot.

And that's it! To create a more colourful scene I'd merged the layers, duplicated the result, applied a Gaussian Blur 4px radius to the copy, and change the copy's Blending mode to Overlay with an Opacity set to 75%.

Chapter 14

The hidden power of Photoshop Brush Tool

In this section, I will describe my favourite feature of Adobe Photoshop – Brush tool. To learn all features, you can simply open Brush palette (Window menu → Brushes), change each setting and try the result when you draw a stroke. The first setting is Tip Shape. You can choose from pre-loaded shapes or you can create your own... more on that later!

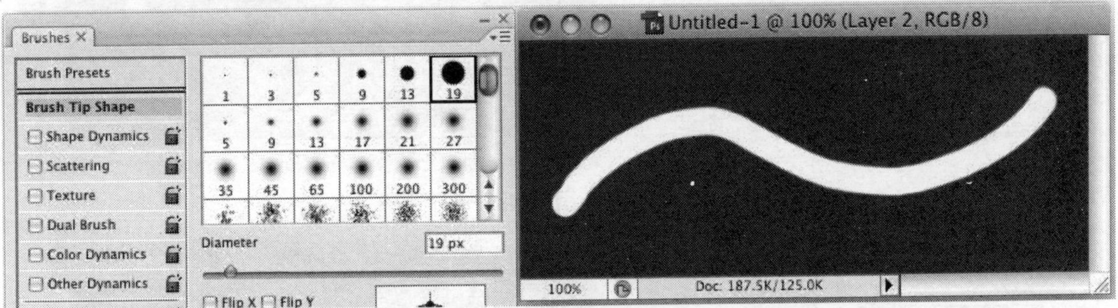

Brush Tip Shape has one interesting setting – Spacing. It is usually around 20-25% but when you set it larger than 100-150% you will get very different result.

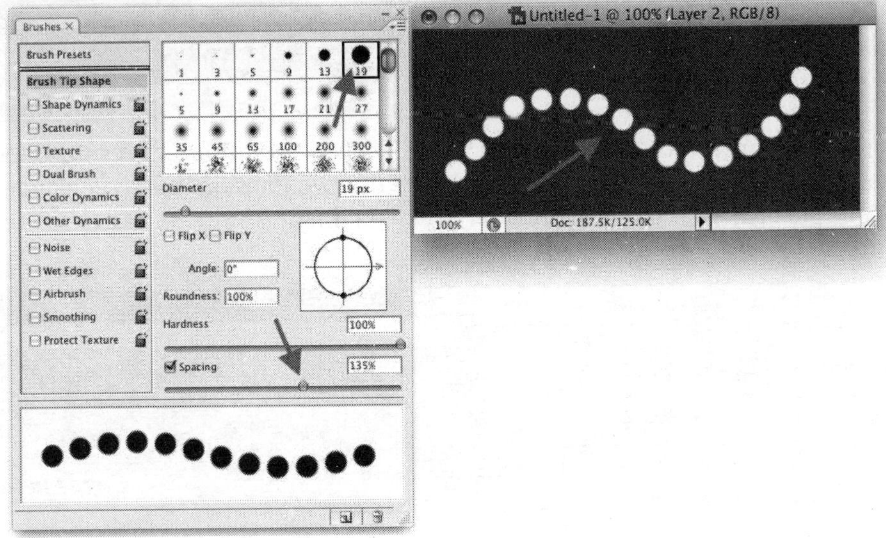

Using Shape Dynamics checkbox, you can randomize sizes and angles of brush dots.

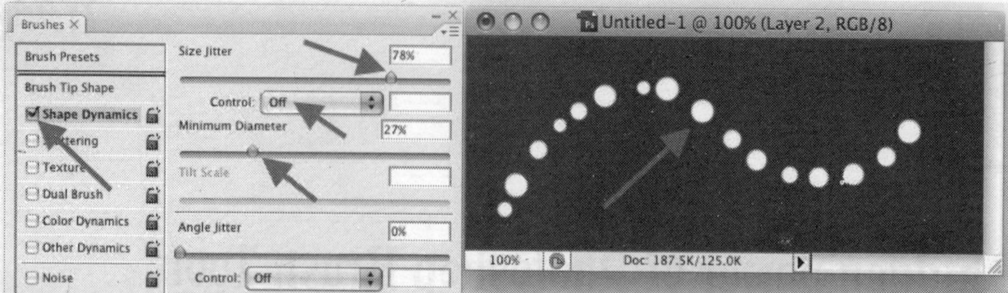

Using Scattering, you can randomize locations of brush dots – as you draw a straight stroke, dots are added randomly around your mouse.

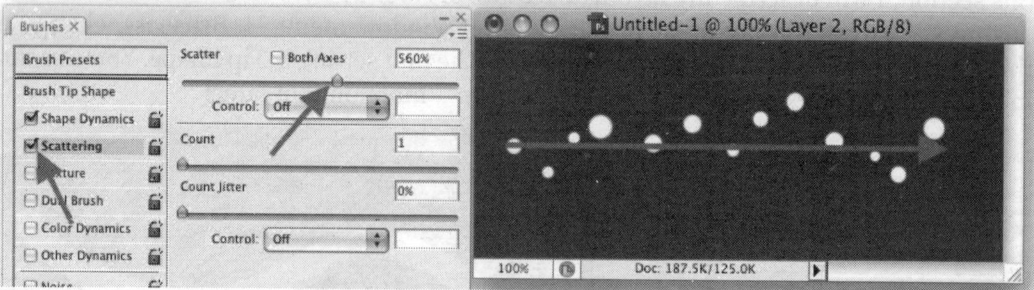

You can use Count setting to control amount of dots.

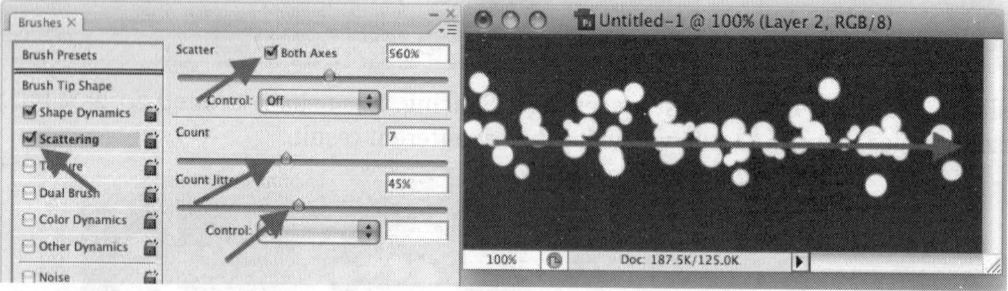

Dual Brush is a very interesting feature, which will get you very different results depending on which brush and which mode you choose. Compare the two lines on this screenshot – first line made with simple brush, second – with Dual Brush enabled.

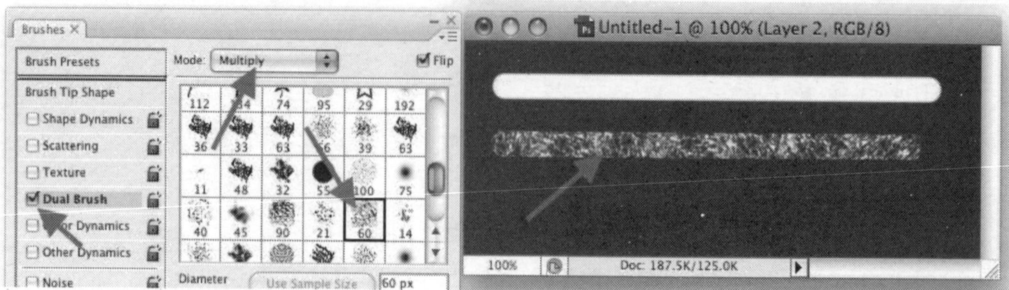

You can use Colour Dynamics to randomize (or fade, or control with tablet pen) brush colour. I do not use this often, though.

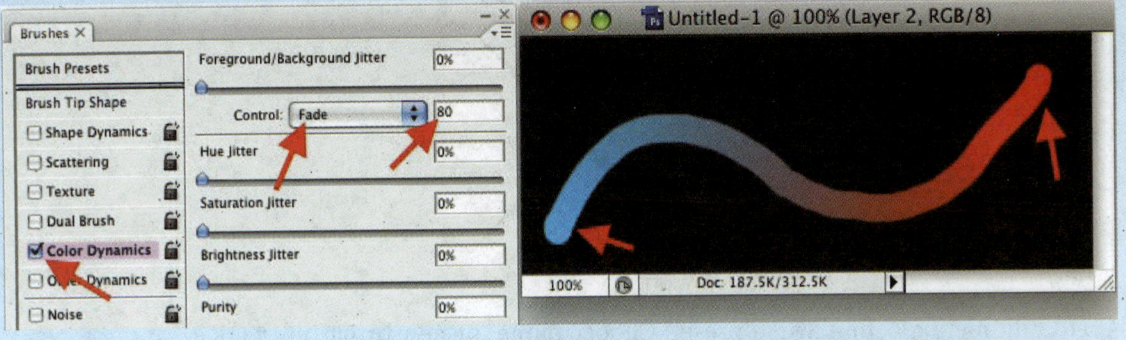

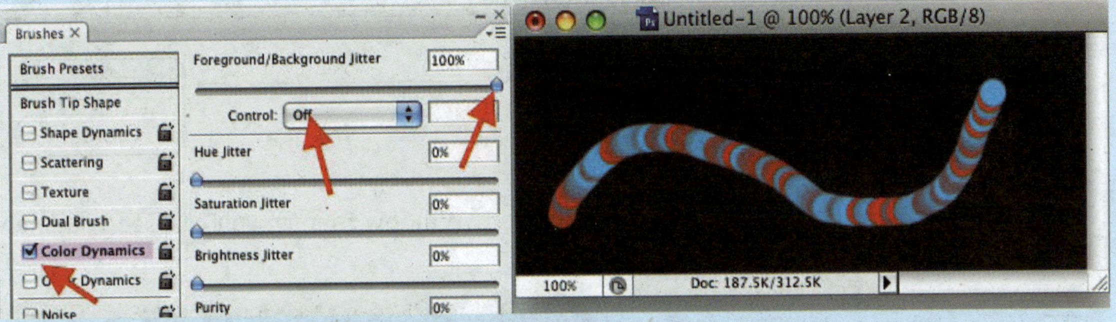

Wet Edges is a simple and self-explanatory feature.

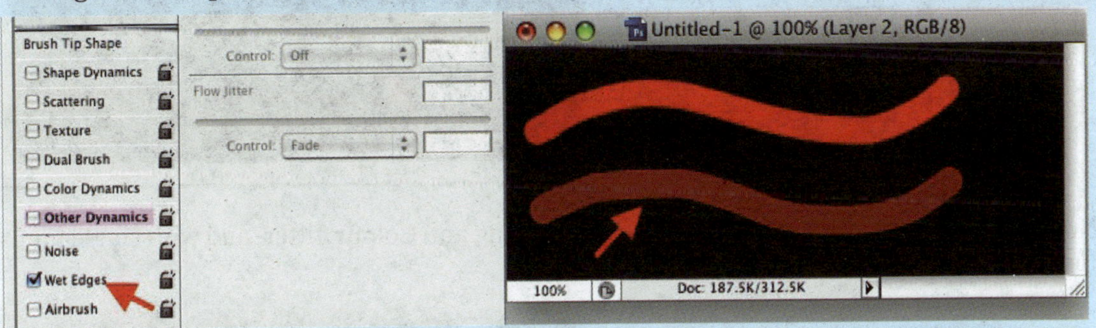

The most exciting thing is that you can easily create your own brush. Let's make a star brush for example. Create new image with transparent background (square for our star). Set foreground colour to Black, switch to Shape tool (U), select Polygon tool on toolbar, open Polygon options, check Star checkbox, set Indent sides = around 90%, and sides = 4.

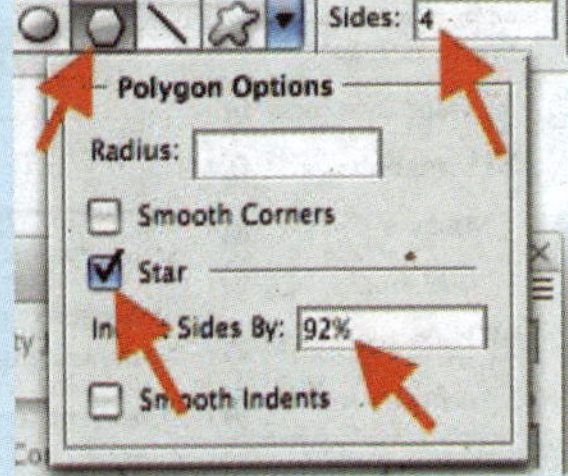

Draw a shape, rasterize it (Layer - Rasterize - Shape). Select all (Ctrl-A).

Go to Edit menu; Define Brush preset. Choose name for new brush, click OK.

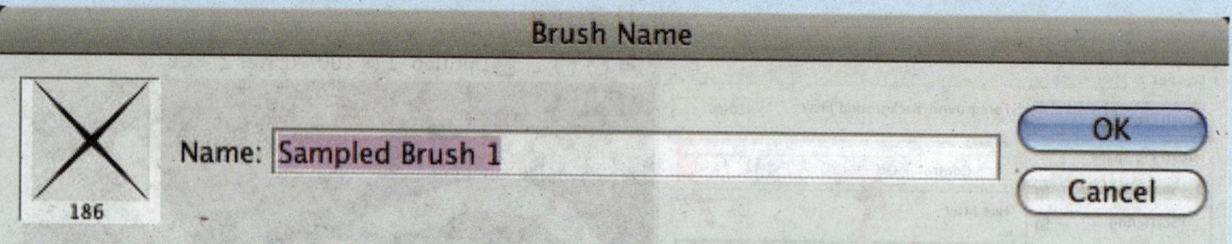

Now, when you open Brushes palette window (from Window menu), you can see your new brush in Brush Tip Shape list.

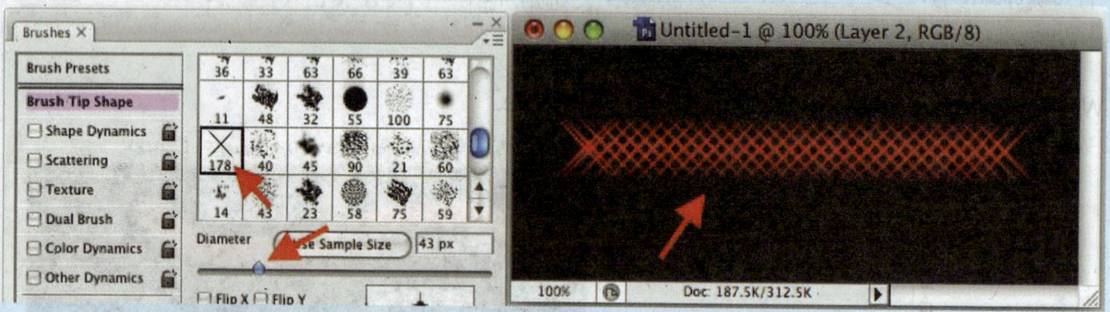

Now you can enable and adjust Size Jitter, Scattering and Colour Jitter, and with single mouse move, get result such as this!

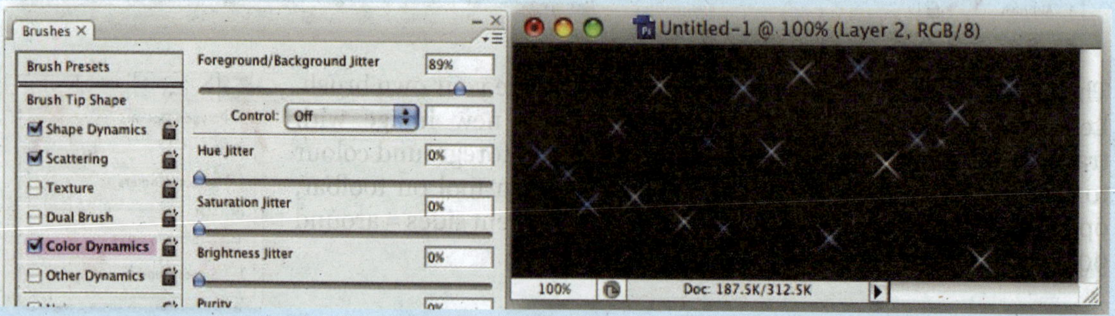

Another example: I took the shape of snow flake, created brush preset from it. With Size Jitter, Scattering and Colour Jitter, this is what single brush stroke looks like.

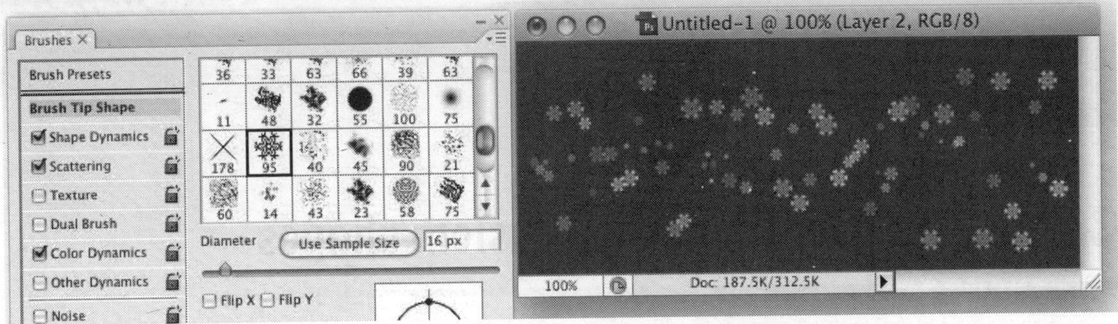

An another example: heart-shaped brush. Again, this screenshot made with only one brush move!

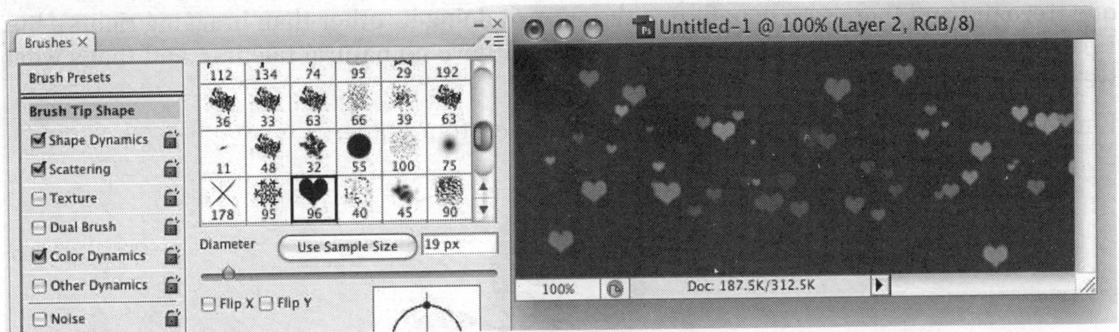

Create your own Photoshop custom shapes

In this section, we're going to create our custom shape by tracing around an object in an image. If you have a natural talent for drawing and can draw your shape freehand without needing to trace around anything, great! There's no difference between tracing an object or drawing one freehand and there's no benefit to either way of doing it (other than bragging rights), but I personally find it easier to trace around objects (I have no natural talents), and that's what we'll be doing here.

I'm going to turn Mr. Gingerbread Man here into a custom shape:

Step 1: Select the Pen Tool

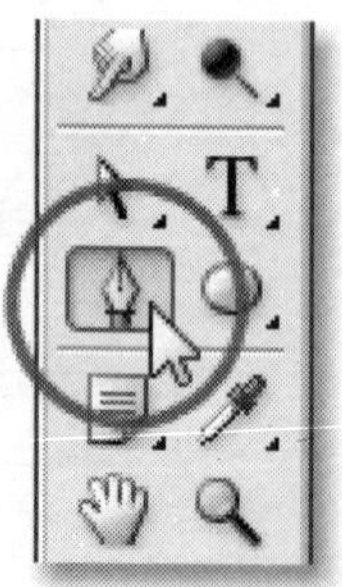

Select the Pen Tool

As I mentioned, you *can* create custom shapes in Photoshop using the basic Shape tools like the Rectangle or Ellipse Tool, but try tracing our gingerbread man with those tools. What we really need is the Pen Tool, so select it from the Tools palette.

You can also select the Pen Tool by pressing the letter P on your keyboard.

Step 2: Select the "Shape Layers" Option in the Options Bar

With the Pen Tool selected, look up in the Options Bar at the top of the screen. Over on the left, you'll see a group of three icons:

The three icons in the Options Bar which allow us to select what we want to do with the Pen Tool

These icons represent what you can do with the Pen Tool. The icon on the right is grayed out, and that's because it's only available when we have one of the basic Shape tools selected (the Pen Tool and the Shape tools share most of the same options in the Options Bar). The icon in the middle is used when we want to draw paths, but that's not what we want to do here. We want to use the Pen Tool to draw shapes, and for that, we need to select the icon on the left, which is the Shape layers icon:

Select the "Shape layers" icon to draw shapes with the Pen Tool

The "Shape layers" option is selected by default whenever you grab the Pen Tool so you probably won't need to select it yourself. It's a good idea though to check and make sure it's selected before you begin drawing your shape.

I should point out here that there's no difference between drawing paths with the Pen Tool and drawing shapes with it. Both are created exactly the same way, by clicking to add anchor points, then dragging out direction handles if needed to create straight or curved path segments. In fact, regardless of whether you're "officially" drawing shapes or paths, you're drawing paths. The difference is that with shapes, Photoshop fills the path with colour, even as you're drawing it, which is what allows us to see the shape.

This is actually going to create a bit of a problem for us, as we'll see in a moment.

Step 3: Begin Drawing Your Shape

Now that we have the Pen Tool selected along with the "Shape layers" option in the Options Bar, we can begin tracing around the object. I'm going to start by tracing around the top of the gingerbread man, clicking with the Pen Tool to place anchor points and dragging out direction handles to create curved path segments around the side and top of his head. We can see the anchor points and direction handles in the screenshot below, but notice that we also have a bit of a problem. Photoshop is filling the shape with the Foreground colour (mine is currently set to black) as I draw it, blocking the gingerbread man from view:

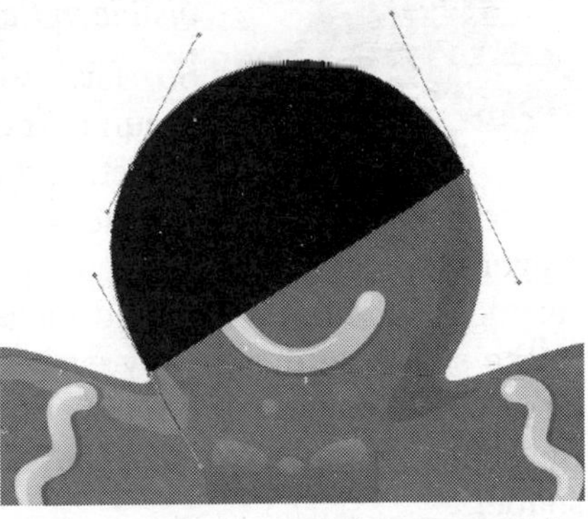

Photoshop fills the shape with the Foreground colour as you draw it, blocking the object from view

We'll fix this problem next.

Step 4: Lower the Opacity of The Shape Layer

To fix the problem of Photoshop blocking our object from view as we try to trace around it, simply go to your Layers palette and lower the opacity of the shape layer. We can see here in my Layers palette that I currently have two layers – the *Background* layer on the bottom which contains my gingerbread man photo, and the shape layer above it, named "Shape 1". I can tell that the shape layer is selected because it's highlighted in blue, so to lower its Opacity, all I need to do is go up to the Opacity option in the top right corner of the Layers palette and lower the value. I'm going to set my opacity to about 50%:

Lower the opacity of the shape layer using the Opacity option in the top right of the Layers palette ➡

Now that I've lowered the opacity of the shape layer, I can see my gingerbread man easily through the shape colour, which is going to make it much easier to continue tracing around him:

The object is now visible through the shape colour after lowering the shape layer's opacity ➡

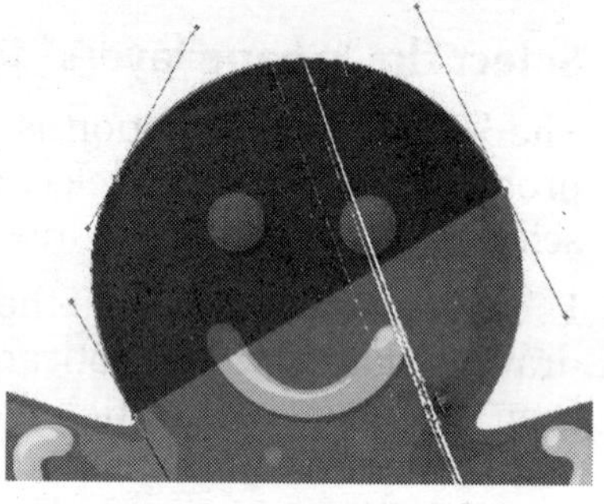

Step 5: Continue Tracing the Object

With the gingerbread man now visible through the shape colour, I can continue tracing around him with the Pen Tool until I've completed my initial shape:

⬅ *The initial shape around the object is now complete*

If I look at the shape layer in my Layers palette, I can now see the shape of the gingerbread man clearly defined:

The shape of the object is now clearly visible in the Layers palette ➡

So far, so good. We've traced around the basic shape of the object, and depending on the shape you're using, this may be enough. In my case though, my gingerbread man shape needs a bit more detail. At the very least, I think we should include his eyes and mouth in the shape, and probably even his bow tie and the two large buttons below it. So how do we add these details to the shape? Simple. We don't! We subtract them from the shape!

We'll see how to do that next!

Step 6: Select the Ellipse Tool

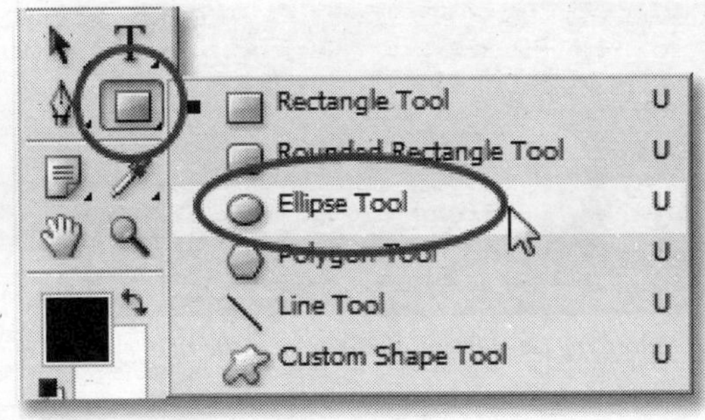

Let's start with his eyes. We could select his eyes with the Pen Tool if we wanted, but since they're round, we'll be able to select them more easily using the Ellipse Tool. Select the Ellipse Tool from the Tools palette. By default, it's hiding behind the Rectangle Tool, so click on the Rectangle Tool, then hold your mouse button down for a second or two until the fly-out menu appears, and then select the Ellipse Tool from the list:

Step 7: Select the "Subtract From Shape Area" Option

With the Ellipse Tool selected, look up in the Options Bar and you'll see a series of icons grouped together that look like little squares combined in different ways. These icons allow us to do things like add a new shape to the current shape, subtract a shape from the current shape, or intersect one shape with another. Click on the third icon from the left, which is the Subtract from shape area icon:

Click on the "Subtract from shape area" icon in the Options Bar

Step 8: Drag Out Shapes to Subtract them from the Initial Shape

Now that we have the "Subtract from shape area" option selected, we can begin adding little details to our shape by essentially cutting holes out of it. I'm going to begin by dragging an elliptical shape around his left eye:

Dragging an elliptical shape around the left eye ➡

When I release my mouse button, the elliptical shape around the eye is instantly subtracted, or "cut out" from the initial shape, creating a hole for the eye. The left eye from the original image on the *Background* layer below it is now showing through the hole:

The left eye has now been "cut out" of the initial shape, allowing the eye from the original image below it to show through ➡

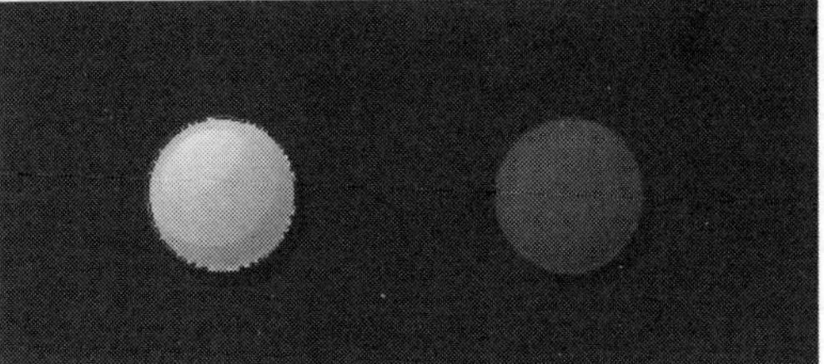

I'll do the same thing for the right eye. First, I'll drag an elliptical shape around it:

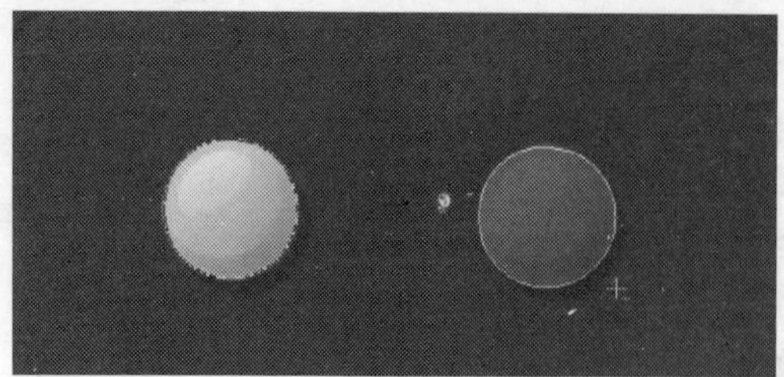

Dragging an elliptical shape around the right eye

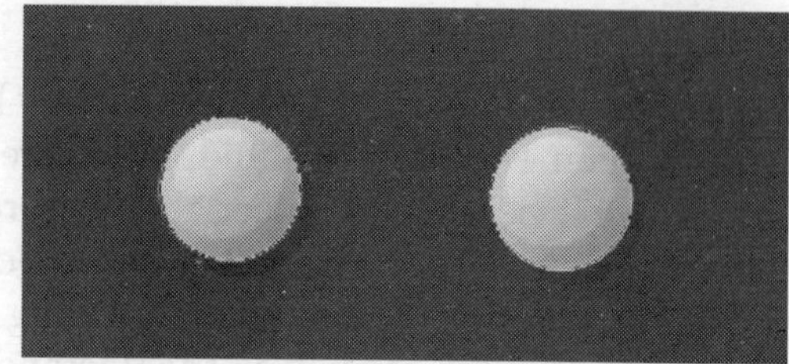

A second hole is now cut out of the initial shape, creating the second eye

And as soon as I release my mouse button, a second round hole is cut out of the initial shape, creating the second eye, again allowing the original image above right it to show through.

Since the two buttons below his bow tie are also round, I can use the Ellipse Tool to cut them out of my shape as well. First, I'll drag a shape around the top button.

Releasing my mouse button subtracts the shape from the initial shape, creating a hole for the button and allowing the image below it to show through.

And now I'll do the same thing for the bottom button, first dragging my shape around it.

And when I release my mouse button, a fourth hole is created in the initial shape.

Dragging an elliptical shape around the top button

A second hole is now cut out of the initial shape, creating the second eye

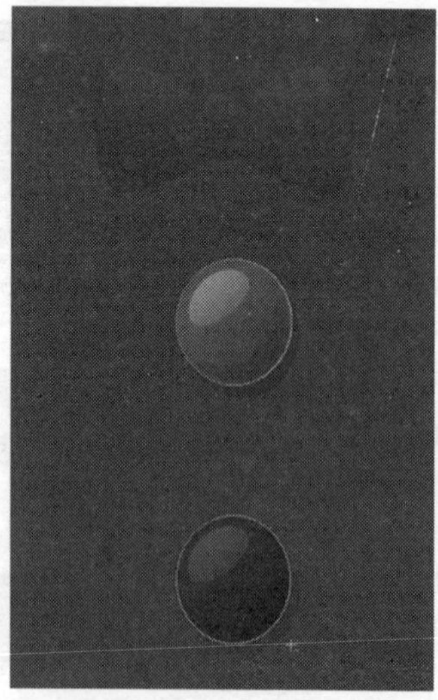

Dragging an elliptical shape around the bottom button

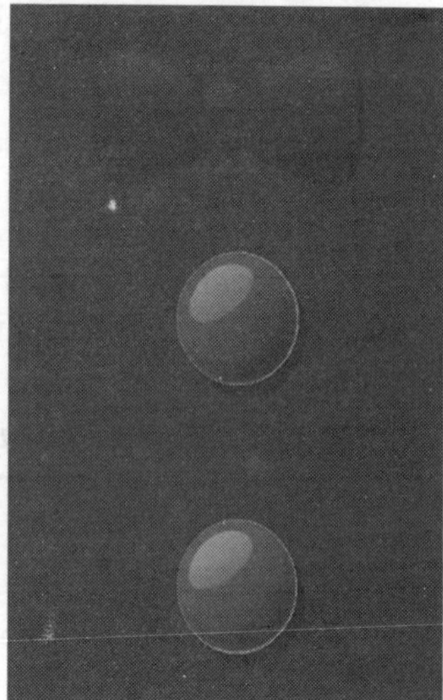

Both buttons have now been cut out of the initial shape

If I look at my shape layer's preview thumbnail in the Layers palette at this point, I can see the two holes for the eyes and the two holes for the buttons that I've cut out of the shape:

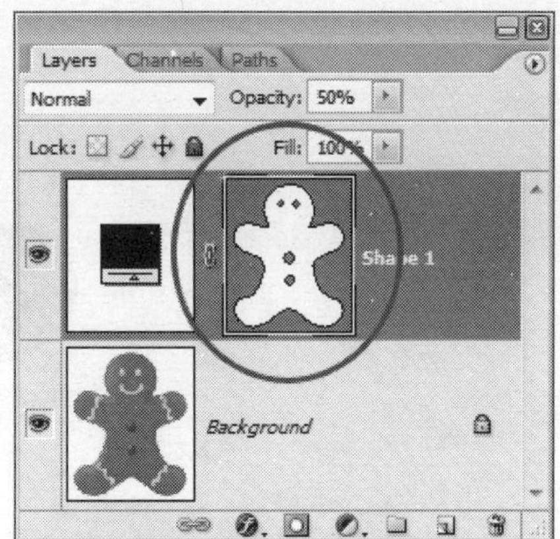

The shape layer's thumbnail now shows the holes cut out of the shape for the eyes and buttons ➡

We're going to switch back to the Pen Tool to add the remaining details to the shape next!

Step 9
Subtract Any Remaining Details from the Shape Using the Pen Tool

I'm going to switch back to my Pen Tool at this point because I have a few more details I want to add to my shape that I won't be able to select with the Ellipse Tool.

I want to add his mouth to the shape, as well as his bow tie, so with my Pen Tool selected and the "Subtract from shape area" option still selected in the Options Bar, I'm simply going to trace around his mouth and bow tie to subtract them from my initial gingerbread man shape.

Here, we can see the paths I've drawn around them, along with the original gingerbread man image showing through the holes I've created:

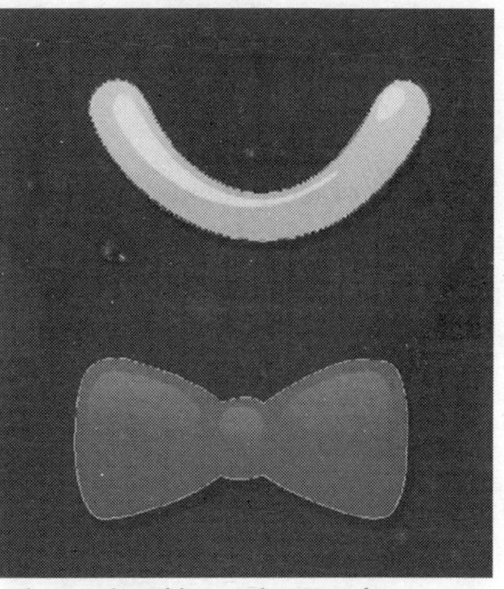

The mouth and bow tie have now been cut out of the initial gingerbread man shape using the Pen Tool

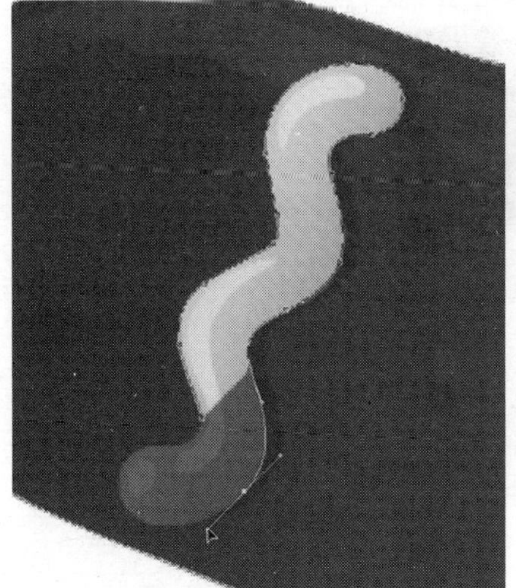

Subtracting the row of icing sugar along his left arm with the Pen Tool

Let's finish off our gingerbread man shape by subtracting those squiggly rows of icing sugar from his arms and legs. Again, I'll use the Pen Tool for this. Here, I'm drawing a path around the icing sugar along his left arm, and we can see the shape of the icing sugar being cut out of the initial shape as I go:

I'll finish tracing around this one, and then trace around the other three as well until all four rows of icing sugar have been subtracted from my initial shape:

The rows of icing sugar along with his arms and legs have now been subtracted from the initial shape.

If we look again at the shape layer's thumbnail in the Layers palette, we can see more clearly that all four rows of icing sugar, along with his eyes, mouth, bow tie, and buttons, have now been cut out of the shape:

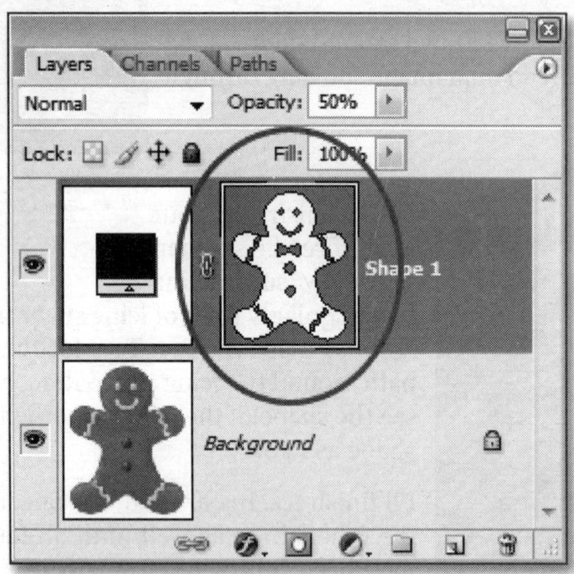

The shape layer thumbnail in the Layers palette showing all the details that have been cut out of the initial gingerbread man shape

At this point, I'd say the gingerbread man shape is complete! We've used the Pen Tool to trace around the outside of him, creating our initial shape, and then we used a combination of the Pen Tool and the Ellipse Tool, along with the "Subtract from shape area" option, to cut out all the smaller details in the shape.

Step 10: Increase the Opacity of the Shape Layer Back to 100%

Now that we're done tracing around the different parts of our object, we no longer need to see the original image through the shape, so go back to the Opacity option in the top right corner of the Layers palette and set the opacity value back to 100%:

Increase the opacity of the shape layer back to 100% ➡

I'm also going to hide my *Background* layer temporarily by clicking on its Layer Visibility icon (the "eyeball" icon) so we can see just the shape by itself against a transparent background. You don't have to hide your *Background* layer if you don't want to. I'm only doing this to make it easier for us to see the shape itself:

Clicking on the "Layer Visibility" icon for the Background layer to hide it temporarily from view ➡

With my original image on the *Background* layer now hidden and the opacity value of my shape layer set back to 100%, here's the gingerbread man shape I've created:

The completed gingerbread man shape, showing against a transparent background

After all that work, we have our shape! We're not done yet though. We still need to define it as a Custom Shape, and we'll see how to do that next!

Step 11: Define the Shape as a Custom Shape

To define our shape as a Custom Shape, first make sure your shape layer is selected in the Layers palette. Also, you'll need to make sure that the shape layer's preview thumbnail is selected. You can tell that it's selected because it will have a white highlight border around it, and you'll also be able to see your path outlines around your shape in the document. If the preview thumbnail does not have a highlight border around it and you can't see your path outlines, simply click on the thumbnail to select it:

Click directly on the shape layer's preview thumbnail to select it if needed ➡

Note....

If you ever need to hide the path outlines around your shape, simply click on the shape layer's preview thumbnail again to deselect it.

With the shape layer and its preview thumbnail selected, go up to the Edit menu at the top of the screen and select Define Custom Shape:

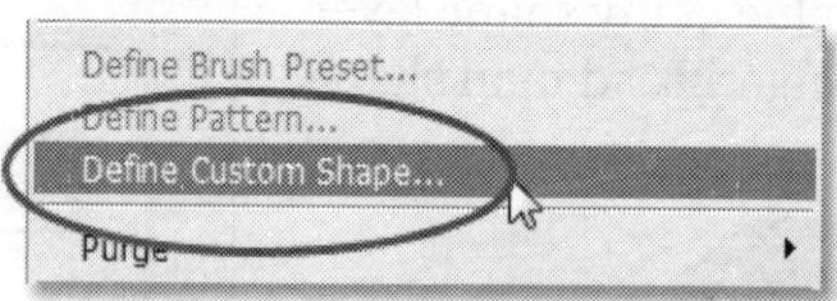

Go to Edit > Define Custom Shape

Photoshop will pop up the Shape Name dialog box, asking you to enter a name for your shape. I'm going to call my shape "Gingerbread Man":

Enter a name for your shape into the "Shape Name" dialog box

Click OK when you're done to exit out of the dialog box, and your Custom Shape is now ready for action! You can close out of your Photoshop document at this point since we're done creating and saving our shape. Now we're going to see where to find it and how to use it!

Step 12: Open a New Photoshop Document

Open a new blank Photoshop document by going up to your File menu at the top of the screen and choosing New.... This brings up the New Document dialog box. For the purpose of this lesson, you can choose any size you want for your document. I'm going to choose 640x480 pixels from the Preset menu:

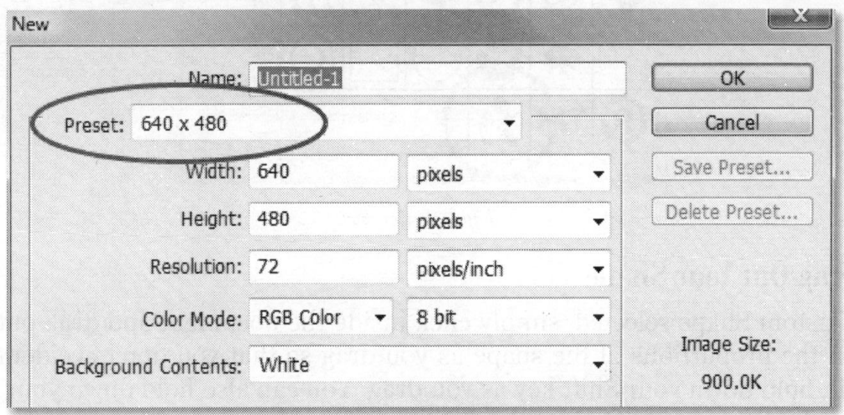

Create a new blank Photoshop document

Step 13: Select the Custom Shape Tool

With your new blank Photoshop document open, select the Custom Shape Tool from the Tools palette. By default, it's hiding behind the Rectangle Tool, so click on the Rectangle Tool, then hold your mouse button down for a second or two until the fly-out menu appears, and then select the Custom Shape Tool from the list:

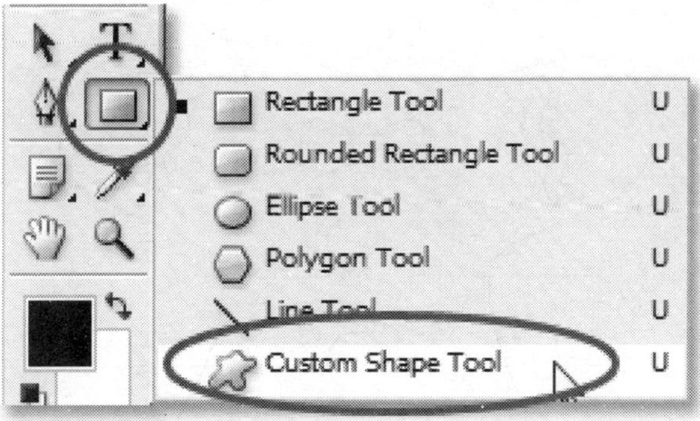

Custom Shape tool

Step 14: Select Your Custom Shape

With the Custom Shape Tool selected, right-click (Win) / Control-click (Mac) anywhere inside your Photoshop document. You'll see the Shape selection box appear, allowing you to select any of the currently available Custom Shapes. The shape you just created will appear as the very last shape in the selection box. Simply click on its little thumbnail to select it:

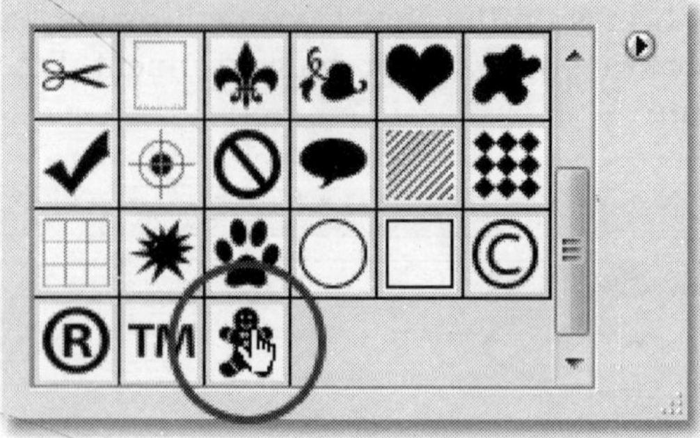

Shape selection box

Step 15: Drag Out Your Shape

With your Custom Shape selected, simply click inside the document and drag out the shape. To constrain the proportions of the shape as you drag so that you don't accidentally distort the look of it, hold down your Shift key as you drag. You can also hold down your Alt (Win) / Option (Mac) key if you want to drag the shape out from its centre. If you need to reposition your shape as you're dragging, simply hold down your spacebar, drag the shape into its new location, then release your spacebar and continue dragging out the shape.

As you're dragging out the shape, you'll see only the basic path outline of the shape appearing:

The basic path outline of the shape appears as you're dragging out the shape

When you're happy with the size and location of the shape, simply release your mouse button and Photoshop fills the shape with your current Foreground colour (mine happens to be set to black):

Release your mouse button and Photoshop fills the shape with colour

We're going to finish things off by looking at how to change the colour of our shape, along with how to resize and rotate it, next!

Step 16: Double-Click On the Shape Layer's Thumbnail to Change the Shape Colour

There's no need to worry about the colour of your shape when you're dragging it out and adding it to your document. Photoshop will automatically fill the shape with whatever colour you currently have selected as your Foreground colour, but if you want to change the shape's colour at any time, just double-click on the shape layer's thumbnail; not the shape preview thumbnail on the right (which is technically called a vector mask thumbnail). You want the thumbnail on the left, the one that looks like a colour swatch with a little slider bar underneath. Double-click on it to change the shape's colour.

This will bring up Photoshop's Colour Picker. Choose a new colour for your shape with the Colour Picker. I'm going to choose a brown colour for my gingerbread man.

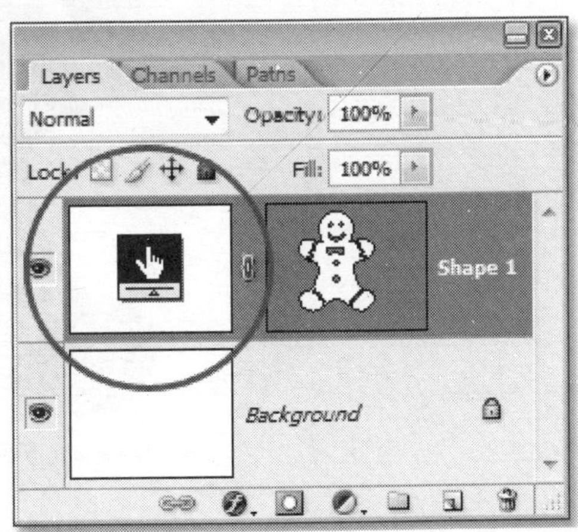

Double-click on the shape layer's thumbnail (the colour swatch thumbnail) on the left to change the shape's colour

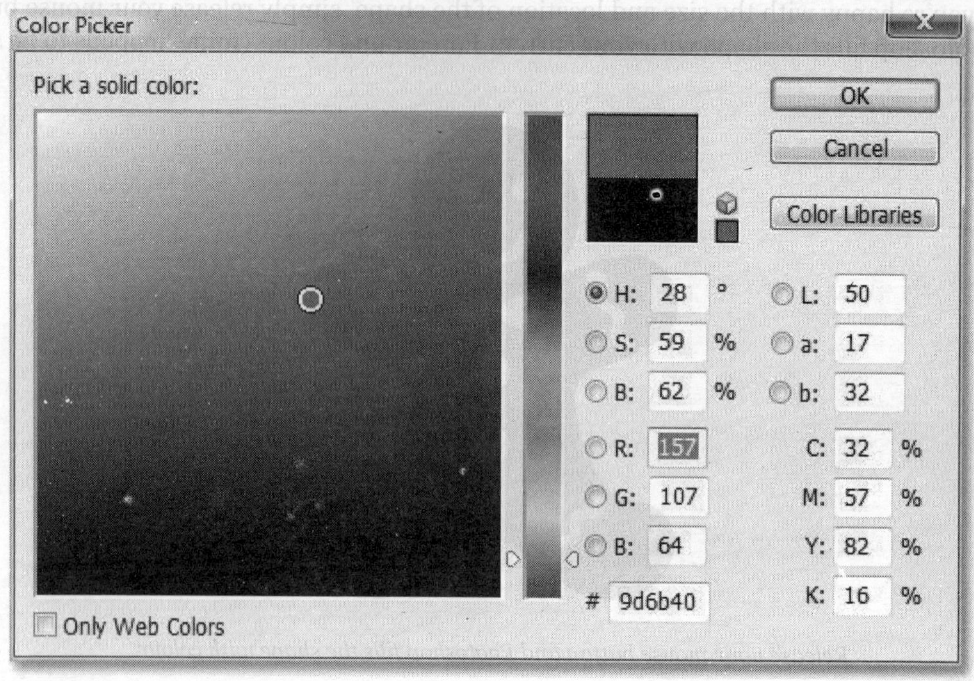

Use the Colour Picker to choose a new colour for your shape

Click OK when you're done to exit out of the Colour Picker, and the new colour is applied to your shape:

The colour of the shape has now been changed

You can change the colour of your shape whenever you need to, and as many times as you want!

Step 17: Resize the Shape if Needed with Free Transform

Colour isn't the only thing you don't have to worry about with shapes. One of the great things about working with shapes in Photoshop is that they use vectors instead of pixels, which means you're free to change the size of them whenenever you want, as often as you want, without any loss of image quality. If you decide you need to make your shape larger or smaller at any time, simply select the shape's layer in the Layers palette, then use the keyboard shortcut **Ctrl+T** (Win) / Command+T (Mac) to bring up Photoshop's Free Transform box and handles around the shape. Resize the shape by dragging any of the corner handles. Hold down Shift as you drag the handles to constrain the proportions of the shape, again so that you don't accidentally distort the look of it. You can also hold down Alt (Win) / Option (Mac) as you drag the handles to resize the shape from its centre:

Resize the shape by dragging any of the Free Transform handles

To rotate the shape, simply move your mouse anywhere outside of the Free Transform box, then click and drag your mouse to rotate it:

Click and drag your mouse anywhere outside of the Free Transform box to rotate the shape

Press Enter (Win) / Return (Mac) when you're done to accept the transformation and exit out of Free Transform.

You can add as many copies of your custom shape as you like to your document, changing the colour, size and rotation of each one as needed. Each copy of the shape will appear as its own separate shape layer in the Layers palette. Here, I've added several more copies of my Gingerbread Man shape to my document, each one set to a different colour, size and angle. Notice how no matter what size you make them, they always retain their sharp, crisp edges:

Add as many copies of your custom shape as you like to your design, changing the colour, size and angle of each one. And there we have it! We've created an initial shape by tracing around an object with the Pen Tool. We "cut out" little details in our shape using a combination of the Pen Tool and the Ellipse Tool, both set to the "Subtract from shape area" option in the Options Bar. We saved our shape as a Custom Shape using the "Define Custom Shape" option in the Edit menu. We then created a new Photoshop document, selected the "Custom Shape Tool", selected our shape from the Shape selection box, and dragged out our shape inside the document. Finally, we saw how to change the colour, size and angle of the shape any time we want.

Chapter 16

Using palettes in Photoshop

In Photoshop, palettes are used to help modify and monitor your documents. An understanding of how to use, organize, and adjust palettes is essential in learning how to use Photoshop.

The Palettes

In order to show you how big of a role palettes play in Photoshop, simply **Press Tab** in Photoshop to hide all palettes. Palettes include everything from the toolbox, to the option bar, to the layers and colours windows.

In this lesson, you'll learn how to:

- Arrange palettes
- Resize, show and hide palettes
- Close, Open, and Reset palettes
- Use options inside of palettes

Arranging Palettes

It's possible to arrange palettes to your personal taste. Doing so can help increase your efficiency by moving your most frequently used palettes to a more accessible part of the screen.

To **move a palette** to a separate palette group, or into a palette group of its own, drag and drop that palettes tab into another group, or anywhere else in the work area.

To **move a palette group**, drag the title bar of that palette with your mouse, and release when it is positioned as you see fit.

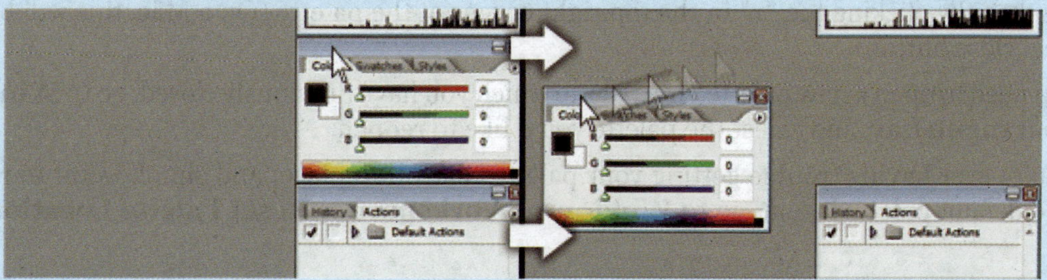

You can also **Dock Palettes** to one another by having their upper and lower edges meet one another. When a palette is docked to another, it will snap into place.

Resizing, Showing, and Hiding Palettes

Perhaps you're working with a palette with a large number of styles, colours, or layers, all of which you like to be accessible at the same time. You can resize many of the palettes by dragging the bottom right corner out to whichever size you prefer.

If you want to hide (minimize) a palette that you're not currently using to save up on space, simply **double click** that palettes tab. Likewise, you can expand a minimized tablet by double clicking the tab again.

Closing, Opening, and Resetting Palettes

If you have some tablets open that serve no use to you for your current work, it's possible to close them by clicking the "x" in the top right corner of the palette (On a Mac, this will be the typical close button).

If you need to open a new palette, or a palette which you have previously closed, go to **Window** in your **menu bar**, and select the palette you'd like to reopen.

If you're ever having trouble getting your palettes back into place, and simply want to revert to the default palette layout, go to **Window > Workspace > Reset Palette Locations** in your **Menu Bar**. This will reset everything back to how you started when you first opened Photoshop.

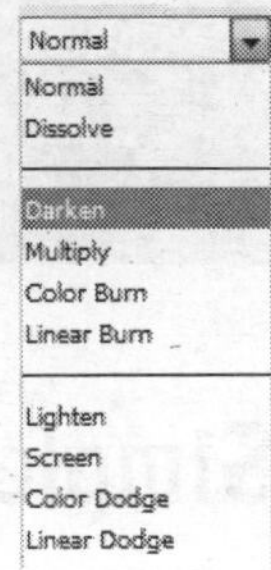

Setting Options in Palettes

Inside palettes, you'll find all sorts of various settings from colour choices, styles, opacity, and other values. We'll discuss how to operate some of these options here.

Drop-down Menus

To operate a drop-down menu, just click the arrow attached to the menu. A list of available inputs will drop down. Click any of these values to select them.

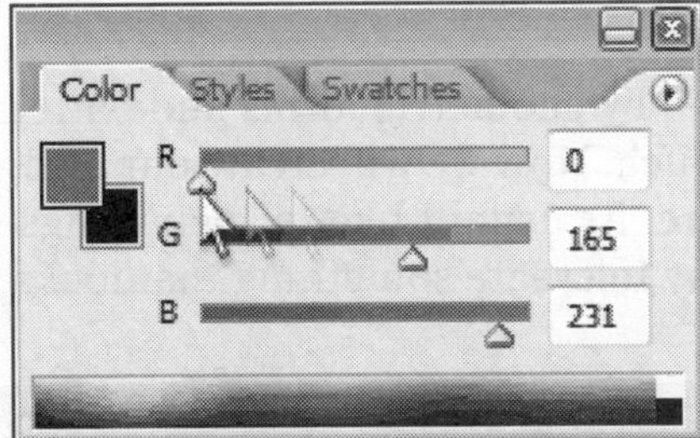

Sliders

Sliders are operated by grabbing a handle by holding down your mouse button over one, and then dragging to your desired value.

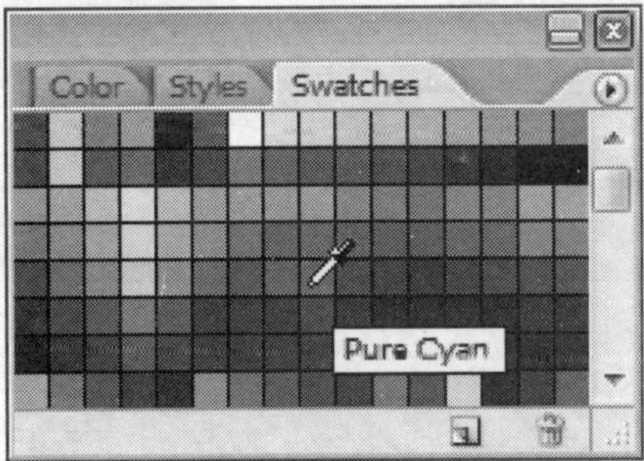

Swatches & Styles

To select a colour swatch, or layer style, simply hover over it with your mouse, and click once with your mouse

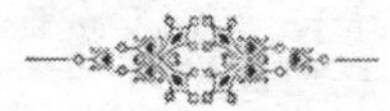

Chapter 1

Simple organic shapes in Photoshop

Lately I seem to be inspired by geometric forms and patterns in general, and especially with a bit of an organic touch. Now we will create our own version because it seems like an interesting thing to explore. As usual I like to keep things simple. So I experimented a bit and I've found an easy way to create something that looks rather complex. Take a look at this...

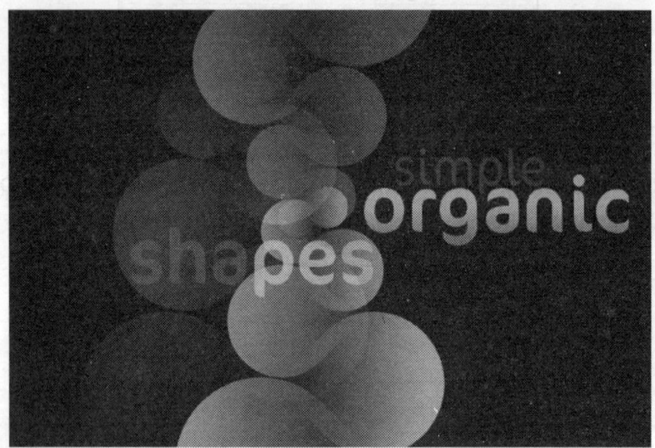

Create the shape

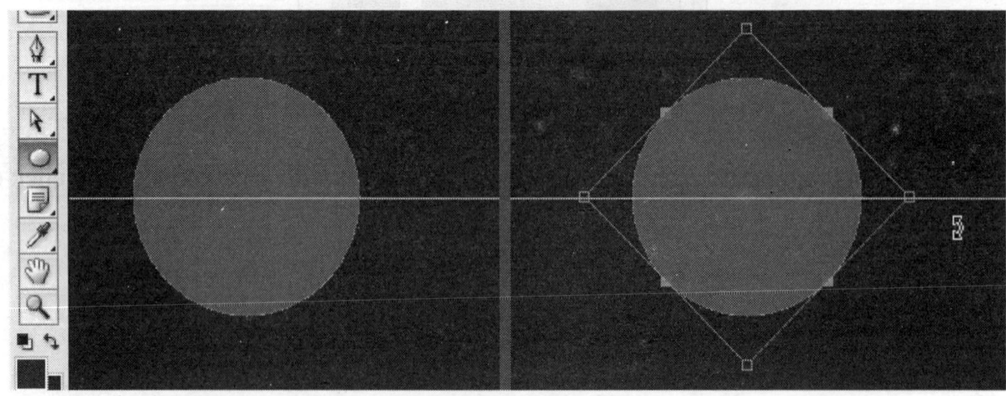

Select the *Ellipse Tool* from the Toolbox. Draw a circle holding down the *Shift Key*. Make sure your *Rulers are turned on*. Go to *View > Rulers* or hit *command/control + r*. Drag a horizontal guide from the top Ruler to the middle of the circle. Hit *command/control + t* to rotate the circle 45°. Hold down *Shift Key* while rotating the circle or just enter the value of 45 degrees in the rotate option field in the Toolbar at the top.

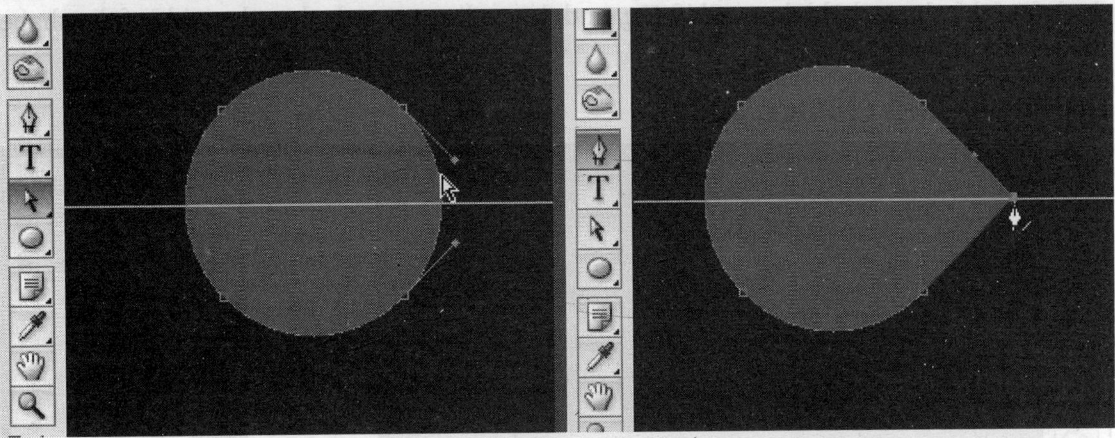

Select the *Direct Selection Tool* (white arrow) from the Toolbox. Click on the right segment of the path of the circle and hit the *Delete Key*. Now select the *Pen Tool* and click in the top right point of the circle where you have just deleted the segment of the path to redraw this part as shown above in the image on the right. Hold down the *Shift Key* and click somewhere on the guide so that you draw a perfect 45° line. Click in the bottom right point of the circle shape (that now looks more like a drop of water laying on its side).

Add Linear Gradient Mask

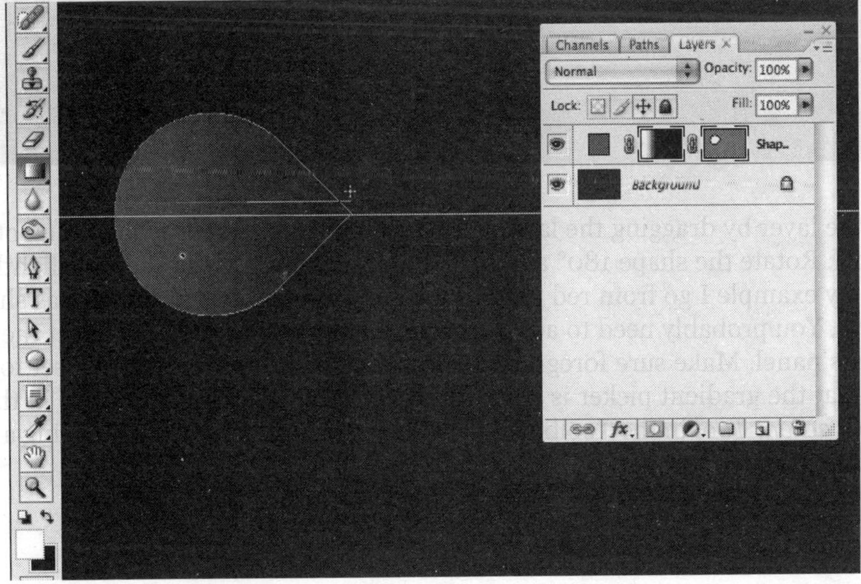

Add a mask to the layer, by first selecting the layer and then clicking the *Add a mask* option button at the bottom of the Layers panel. Make sure foreground and background are respectively set to white and black. Hit the *D Key* once and if needed use the *Switch foreground and background* arrows, so white is your foreground. In the Toolbar make sure the gradient picker is set to *Foreground to Background*. Select the *Gradient Tool* from the Toolbox and click on the left of the shape, hold down *Shift Key* and drag a line towards the other side of the shape. Release the mouse.

Duplicate and change colour

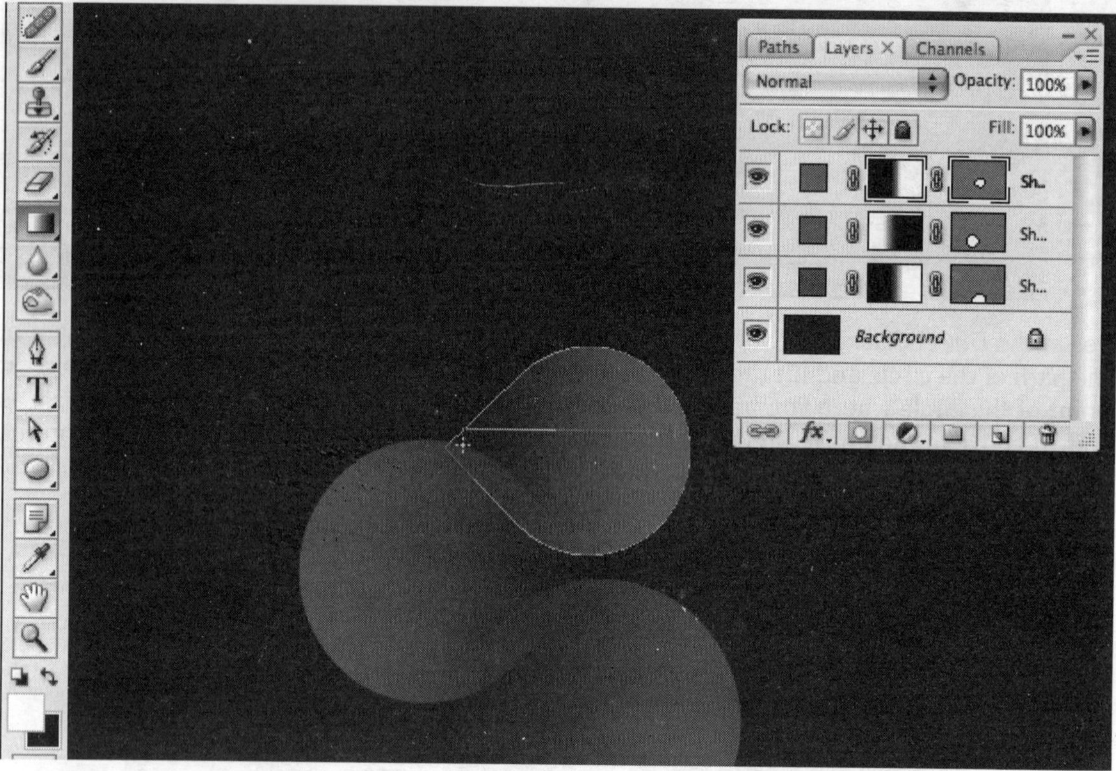

Duplicate the layer by dragging the layer over the *Create new layer* icon at the bottom of the Layers panel. Rotate the shape 180° and scale it a little bit. Give the shape a slightly different colour. In my example I go from red to hot pink and purple. Move it in place as shown in the image above. You probably need to adjust the gradient mask again. Just select the mask icon in the Layers panel. Make sure foreground and background are respectively set to white and black and that the gradient picker is set to *Foreground to Background* again in the Toolbar. Select the *Gradient Tool* in the Toolbox. Hold down the *Shift Key* while dragging a horizontal line, this time from left to right.

Build a 'pile' of shapes

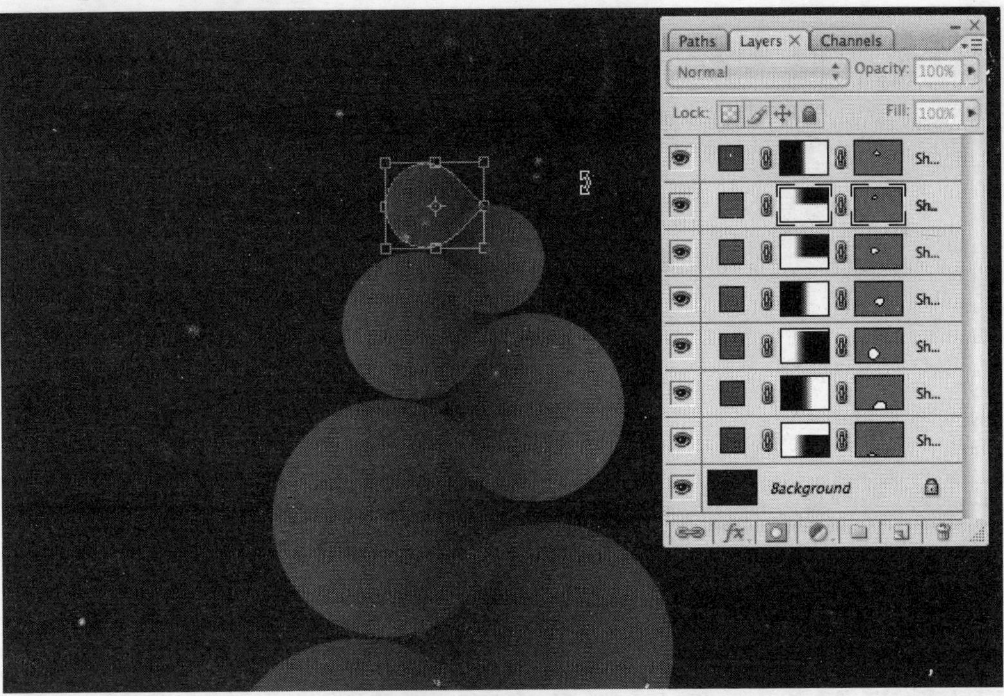

Repeat the previous step until you've created a pile of shapes as shown in the image below.

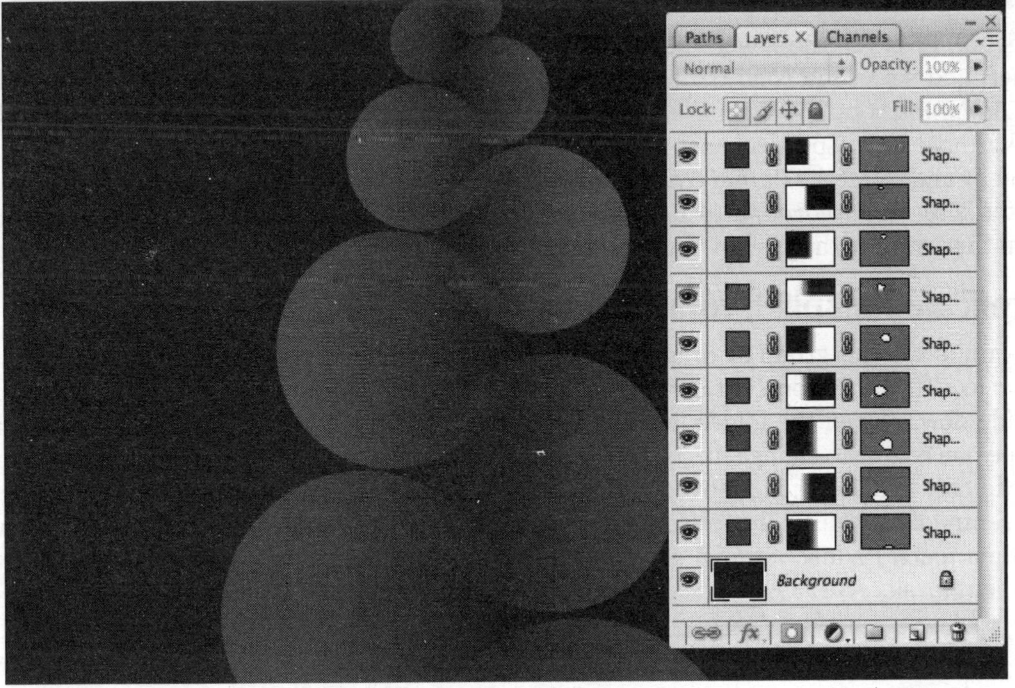

Group in a Layer Set and add a Radial Gradient Mask

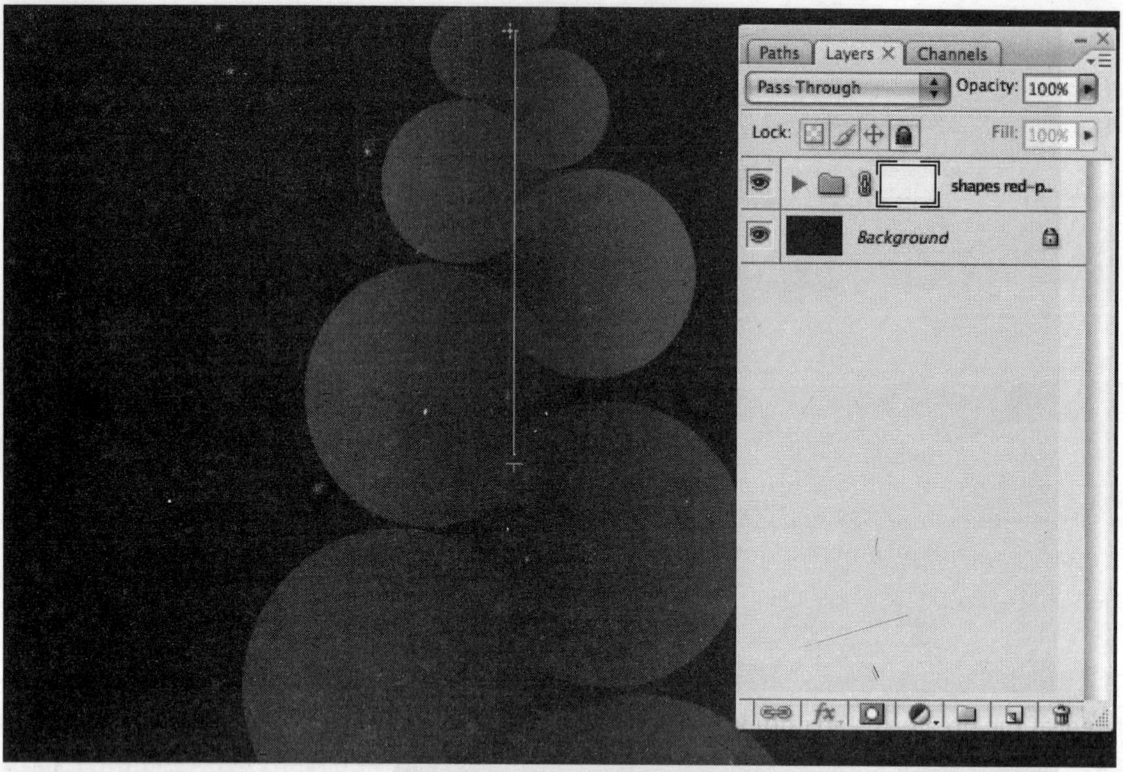

Select all layers in the Layers panel. Go to the panels menu (located at the top right of the panel) and select the *New Group from Layers...* option. Enter a name and click OK. Click the *Add a mask* option button at the bottom of the Layers panel. Make sure foreground and background are respectively set to white and black again. Select the *Gradient Tool* from the Toolbox and select the *Radial Gradient* option at the toolbar at the top. Make sure the gradient picker is set to *Foreground to Background* again. Drag a vertical line (hold down *Shift Key*) from the centre of the pile towards the top.

Duplicate the 'pile', rotate and re-colour

Now duplicate this group by dragging the folder icon in the Layers panel over the *Create new layer* icon at the bottom. Hit *command/control + t* and enter a value of 180° to turn the pile upside down. Open the folder icon in the layer to reveal the layers. Double click each layer shape one by one to change its colour. I started with green for the smallest shape and changed it gradually to blue. Then I moved my pile upwards so that the smallest shape is somewhere in the centre of my canvas. I duplicated my green-blue pile, rotated it 180° and moved it in place. As final touch I added a radial gradient in the background, using a solid colour and a radial gradient mask.

Using Pen tablets in Photoshop

Getting Started

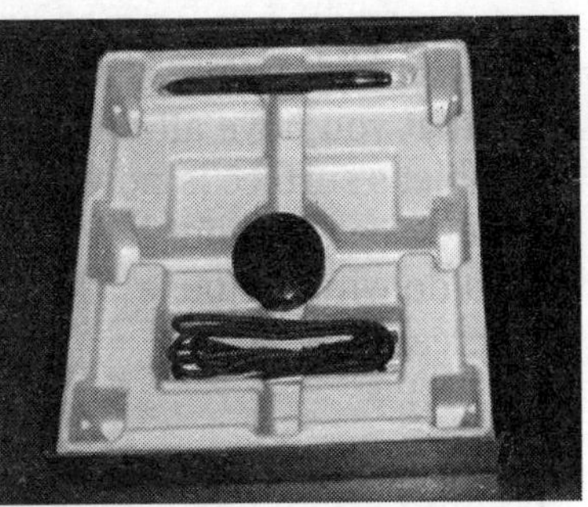

We are using Wacom's Bamboo tablet pictured above as the reference tablet for this lesson. Once you unwrap your newly purchased pen tablet you should usually find in the box the *tablet* itself, a *tip sensitive pen*, and the *installation CD* required to run the tablet features on your computer. If you plug your tablet instantly without installing the necessary drivers it will still work, but it will only support mouse features and not advanced tablet features such as pen pressure sensitivity that controls brush stroke's depth or thickness. Install the software that came on the CD to make sure that all the features get supported.

Windows Vista always comes with tablet pc friendly programs for pen usage training and writing recognition. You can access those programs by going through *Start Menu>All Programs>Tablet PC*. Those programs will help you get accustomed to using the pen tablet across Windows Vista as well as personalizing your pen's handwriting for system recognition.

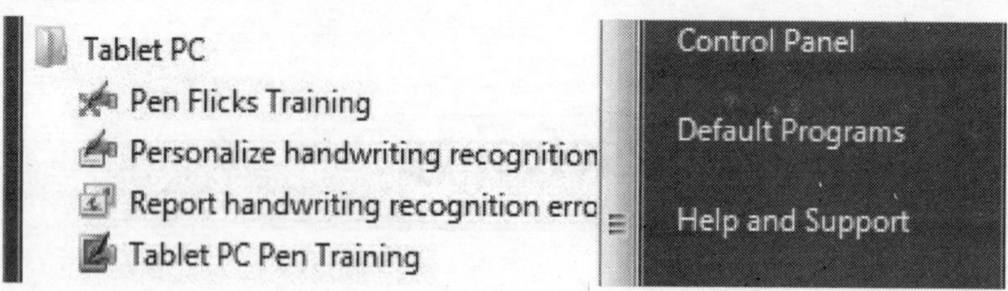

Setting Up Your Tablet

Now that you have all the drivers installed and the pen tablet identified, you can notice that the tablet's surface is now proportional to your screen, which means you can point anywhere on the screen without having to pick the pen up and drag it to the position the same way you would do with a mouse. The illustration below explains how the Pen Tablet is proportional to the screen.

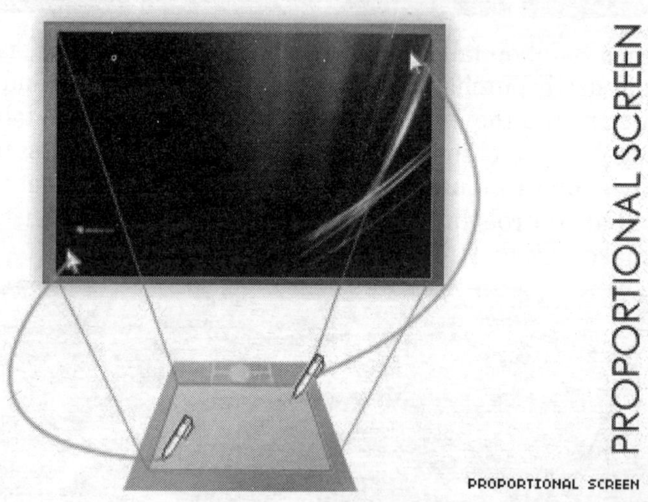

PROPORTIONAL SCREEN

Before getting using the tablet on programs, you are going to need to set up some setting to use the tablet's pen more conveniently. A new folder is usually created in your *Programs Menu* that contains tablet preferences programs installed in the previous step. For Wacom

Tablet users, open up the program which brings up the Tablet's Properties and the pen tablet's settings window should appear.

Configuration settings will differ from one tablet to another; however, the most important feature that you need to play around with is the *Tip Feel* or what is occasionally called the Firmness. You will need to configure this property to determine how hard you have to press to make a thick line when you draw. The higher the firm the harder you have to press to make your lines thicker, the lower the firmness (more softness) the easier it is for you to get a thicker line when you draw.

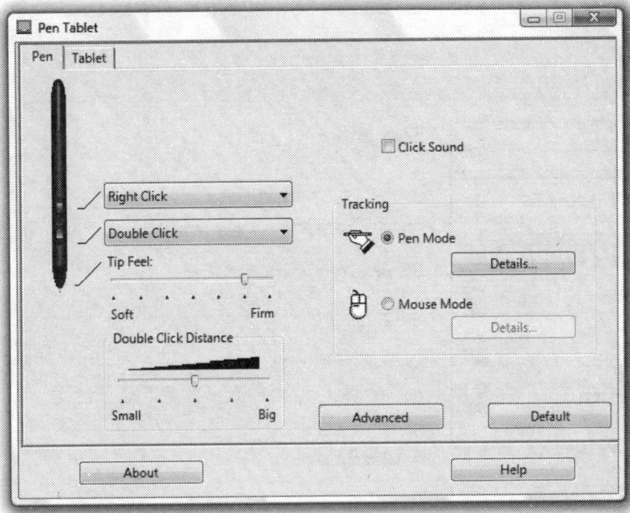

All other settings will differ from one tablet to the other and most of them are self-explanatory. It is worth noting that you may have configurable shortcut buttons which can be very helpful.

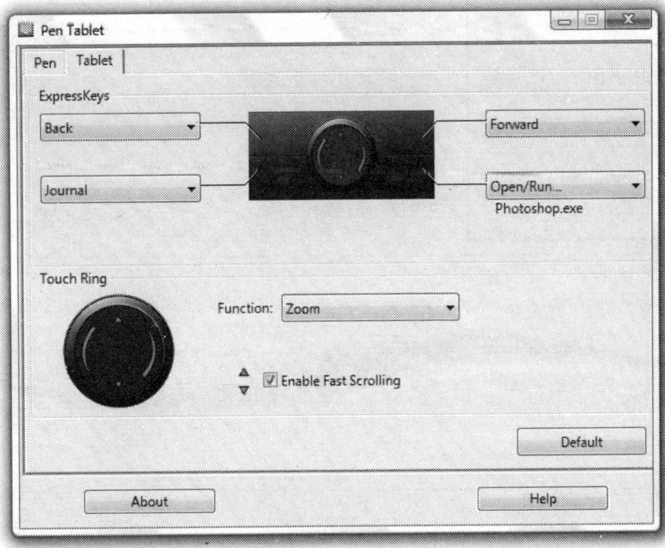

These were the global settings of the pen tablet. We will now configure Photoshop so that it recognizes our pen tablet input.

Adjusting Pen Settings in Photoshop

Even if you do configure the global settings of your pen tablet, Photoshop will have to be configured personally to actually make use it. To do so, open up *Adobe Photoshop* and then create a *New Document* of any size by going through *File>New*. Go through *Window>Brushes* to open up the *Brushes Panel* and click on *Shape Dynamics*. You will then have to change the *Control* under *Size Jitter* to *Pen Pressure* and that should do it!

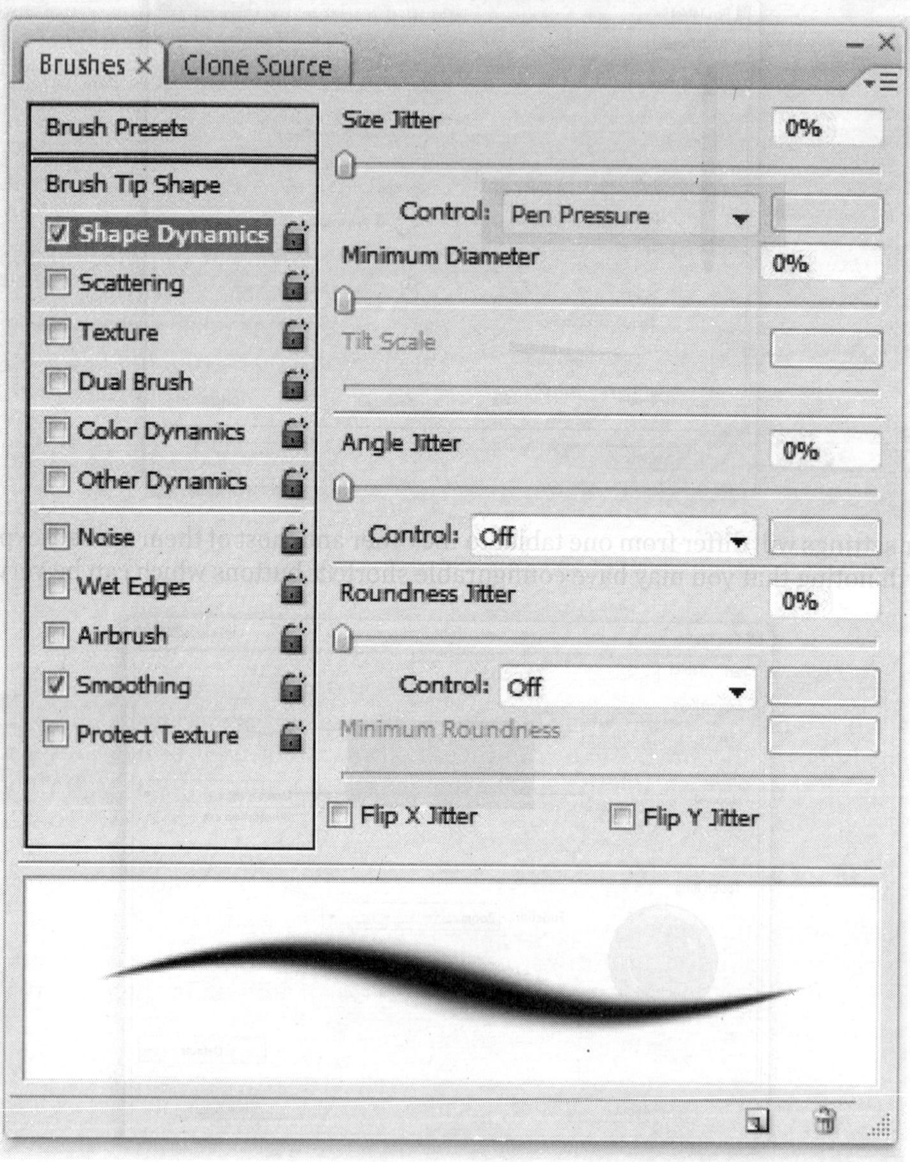

If you now try to draw using any of the brushes you will notice that the line gets thicker the harder you press the pen against the tablet. The screenshot below explains how the lines thicken when more pressure is applied using an *Air Brush* of *20px diameter*.

Here is an example of how this technique differs from normal brush settings using the same *20px Air Brush*.

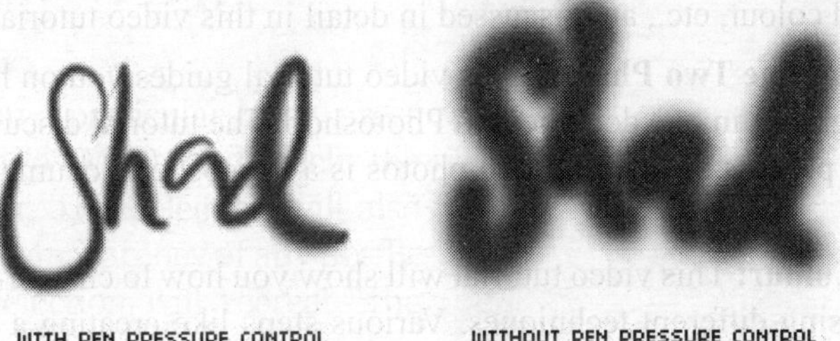

These were the essentials for getting your tablet working with Photoshop. Always remember that mastering the pen table will require plenty of practice and like any other skill, so do keep on drawing regularly to shapc up your talent!

Audio Tutorials in Youtube

Youtube Link: https://www.youtube.com/watch?v=v1-ibFK6QYE

The book comes with a Youtube containing 6 Video Tutorials for better understanding of some useful applications discussed in the book.

1. **Colour Setting in Photoshop**: This video tutorial familiarizes you with colour setting in Photoshop. The tutorial shows the methods of colour setting, such as how to make custom changes to Working Spaces, Colour Management Policies, Missing Profiles, and saving those changes you have made, etc, step by step.
2. **Introduction to Layer Masks:** This tutorial will show you how to work with layer masks in Photoshop. Different steps such as unlocking the layer, applying masks, changing foreground and background colour, etc., are discussed in detail in this video tutorial.
3. **Merge and Combine Two Photos**: This video tutorial guides you on how to merge and combine two photographs in one document in Photoshop. The tutorial discuses different techniques involved in the process of merging two photos is a Photoshop document in detail with proper directions.
4. **Change Hair Colour:** This video tutorial will show you how to change hair colours of a person in Photoshop using different techniques. Various steps like creating a new layer, adding new colours, adjusting hue/saturation, etc., are discussed step by step.
5. **Change lip Colour:** In this video tutorial you will see how to change lip colour of a person using various techniques in Photoshop. Every step is discussed in detail.
6. **Change Eye Colour:** This video will teach you how to use Photoshop's techniques to change the eye colour of a person. You will get step by step instructions for every step.

Comprehensive Computer Learning

Windows 8

V&S PUBLISHERS

What You Need to Know About Windows 8

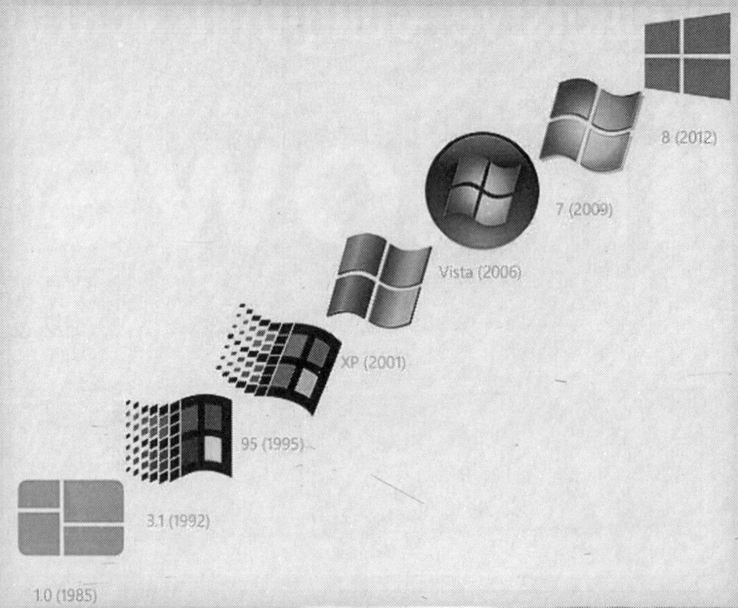

Back in 1991, Microsoft released their first version of Windows, a mouse-driven graphical user interface that revolutionised the way we use computers, both at home and at workplace.

Now, in 2012, they hope to stage a new revolution with Windows 8, perhaps Microsoft's most daring release yet. Featuring an unusual **Tile-Based Start Screen** that's optimized for touchscreen devices, Windows 8 will be available on new computers, laptops, ultrabooks, hybrid tablets and even a new range of Microsoft-branded, iPad-style tablet called **Microsoft Surface** and mobile phones also.

Whichever device you end up running Windows 8 on, you'll need to know a few things. First, how are you going to get the data from your current operating System to the new one? Second, you'll probably be wondering where the famous Microsoft desktop has gone. Finally, you might be wondering just what is going on? Why did Microsoft discard the Start menu?

Upgrading from Windows XP or Windows Vista or Windows 7

If you're upgrading, and you're already using Windows Vista or Windows 7, the new version of Windows offers an Upgrade option. This enables you to manage the transfer of data with little or no trouble – Windows 8 will effectively upgrade the existing OS without damaging your data – although you should backup your vital files anyway, just in case.

If you're upgrading from Windows XP, the process is a little different. Windows 8 cannot upgrade Windows XP in the same way in which it can Windows Vista and 7, in which case you will need to use a more detailed and drawn out process for saving your data and migrating it to the new operating system.

Where's the Desktop Gone?

So you've installed Windows 8. At least, you thought you installed Windows, but what you see doesn't look at all familiar.

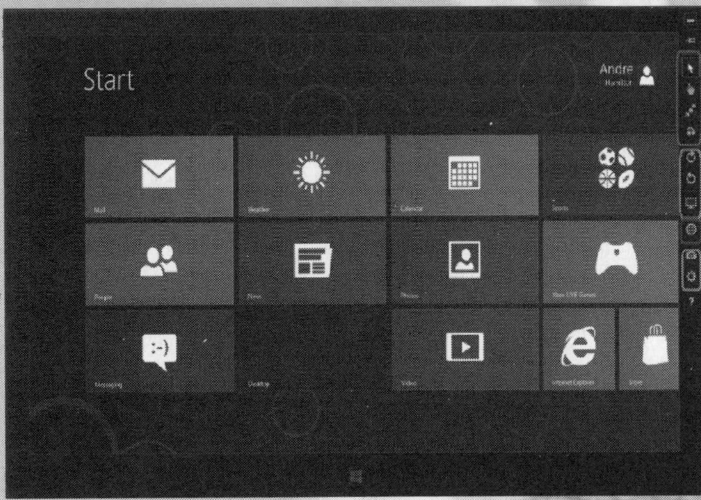

One of the most striking developments in the new version of Windows is the way in which the desktop – the area hosting the Start button, taskbar and icons in previous releases – has been demoted in favour of a new Start screen, Complete with tiles that can be clicked or tapped (depending on your hardware) to launch apps and adjust settings.

Have no fear, however – the old Desktop is still available. Indeed, it can be reached by tapping one of the tiles. While viewing the Desktop feels and looks like classic Windows, note that there is no Start button – all tasks related to this feature will need to be performed via the Start screen or by setting up some shortcuts on the Desktop.

Windows 8 Devices

There are many types of computer hardware capable of running Windows 8. First and foremost is the standard desktop computer. If your PC is capable of running Windows Vista, chances are it will run Windows 8. There are even some older computers stuck on Windows XP that can run Windows 8 effectively!

Similarly, existing laptop computers and ultrabooks will also be able to run Windows 8 – thanks to useful touchpad gesture apps, Windows 8 might actually be better for smaller systems than Vista or Windows 7 were. Despite this, Windows 8 is really intended for new devices. The reason for this is simple: the change in focus for the Start screen means that fingers are recommended, if not required. As a result new PCs shipping with Windows 8 will come with touchscreens and/or mice with gesture recognition tools, new Mac OS X-style touchpads will become available and laptops will almost all become hybrid devices, with pivoting touchscreen displays.

Microsoft aren't entirely playing nice with their traditional partners, the hardware makers – they've announced the release of a new tablet, Microsoft Surface, which will come in two flavours.

That's a big step for a company that doesn't usually make hardware. Windows 8 is designed to work on devices powered by a low-power ARM processor (found in typical Android and Apple tablets) as well as typical Intel x86 based processors (which is what most desktop, laptops and ultrabooks today use). Surface is seen as a competitor to Android and iOS tablets, and Windows 8's app store and tile–based interface are a big part of that.

With this in mind, there will be no shortage of suitable computers and tablets to run the new operating system! It should also be noted that a Windows 8 device powered by an ARM processor will be unable to run legacy Windows software, such as games and older versions of Microsoft Office. That software is Intel-only.

The Windows 8 User Interface

The major difference between Windows 8 and previous releases – the tile-based UI – means that you will need to spend a bit of time getting used to the Start screen. No longer will you need to click a Start button and browse the Programs list, or use the search function – at least not the way you're used to. Instead you will need to find a new way in which to perform tasks that have become ingrained, hard wired into your brain.

Understanding Metro

Probably the best route to understanding how to use Windows 8 is to forget that you're using Windows at all. There are various ways in which you can interact with the system, but few of them require you to click and drag, open properties or make any adjustments to the layout of the Start screen (although this is possible). Gaining familiarity with the tiles and the navigation is important, as is being aware of the **"charms"** – a hidden array of menu items. You'll need to move your mouse pointer to (or tap) the top or bottom right of your Windows 8 display to reveal the **Charm Bar**. If you are using a device with a keyboard, pressing WIN+C will also open the Charm Bar.

Appearing on the right-hand side of the screen, the Charm Bar provides other features and functions:

- **Search** – like the Windows 7 Start menu, simply type to find what you're looking for. When an app is open, Search will focus on that software rather than the computer itself. For a full computer search, use the tool from the Start screen. Note also that you can commence a search from the Start screen by simply typing – the Search tool will open as a result. Also note that Search can be used to find Desktop-based Windows items.
- **Share** – apps with sharing permissions can be used to share information such as links. Note that this cannot be used in desktop mode, only via the Metro browser.
- **Start** – this is yet another option to open the Start screen, along with the menu in the lower-left corner, or by pressing the Windows key on a hardware keyboard.
- **Devices** – settings for peripherals such as second/external monitors can be adjusted.
- **Settings** – Audio, Brightness, Wi-Fi, Power, Notifications and Language are all accessed from here. The **More PC Settings** link will enable you to access more options in the control panel. The Settings option will display settings for individual apps while they are active.

These options are displayed **Metro-style.** On the left side of your display, the date, time and battery and wireless networking information will also be displayed.

Note that many apps (native and third party) will have their own context menus. These menus can be accessed by right-clicking with the mouse.

Launch and Install Apps, Multitasking

One of the strengths of Windows 8's tile-based user interface is that the applications that are installed can be easily accessed. Another is that adding new apps is a case of tapping the Store tile and finding what you need to use. Multitasking remains a key element of Windows, although in the new-look Windows you'll notice that things have changed somewhat.

Meanwhile, any *legacy software* – applications and utilities designed initially for older versions of Windows – can be installed via the Desktop.

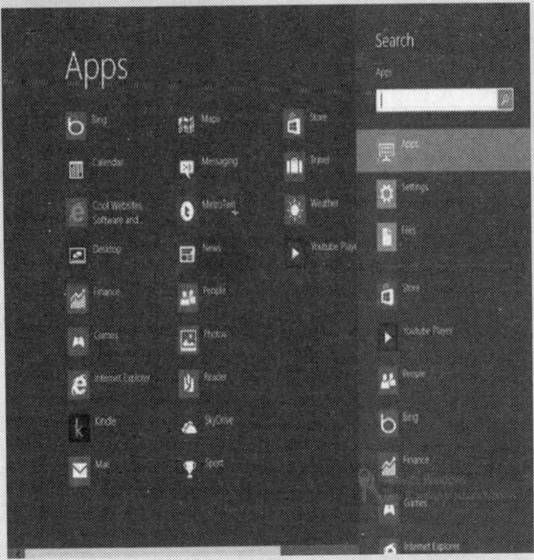

Launching Apps

You'll be stuck running applications in Windows 8 without knowing where your favourite applications can be loaded from. To find your applications, open the **Charm Bar** and click or tap **Search**. This will display the search pane on the right with the Apps list taking up most of the screen to the left of this. You'll be able to scroll left and right through the Apps list, while the search function will help you to quickly find the app you're looking for. You'll be able to open an app by tapping or left clicking.

The Apps List can also be opened from the Start screen by right-clicking or long-tapping and selecting **All Apps**.

Switching Between Applications

As ever, switching between running apps is possible by holding **ALT+TAB** on your keyboard. This will display the task switcher window in the center of the screen, enabling you to select the open app you wish to use. You might also use the **WIN+TAB** keyboard combination, which displays a list of open apps to switch between.

If you're not using a mouse and keyboard – that is, you're using a tablet or other touchscreen computer – you'll find that switching between application is done by swiping left across the display in order to find the app you wish to use. Tapping the top left corner of the display is also an alternative. A quicker way is often to head back to the Apps List and select the desired application again.

Closing Apps

One of the difficulties of Windows 8 is that the method used for closing apps isn't obvious. It is very effective, however. To close an app you will need to use your finger (or mouse pointer) to drag the app down, and discard it. This is done by placing your finger at the top of the display where you should see a small hand icon appear; drag your finger from the top edge of the display to the bottom, where the app will shrink and fade away! The same action can be performed with a mouse.

If you run into problems, you can call on the redesigned Task Manager to get you out of trouble. This will open in Desktop mode, however, but can be used to quickly close unresponsive apps. Note that it isn't optimised for fingers!

The Windows 8 Store

Available via the appropriately labelled tile, the Store will enable you to install apps, games and utilities for the Metro side of Windows 8. Although software can be installed through the desktop, the main way to install a new app in Windows 8 is to head to the Store, one of the first icons you will see on the Start screen. Launching the Store will provide access to a range of free and premium apps and games, similar to the Apple App Store or Google Play on Android. These apps and games have all been designed specifically to work under Windows 8, which means that they will be unavailable via the Desktop mode.

Use Your Windows Account

Key to your ability to access the Windows 8 Store is your Windows account. This might be a Hotmail account, a Windows Live Messenger account, even an MSDN or Xbox Live account. Either way, you will need to use this to access the store, whether you have setup Windows 8 to use this account as your login or not. There is a simple reason for this: some apps are free, others are not. If you wish to purchase an app, you will need to have a credit card attached to your Windows Live account. A credit or debit card can be added to your account via **Settings > PC Settings > Users > More account settings online > Billing**. Note that if you already have a payment card associated with your account, this will be used unless a new one is added.

Finding, Reviewing and Buying an App

There are different ways of finding new apps in Windows 8. First, you might select the Store tile, and take a look at what is on offer in Spotlight. This lists the most interesting new apps, free and paid, while scrolling right will display interesting options from other categories, such as Games, Social apps, Music and Video, Sport, and many more. Each of these options can be opened and browsed, while the search tool will help you find what you're looking for.

Once you tap into the app or game itself, you will find a list of details about the app, such as its reviews star rating, the permissions it requires and recommended minimum age of the user (useful for video games). The Overview screen will provide a summary of the app; Details provides more information, such as detailed permissions and features, while Reviews provides a record of the thoughts of other users of the app. Images from the app are also displayed, which can be scrolled through. If you have downloaded an app, you will be able to return to its Store screen and leave your opinions and rating via the Write a Review link. Doing so is important – this is a new software ecosystem and other Windows 8 users may benefit from your thoughts when choosing an app or game. Adding a free app to Windows 8 will require you to tap Install on the app's description page. If the app in question has a price listed, tap **Buy** instead to proceed with the purchase. Note that some paid apps will offer a **Try** option, with a short trial period for you to use the software.

Updating Apps

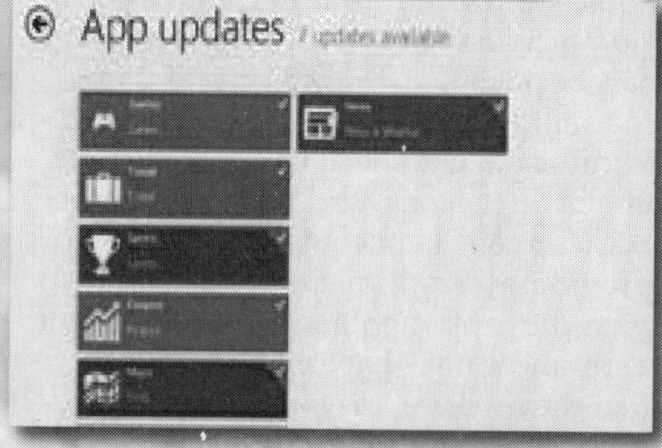

You'll also notice that the Store will display a notification in the top-right of the screen informing you that apps can be updated. This can be done by right-clicking and selecting **Update > Install**, ensuring that the apps you want updating are selected.

Windows 8 system requirements

If you want to run Windows 8 on your PC, here's what it takes:

- Processor: 1 gigahertz (GHz) or faster with support for PAE, NX, and SSE2
- RAM: 1 gigabyte (GB) (32-bit) or 2 GB (64-bit)
- Hard disk space: 16 GB (32-bit) or 20 GB (64-bit)
- Graphics card: Microsoft DirectX 9 graphics device with WDDM driver

Additional requirements to use certain features:

- To use touch, you need a tablet or a monitor that supports multitouch
- To access the Windows Store and to download and run apps, you need an active Internet connection and a screen resolution of at least 1024 x 768
- To snap apps, you need a screen resolution of at least 1366 x 768
- Internet access (ISP fees might apply)
- Secure boot requires firmware that supports UEFI v2.3.1 Errata B and has the Microsoft Windows Certification Authority in the UEFI signature database
- Some games and programs might require a graphics card compatible with DirectX 10 or higher for optimal performance
- Microsoft account required for some features
- Windows Media Center license sold separately
- BitLocker To Go requires a USB flash drive (Windows 8 Pro only)
- BitLocker requires either Trusted Platform Module (TPM) 1.2 or a USB flash drive (Windows 8 Pro only)
- Client Hyper-V requires a 64-bit system with second level address translation (SLAT) capabilities and additional 2 GB of RAM (Windows 8 Pro only)
- A TV tuner is required to play and record live TV in Windows Media Center (Windows 8 Pro Pack and Windows 8 Media Center Pack only)
- Free Internet TV content varies by geography, some content might require additional fees (Windows 8 Pro Pack and Windows 8 Media Center Pack only)